Sheela Rohekar, a Bene Israel Jew is probably the sole-living Jewish Hindi author. In 1978, her first Hindi novel, *Dinat*, was published, followed by *Taviz* (2005), *Miss Samuel: Ek Yahoodi Gatha* (2013), and *Pallipaar* (2022). She has been awarded the Yashpal Award for *Dinat,* the UP Hindi Sansthan's Premchand Award for *Miss Samuel,* and the Pen of the Year Award by *The Hindustan Times.*

Madhu Singh is a professor at the Department of English and Modern European Languages, University of Lucknow. She has translated G.N. Devy's *A Nomad Called Thief: Reflections on Adivasi Silence* into *Ghumantu Hai, Chor Nahin: Adivasi Maun Par Vimarsh* (2017) and Ramchandra Singh's memoir, *Thirteen Years: A Naxalite Jail Diary* (2018).

Miss Samuel A Jewish-Indian Saga

Sheela Rohekar

Translated by Madhu Singh

SPEAKING TIGER

SPEAKING TIGER BOOKS LLP
125A, Ground Floor, Shahpur Jat, near Asiad Village,
New Delhi 110049

Originally published in Hindi as
Miss Samuel: Ek Yahoodi Gatha by Bharatiya Jnanpith in 2013
First published in English in paperback by Speaking Tiger Books in 2024

ISBN: 978-93-5447-758-4
eISBN: 978-93-5447-965-6

10 9 8 7 6 5 4 3 2 1

Typeset in Minion Pro by SÜRYA, New Delhi
Printed at HT Media Ltd, Greater Noida

Contents

FOREWORD

On Translatability and the Space In Between

I very well remember my personal discovery of Sheela Rohekar's novel *Taviz* more than a decade ago. The great connoisseur of world literature and translator Vishnu Khare, who unfortunately passed away in September 2018, had hinted that *Taviz* was worth reading. I knew I could rely on his recommendations.

A few pages in, I got completely immersed in the novel, its narrative and the subject of *Taviz*: the flashbacks, the plot meandering here and there, back and forth in time, but at the same time, the seriousness of this voice, and its psychological insight into a wide range of characters. It is a very personal narrative on the tragic fate of a Hindu-Muslim interreligious marriage, on the space in-between of the personal and the collective, and structural as well as physical violence—and finally, murder.

Essentializing the other is the first step towards violence. The argument inevitably goes like this: You argue like this because you are different. Unity in diversity is fine, but it does not fit the identity the other incorporates. Discrimination is a form of structural violence and can turn into direct violence on occasion. Those who fall out of conventional frames of how social, cultural and religious identities should become visible can become a target. Isn't it strange how the trimming of a beard, the style of a pyjama, and the way you pronounce certain Arabic words should once and for all establish communal identity?

Sheela Rohekar questions these identities. There is a strong tendency in middle-class society to define religion as a kind of individual comfort zone. Sheela-ji's religion is beyond that. The disbanded amulet (i.e., taviz) that was once given to the Hindu by a Muslim Pir as a token of love two generations ago turns into the symbol of a society that is losing its competence to deal with diversity.

I immediately felt that *Taviz* was an important novel in the world of Hindi literature. It immediately struck me that Sheela-ji's construction of the plot had a personal element in it. The narrative is more than just a detached view of identity by a contemporary secular author. Of course, the relationship of an author to her or his narratives is always complex. A certain degree of detachment is always there. At the same time, the personal is involved and eventually reveals itself. After reading *Taviz*, my fundamental quest was how Sheela-ji relates herself, as a person, to her fiction. This was what we discussed during a wonderful afternoon in spring 2007, I think, when I had the pleasure to meet her for the first time in her and her husband's flat in Gomti Nagar in Lucknow.

I cannot but see a repercussion of minority Jewish sensitivity even in *Taviz*, and these repercussions are evident in *Miss Samuel: Ek Yahoodi Gatha*, which, in a way, is a continuation of the subject that *Taviz* dwells upon. Both novels focus on the question of belonging and estrangement in the in-between space, the subtle forms of discrimination in Indian society, and the binary of inside and outside within communities.

Writing on the diminishing Bene Israel means writing

on a tiny and shrinking identity in the middle of a torrent of modernity and modernization. Antisemitism may have never threatened the Jews in their long history in India, but the option of emigration is too strong a temptation for many in India to resist. In the case of the Jews of India, emigration has particularly bitter effects since it leads to the loss of an important piece in the mosaic of religions in India. The shrinking in numbers is threatening the very existence of the community itself, and Parisar—the old people asylum—of the novel is, in a way, a last refuge. The ladies in Parisar look more into the past than towards the future. The Jewish religion is quickly losing ground in India.

Maybe it was not fair when I called the novel a swansong on Jewish identity in India and South Asia in an essay published some years back. *Miss Samuel: A Jewish-Indian Saga* is not only about Jewish identity; it goes much further. It is, I think, firstly on contemporary Indian identity as such and on the layers of meanings of the famous 'unity in diversity'. How much diversity does the modern nation-state allow, and how much unity is essential for India?

Parisar is not at all a closed space. It opens to new forms of solidarity among abandoned elderly women, an open space made up of their lived experiences. Old ladies of different faiths and identities leave their frustration within a patriarchal society behind to discover what friendship, love and solidarity actually mean.

The question raised here is how a society with its traditional mix of identities can live together, how it can deal with differences, and discover the interreligious space. Curiosity and consolation are two important modes of building bridges between individuals as well as communities. In a way, Parisar is a model of a tolerant society that not only accepts differences but even respects, maintains and transcends them at the same time. Everyone has her or his samskaras (acquired faculty), which enables us to perceive and judge the world.

It is significant how Sheela-ji turns towards a more positive connotation of the meaning of identity in *Miss Samuel* compared to *Taviz*. Religious identity is not necessarily threatening in the later novel. It opens new spaces, it shapes narratives, and it establishes bridges towards the other, beyond the subtle regime of trained behaviours in the social space outside Parisar.

There is not much Hindi writing by Jews in India. However, there is another important novel, *Shulamith* by Meera Mahadevan, written originally in Hindi in the 1960s during the ongoing emigration of the Bene Israel and published in English translation in 1975. That novel was composed in a historical moment when the Bene Israel and other Indian Jews were under the pressure of having to decide to stay in India or follow the Zionist call to Israel. Most Indian Jews finally settled in Israel after 1964, when the Head Rabbinate accepted the Jewish identity of the Bene Israel.

Almost fifty years later, *Miss Samuel* is an epic narrative of another epoch. The mass emigration of the Indian Jewry is a given fact, and only very few returned—like the English author Esther David, who describes her return to India as her real 'aliyah' (return to the mother country, i.e., Israel).

It is extremely fortunate that my colleague Madhu Singh agreed to translate this great work of novel writing into Hindi. She is deep into the art of translation, and she knows a lot about Judaism. Her sensitive translation of Sheela Rohekar's Hindi, with its underlays of Gujarati and Marathi, is a fine example of the art of translating, of a successful 'interpretative performance', a wonder in understanding a complicated narrative and a transfer of meaning from one linguistic discourse into another.

In a way, a translation inevitably falls short of some of

the deeper layers of meanings of the original text. However, some people believe that English is different; English opens up to transform the rough into the refined, the rural into the cultured, and the regional into the globalized, but I choose to disagree. Sheela Rohekar's Hindi original is refined, cultured, and very much globalized. The language does not create the novel—rather, it's the other way around. The novel designs its language—and every translation is more than just a rendering in another language. It is a recreation.

Globalization does not mean that we all have to turn into one and the same people with the same language, customs, and tastes in a completely secular space in the way Max Weber used the term. Anything that bears literary quality is translatable. The translatability of cultures is a constant revelation. I think this is what globalization should be about. Sheela Rohekar's novel *Miss Samuel* is a key novel to understanding not only Indian-Jewish identity but also Indian identity and its challenges in the twenty-first century.

Heinz Werner Wessler
Professor, Institute for Linguistics and Philology
Uppsala University (Sweden)
November 2019

Translator's Note

In 2013, *Miss Samuel: Ek Yahoodi Gatha*, a Hindi novel based on the life of a minuscule Jewish community, the Bene Israel ('Children of Israel' in Hebrew) of Western India, was published by Bharatiya Jnanpith, New Delhi. The writer was Sheela Rohekar, a Bene Israel Jew who speaks Marathi and Gujarati but writes primarily in Hindi. The novel was a fascinating account of the lives of six generations of a Bene Israel family, their fears and apprehensions and their cherished dream of 'aliyah'—a return to the Promised Land of Israel. After reading the novel, I felt it needed a larger audience not only because the Bene Israel story was relatively unknown but also because it touched the lives of those who were displaced and relocated across the world by circumstances, compulsions or choice. Their struggle to assimilate with the mainstream for over twenty centuries and to maintain a distinct identity was sensitively evoked. They experienced an identity crisis because in the caste-entrenched society of India, for a long time, people did not know who Jews were and often mistook them to be Christians or Muslims. So, one of the many reasons to translate this book—though certainly not the only one—was to allow a wider readership to be touched by Sheela Rohekar's work.

Miss Samuel is no ordinary story but a saga of belonging and not belonging, of being home and un-homed, and more importantly, a tale that touches that substratum of human consciousness, which transcends the categories of caste, class, race, religion or nation. The eponymous protagonist, Miss Samuel's unsuccessful struggle to fit into a majoritarian Hindu society and the plight of being an unmarried woman in India who spends her last days in the old age home—Parisar—will touch the readers' hearts and souls. Here, the term 'parisar' has multiple connotations. It is an old age home meant for women who have been cast off by their children. It also means an empty, forlorn space around a building, an unclaimed open space near a house, a neighbouring area, and even death. Metaphorically speaking, all these connotations indicate physical distance and isolation.

Who are the Bene Israel? When and under what circumstances did they arrive in India? Are they diaspora Jews or 'native converts'? How similar or different are they from the world Jewry? Such questions about their Jewish identity have led to some historical, sociological, anthropological and ethnographic research over the years. Although representing a microscopic segment of the Indian population, the Bene Israel is one of the largest and oldest of the three major Jewish communities of India, the other two being the Cochin Jews of the Malabar Coast and the Baghdadi Jews of Bombay and Calcutta. According to Joan G. Roland, the Jews of India have always aroused curiosity because of the legendary long-term residence of the Bene Israel and the Cochin Jews in India, the commercial and philanthropic activities of the Baghdadi Jews, and the security enjoyed by all.* Scholars like Roland, Shalva Weil and others agree that India is perhaps the one country where the Jews have maintained their identity without ever being exposed to antisemitism at the hands of their host.

*Roland, Joan G. *The Jewish Communities of India: Identity in a Colonial Era*, 2nd Edition, (London: Routledge, 1998)

Sheela Rohekar acknowledges the grace of the host country but at the same time points at their alienation and isolation from the mainstream in her novel:

> 'Despite acclimatizing to the earth, water and air of this country, the Jews are in such a minority that they have no voice of their own. So, they have no say in Indian politics or culture. Since they landed in this country which gave them shelter, they have remained either mute or short-sighted outsiders!'
>
> —*Miss Samuel;* Chapter 16, Page 207

The Bene Israel increased steadily from 6,000 in the 1830s to 10,000 by the turn of the century. At their peak in 1948, they numbered 20,000. With the formation of the nation-state of Israel in 1948, the exodus of the Jews of India took place on a very large scale. So, by 1961, the Bene Israel number had declined to 16,000. Over time, more of the community emigrated, till, at the beginning of the twenty-first century, approximately 50,000 members lived in Israel, whereas around 5,000 remained in India, mainly in Mumbai. This includes a population of a little over 200 members in Gujarat.

Shalva Weil mentions that before 1948, the Bene Israel showed little interest in Zionism. They had even declined the invitation to the First Zionist Congress, held in Basel, Switzerland, in August 1897, which was arguably the most significant Jewish assembly since antiquity. According to the community, the resurrection of Israel was not a human concern. However, after the founding of the Zionist Organization in Bombay in 1920, they expressed full sympathy to the Zionist cause.

The Bene Israel have lived in India for more than 2,000 years and claim descent from the ten lost tribes of Israel. They hold that their ancestors fled the persecutions of Antiochus

Epiphanes around 175 BC or later and were shipwrecked near the village of Navagaon along the Konkan coast near Bombay.* The Jewish philosopher Maimonides, in a letter written 800 years ago (1200 AD), briefly mentioned a Jewish community living in India. Though the exact date of their arrival in India and their origins are conflicting, fractured and shrouded in historical uncertainties, the antiquity of their Jewish past may still be established.

After they had settled down permanently in the Konkan villages of Western Maharashtra, they were called 'Shaniwar Telis' or Saturday oil pressers—a relatively low-caste designation—by the local population because they refrained from working on Saturday, the Jewish Sabbath.† Later, they also farmed their land, peddled produce, and took up petty jobs as carpenters, masons, mechanics, tailors, etcetera, with a majority working as clerks in government offices and private firms. With time, they adopted Hindu names similar to their Biblical names and took up Marathi surnames such as Rohekar, Penkar, Palkar and Ashtamkar by adding the suffix '-kar' to the villages and towns they came from, such as Roha, Pen, Pali or Ashtam. They adopted Marathi, the local language, as their mother tongue and, to outsiders, became physically indistinguishable from the local population. Within village society, the Bene Israel were clearly differentiated from others because they adhered to Judaism. Tradition recounts that they forgot all Hebrew prayers except the 'Shema Yisra'yel…' (Hear, O Israel…). However, they observed the Sabbath, celebrated major festivals, circumcised their sons on the eighth day after

---

*Weil, Shalva. 'Indian Judaic Tradition', *Religions of South Asia: An Introduction*, ed. Sushil Mittal and Gene Thursby, (London, Routledge, 2006)

†Kehimkar, Haleem Samuel. *The History of the Bene-Israel of India*, (Tel Aviv: Dayag Press, 1937)

their birth and performed most of the prescribed offerings mentioned in the Bible.

The earliest recognition of the 'Shaniwar Telis' as a Jewish community was by one David Rahabi, who was instrumental in bringing the Bene Israel into contact with other Jews in India. However, neither his exact origin nor the date of arrival is certain: he may have been a Cochin Jew who came in the eighteenth century from the Malabar region in South India, although the Bene Israel records his arrival as far as 1000 AD. According to Bene Israel legends, Rahabi requested the women to prepare him a fish meal to test their claim of Jewishness. When they separated the fish with fins and scales from the non-kosher fish to cook, recognizing their vestigial Jewish customs, Rahabi was convinced of their Jewish identity and agreed to instruct them in the tenets of Judaism.

Interestingly, the overtones of a caste system were also present among the Bene Israel. These were once quite apparent in relationships within and between the Jewish communities, but with the changed times, intermarriages between them became common. Like the endogamous caste-like groups of 'black', 'white' and 'brown' Jews in the Cochin Jews, the Bene Israel also distinguished between the two sub-castes: 'kala' (black) and 'gora' (white) Jews. The 'kala' Jews were those who were believed to descend from non-Jewish mothers or from those who had been converted. The 'white' Jews among the Cochin Jews and the Bene Israel treated the 'black' Jews as inferior and, at times, as untouchables.

Similarly, the Baghdadi Jews also adopted caste-like attitudes towards the Bene Israel because of their lack of ritual orthodoxy and supposed 'ancestral impurity'.* It is said that there was no difference in physical appearance between the

*Roland, *The Jewish Community of India*, 1998

two groups, although the 'black' Jews are considered to be the progeny of union with local non-Jews. Nevertheless, the terms 'gora' and 'kala' may have at one time reflected a distinction of colour, but now, as Sheela Rohekar states, the distinction has gradually faded, and the 'gora' and 'kala' Jews have marital relationships. In fact, there have been such marriages among her own immediate family members.

By the end of the eighteenth century, under British influence, the first Bene Israel began moving from Konkan villages to Bombay (Mumbai). Unlike the Baghdadi Jews who arrived in India in the early eighteenth century and soon dominated cotton, Bombay yarn, opium, tea, jute, spices and indigo trade, and entered merchant banking, insurance, real estate and manufacturing in full swing to become prosperous and influential, the Bene Israel found themselves in the military and police services as they had traditionally served in the Maratha armies. The Bene Israel embraced military service in the Sepoy regiments, first for the East India Company and later in the Bombay Army. As the male members of the community enlisted in big numbers because they lived within a major recruiting area, they were deployed in imperial wars in Persia (1855-1857), China (1856-60) and Abyssinia (1867-1868). As a group, they remained loyal to the British in the Mutiny of 1857.

By the end of the nineteenth century, with a change in the British policy of army recruitment, they shifted their attention to ancillary services such as supply, works, accounts, education, and medicine. The spread of English education brought them closer to the mainstream Jews and reduced their dependence on Christian missionaries for religious instruction and sustenance. As a result of the opportunities offered to the Bene Israel by the British at the end of the nineteenth century, the Bene Israel families began to emigrate to other centres as far as Burma and Aden. By the twentieth century, groups of Bene Israel had moved to the hill stations along the railway lines. A large part of the community settled in Karachi, now in Pakistan. In 1921, a Bene Israel synagogue was established in Pune, and in 1934, another was built in Ahmedabad. In 1956, the Judah Hyam Prayer Hall was opened in New Delhi.

As mentioned earlier, in 1948, the Bene Israel began to immigrate to Israel, although their integration into Israeli society was not easy. In 1951, a small number of the Bene Israel claimed discrimination and demanded repatriation; after a series of strikes, they returned to India. Most of these Jews re-emigrated to Israel later. Furthermore, some orthodox rabbis in Israel did not recognize the Bene Israel as Jews, and therefore, the Bene Israel faced difficulty marrying other Jews. After 1964, when the religious status of the Bene Israel was finally accepted in Israel, emigration increased. The most popular account of the community is available in Bene Israel historian H.S. Kehimkar's book *The History of the Bene-Israel of India* (1937). Current scholarship has largely continued where Kehimkar left off, with the best-known historian in the field, Nathan Katz, producing an account of Jewish history in the Indian subcontinent, which classifies Indian Jews into racially and culturally distinct communities—the Cochin Jews, the Bene Israel and the Baghdadi Jews. However, there are two other lesser-known Jewish communities in India: the Bnei Menashe of the North-East and the Ben Ephraim, the Telugu-speaking Jews of Andhra Pradesh.

Translating Jewishness: Through Mists of Lost Time

In his essay titled 'Imaginary Homelands', Salman Rushdie pointed out that the word 'translation' comes, etymologically, from the Latin for 'bearing across'. Men coming from one culture and entering another become, in Rushdie's own words, 'translated men,' men who have been 'borne across'. In that sense, Sheela Rohekar is a 'translated woman' as she represents a community which had 'borne across' two different cultures and managed to create a distinct identity of their own. 'Bearing across' the life history of her ancestors, she seeks answers to those questions that trouble her in the novel.

Translation is a silent, solitary process that is done intuitively. It is a close and intimate linguistic and cultural encounter within the soul of the translator. When I started translating the book, a few questions confronted me.

Can a non-Jewish translator translate a writer's Jewishness?

If so, to what extent can a non-Jewish translator adjust, adapt or compromise in order to translate a sensibility and ethos different from her own?

Would it be possible for me to reach out to the implicit subtext that renders a book Jewish, besides the explicit themes?

Will I suffer from the anxiety of authenticity in my translation?

Throughout the 'rewriting' of the book, Sheela Rohekar and I met frequently, had lengthy conversations over the phone and exchanged emails several times. During these interactions and conversations, she opened up, and her stories flowed freely and spontaneously—the stories of her childhood, of her family, of her ancestor who was decorated as Khan Bahadur by the British, the essential characteristics of her community, the influence of the Hindu-Muslim culture on her community, their relationships with other communities, their sense of isolation in a majoritarian context, about characters who were fictional and yet based on real-life characters. Each visit, each telephonic conversation, was a revelation, a moment of disclosure and sharing, a bond of sisterhood, to go deeper into the nuances of her writing and to understand how vulnerable it is to be a Jew. She admitted that only when she kisses the holy Bible and touches the mezuzah the first thing in the morning does she feel that she is a Jew.

With each visit, our working relationship became friendlier, our conversations flowed freely over home-made snacks and tea. All through these exchanges, we negotiated meaning and discussed the chapters as they were written. It was important for me to know what each sentence actually meant in her sometimes dense narration. It was also important to maintain a dialogic relationship between past and present and to weave a thread of continuity into the narrative, which spans multiple timeframes and locations. I tried to infuse the community's Jewishness into English through literal and metaphorical translation, and the writer supported my efforts. At times, I found it quite daunting to match her style, which was experimental—with fragmented sentences, flashbacks, commingling of past and present, her Marathi-Gujarati flavoured Hindi and a profound existential angst evident in her characters.

One of the most crucial aspects of literary translation can be the translator's relationship with the source text (Source Language) writer. Often, translators and authors forge a lasting friendship. Therefore, it is important for the translator 'to choose carefully and select an author with whom there is a sense of empathy…"a sympathetic bond". They cease to exist as separate entities and become one.'* In my case, I shared a 'sense of empathy' with Sheela Rohekar when I started off, and now I share a unique bond of friendship with her. However, during our collaboration as author and translator, although she helped me in getting the contextual and cultural

---

*Bassnett, Susan. 'The Meek or the Mighty: Reapprising the Goal of the Translator', *Translation, Power, Subversion*, ed. Román and M. Carmen-África Vidal, (Cleavedon: Multilingual Matters Ltd., 1996)

connotations right, she trusted me and maintained a healthy 'critical distance' from my rendition of Miss Samuel's life journey.

A great translator from Germany, Ralph Manheim, once famously said that translators are like actors who speak the lines as the author would, if the author could speak English. So, translation in Manheim's formulation is a kind of interpretive performance, bearing the same relationship with the original text as the actor with the script, or for that matter, a performing musician to the composition. How successful or unsuccessful I have been in this endeavour of 'interpretive performance' is for the readers to decide, but for me, this book was a meaningful journey, a journey beyond imaginary borders and of reaching out to others.

Madhu Singh
November 2024

Family Tree

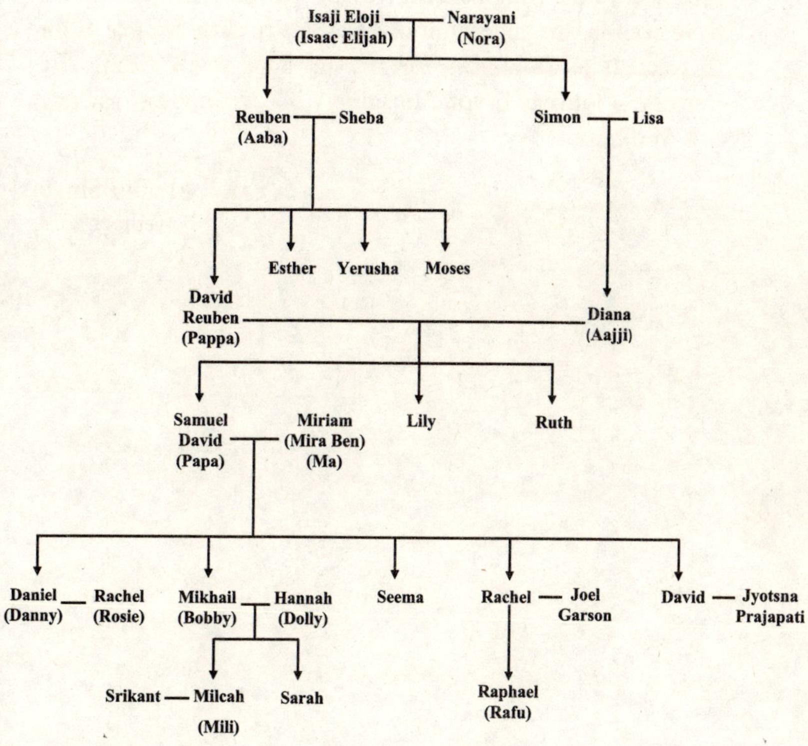
Isaji Eloji
(Isaac Elijah)
Narayani
(Nora)
Reuben
(Aaba)
Sheba
Simon
Lisa
Esther
Yerusha
Moses
David
Reuben
(Pappa)
Diana
(Aajji)
Samuel
David
(Papa)
Miriam
(Mira Ben)
(Ma)
Lily
Ruth
Daniel
(Danny)
Rachel
(Rosie)
Mikhail
(Bobby)
Hannah
(Dolly)
Seema
Rachel
Joel
Garson
David
Jyotsna
Prajapati
Srikant
Milcah
(Mili)
Sarah
Raphael
(Rafu)

Chapter 1

It was a somewhat old-looking house.

The house with many rooms and verandas, constructed in a middle-class colony, belonged to an old Parsi gentleman, Rustamji Daruwalla. The place was known as the Parsi Colony.

The streets were not pitched but paved with large slabs of hilly stones on which plied ikkas, tongas, bicycles, donkeys, horses, and occasionally a motor car.

At the outskirts of the qasbah, which was only a little way away from the house, stood a tall tamarind tree with thick foliage. Before the rains came and even during the first shower of the monsoon, the children of the colony would hang around the tree, greedy for its bright red-brown fruit. An old man used to sit under the tamarind tree, propped against its trunk, selling his ware of roasted gram and groundnut, tamarind, jujube, and peas spiked with star fruit from a tiny makeshift shop of gunny sacks and earthen pots.

There were plenty of toddy palm trees in the qasbah, and every evening, the old man would guzzle down toddy liquor. Then, in an inebriated state, he would sing film ditties mixed with devotional songs in his own *Binaca Geetmala* song series. The children of the colony would wait just for that moment to buy his ware. His intoxication always made him careless. They would give him one-paisa or two-paisa coins, or at the most, a one-anna brass coin, and he would give handfuls of roasted grams and groundnuts without weighing them.

Holding little Rachel's hand, Seema, too, would go and stand before him. 'Give me roasted grams for two paise.'

The old man would lift his eyes and say, 'Arre, Seema bitiya, and you, little doll! Aren't you the Sahib's daughters? Okay, you want some gram? This is for you.'

Seema and Rachel's frock pockets would overflow with the gram, some even spilling out of their fists, but the old man's generosity would not end.

'I have packed some for your brothers, too.'

Seema would put on an innocent face and say okay.

Everyone in the colony knew of the old man's drunken generosity and took full advantage of it. But the poor man never discovered why the kids flocked before his tiny shop only when the sun was down till the end of his life, when he died vomiting—because of the poison in the stale toddy—under the same tamarind tree.

Anyway, the toddy shouldn't be held responsible for his death. No, it was the ferocious ghost that had lived on the tamarind tree for centuries, fearing whom people avoided going near the tree after sunset.

A few days later, after his death, the old man's son—head ceremonially shaven—took his father's place, but by then, the crowd of children had disappeared.

One day, Seema had gone to his shop to buy some gram with her two-paisa coin. Rachel hadn't come along that day. The boy had measured some gram and put it in a packet. Then he had placed a handful of gram in her hand, said, 'Take this, too,' and had caught her outstretched hand and pressed it.

Seema never went to buy gram or groundnuts again.

Miss Seema Samuel has now forgotten the name of the old man. About fifty years have passed since that incident, but she can never quite forget the rented house where she lived when she was twelve.

That house is the first stopover in her memory because it was there that the grandson of their landlord, Rustamji, had arrived with his parents from Bombay to this small town—and had made a bet of a one-rupee silver coin with her.

His name was Sohrab. He was older than Seema by some four years or so.

It was holiday time. Ma had once sent her with Sohrab to fetch mangoes that had been kept to ripen in the upstairs room. Sohrab loved humming tunes. He had sung two lines each from different songs and then come to the song from the film *Jagriti*.

'I bet you can't sing this number correctly—*De di hamein azadi bina khadag, bina dhal.*'

'Of course I can. Do you want to bet?'

'Okay. The bet is for one silver rupee. Pappa gave me one to spend yesterday.'

Seema had sung perfectly as they sat on the veranda stairs in the fading sunlight of the evening.

He kept looking at her, for he had never thought that a small-town 'Gujju' girl like her could ever sing both the stanzas from the HMV record without stopping and that too in perfect Hindi!

'Okay, you win,' he had conceded.

'Now give me my silver coin,' Seema had extended her long, thin hand towards him.

Sohrab had pulled her close to him and had placed his trembling lips over her half-parted ones.

That was the first house stuck in her memory.

The house had some eighteen or twenty rooms, and in the last room on the ground floor, Ma kept her hens. There was a large sitting room with a big cabinet with glass top shelves, containing toys from all over the world and dolls with blinking eyes. Seema and Rachel would look at the dolls longingly, but they were kept under lock and key, and the keys were with the landlord.

Seema had heard from her father that Rustamji Daruwalla was an Anglicized gentleman who mostly stayed abroad. Then Papa had said something to Ma in English, which she couldn't understand completely, but she knew words such as 'another wife' from school. Papa said that Rustamji was a strict disciplinarian who disliked girls going out, so he had educated his younger daughter, Dhanmai, only till the seventh grade. Similarly, he believed that homes shouldn't have full-length mirrors because when girls grew up, they hovered around them all day. Seema was only too happy that their almirah was kept in the drawing room: how would she ever have seen her reflection in those small mirrors hung on the walls in Ma, Papa, and her brothers Danny and Bobby's rooms? It was her mother who would get her ready, turn her around and inspect her from head to toe, and then say, 'Now, it's okay,' and pack her off to school. Seema barely got to look at herself. However, it was also true that not only Seema's but even her mother's heart longed for such almirahs of her grandfather's, seen at her maternal uncles' place!

Watching her reflection in the full-length mirror in the fading light of the evening, she hadn't known at that time that the same fading light would also flow within her, that she would make her own plaits one day, and when no one was watching, she would look at herself in the mirror uninterrupted, till her eyes fell on her lips!

Sohrab had placed a square, brass two-anna coin in her palm and then laughed and said, 'This is the only money that I am left with; the rest I have squandered. Keep it safe. It will remind you of me.'

About four inches taller than Seema, Sohrab had gently rapped her on her head.

She had safely kept that coin for so many years!

Miss Seema Samuel smiles, lying in bed.

In the same large room was a six-sided marble table. An intricately carved plate was at the centre which had a ball-like object, slightly smaller than a football and light grey in colour, but quite heavy. Excitedly, Seema had pointed out to this object and said, 'Look! An ostrich egg!'

Sohrab had laughed till his stomach ached. 'You fool!' he had said, 'How can an ostrich lay such an enormous egg? Silly! This is a dinosaur egg. Bade Pappa had brought it from Africa.'

Seema did not know much about dinosaurs then. She didn't know that the way the dinosaurs had vanished from the earth, she, too, would turn sixty-eight one day and disappear from this world.

That was a long time ago, in Seema's childhood days, when her mother would send Rachel and her to count the hens in the last room of the house in the dark evening. 'Go and see if all the hens have returned to their coop.'

The backyard of the house was also large. There were three toilets at its farthest end—one for the tenants and the other for the landlord, made of concrete. The third, at a slight distance from these, had an iron door.

When she had come to this house, she wasn't 'grown-up' as they would say. She would be very surprised to see Dhanmai using the third toilet every four or five days in a month. But she had not seen Dhanmai's elder sister Tahmina ever coming down. She was kept locked in a room on the upper floor. The window of that room opened across to the window in Seema and Rachel's bedroom, a distance of about ten feet between them. While Rachel generally dozed off by evening, Seema could not help but peep out from her window to hear Tahmina yell and watch her activities in the dim light of the lantern.

Once, Danny had come looking for something in her room and had seen her peeping out. He had told Papa that Seema had been watching an almost-naked Tahmina who was standing before her window.

Seema never forgot that tight slap from Papa.

Miss Samuel turns over with great effort. It seems as if musical strings had become entangled and a discordant note had been struck at the first beat of a melody. She keeps her hand on her eyes. The warmth of her palm flows in through her eyelids but the echo of entangled strings trembled for long.

Miss Samuel's eyes turn towards the windows. The shadow that stands at the window slides fifty years back in time. In the pitch dark of the night, who was it that stood close to Seema's window? Whose whispers had awakened her from sleep? Who was gesticulating at her from the window? In such a big room, in the darkness of the blown-out lantern, the sight that twelve-year-old Seema had seen half-asleep, was it a dream? Or a memory? Or intuition?

Who's there? Papa? Danny? No, it was indeed Papa!

Seema had started having periods but Ma had asked her not to tell anyone and she continued to send her to the common toilet instead of the one with the iron door. Then she would flush it with plenty of water so that the woman who cleared the service latrine wouldn't know.

But water cannot cleanse some acts. Like what had happened that day. As always, Rachel had been too scared to enter the hen room in the dense inky darkness of the evening. She feared that a hen would flutter and perch on her head or shoulder and drop a lot of poop on it out of fear. Naturally, a hen *would* perch on her head as it was small and couldn't fly too high!

In this confusion, scared and sleepy Rachel had dropped

the burning candle right on the back of a fluttering hen. The poor hen had started running in circles! And the fire had swept the other hens, packed close to each other, also into its flames.

Two girls in a circle of fire and their cries—

'Ma!'

Ma had come. She had doused the fire on the hens with her hand and by thrashing them with a cloth. The fire had been put out but the smoke remained.

The smoke had suffocated the room.

When Rachel left, the same smoke had filled the eyes of Ma and Papa. Bobby had closed his eyes. Danny had remained indifferent.

Acrid smoke burns the eyes.

It changes perception.

But its smell burrows within.

The stiff and tired face of Rachel, who was lying on the table, had slowly relaxed, then it had become lifeless and indifferent.

'When inflammable objects don't burn properly or are wet, even then, smoke comes out of them,' thinks Miss Seema Samuel with a bitter smile, turning in her bed. Ma hadn't been able to bear the acrid smell of smoke.

But this happened much later. Then, when Ma looked very pretty, and Papa's shoulders hadn't sagged; when Danny, like a big brother, would keep a tight vigil over Seema's activities; and Bobby, though elder, would take Seema's side and counter Danny, then Seema had heard Tahmina crying out to every passer-by with her hands stretching out of the bars of her window, 'Rumi, Rumiiii!'

Towards the end of her life, even Ma had had started to howl from behind the bars, 'Rachel! Rachel! Bobby!' To Miss Seema Samuel, Ma and Tahmina seemed to fuse into each other. She smiles. How so many and such different things, incidents, and scenes seem to meld into each other, so that one tends to lose the thread of their differences. But some images embed themselves in the mind, not in the eyes, and chase you—all your life. The role of time in fusing images is not much but the trick of a fading memory. They light up in a flash!

That early morning, when the whole house had been asleep, Seema had awoken to the hissing sound of drawn breath. Before the window stood Tahmina, and standing between the two houses was the servant, Ramu. The fly of his shorts was open, and his right hand was stuck inside. He was trying to 'show' something to Tahmina, and she was breathing heavily.

Seeing Seema, he had also turned towards her, winked at her and pointed at his hand. Seema had frozen with fear. Standing at the crossroads of adolescence, she didn't know what to do. By that time, Ramu had unbuttoned his fly; he whistled and pissed in full public view, standing between the two houses. Tahmina had clung to the window bars and laughed but Seema had suffered from such a strange feeling of guilt that she had flopped down on the floor and cried.

Seema could have forgotten this spot of memory among all the other left-behind faded blobs of time, but whenever she saw a familiar pile of tiny stones in a corner near the window of Rachel's and her room, she remembered Ramu.

Miss Seema Samuel opens her eyes and looks at the room. Perhaps it is past midnight. The brightness streaming through the window and the skylight has unrolled over the darkness.

Sohrab had come many days before Tahmina committed suicide by hanging herself from the ventilator. Seema had asked him why Tahmina, his aunt, wasn't allowed to come downstairs.

Sohrab had remained quiet for long and then said, 'She's mad! Pappa doesn't come here because of her; Granny cries and insists that she should be taken to Bombay. My Mama doesn't like anyone.' Then he had become quiet. Seema, too, kept quiet. Then, as if sharing a secret, he had whispered to Seema, 'I also don't like her at all. You know, whenever I go to meet her, she hugs me so tightly that I suffocate. And the number of kisses she plants on my face!'

Sometimes, Rafu, Raphael—Rachel's son—too, would hug Seema like that. It would make her breathless. He was an adult now and had a great deal of strength. Seema would pretend to cry so that he released her. Then, with the innocent surprise of a child, he would ask, 'Why do you cry, Mama?'

Could Seema ever answer him or herself?

Many actions have completely absurd answers. After Bobby's death, Seema's mother had almost slipped into a quagmire. How could her educated and sensible mother sink so deep into depression? Who could ever pull her out of that sinking mire?

By that time, Seema had grown up. She was thirty or thirty-two. Her tender dreams were made of little houses, clouds, flames of fire, and sometimes, a snatch of melody. But in the wilderness of Ma's heart, they staggered and got lost, like Sohrab's two-paisa brass coin had been lost in the backyard at home. Seema had cried her heart out at that time. Papa had given her a four-anna coin, but Seema had thrown it away—'How does one know where the coin got lost in this huge yard?' Bobby had found the coin and given it to her, 'Here! Take your coin.'

'Seema, didn't Sohrab give it to you?' Rachel had asked while looking for it.

Seema was self-conscious, 'Silly, we have already found it. What are you searching for now in the dust?'

Six-year-old Rachel had swung Seema around and said, 'I like Sohrab very much. When I am big—as big as Dhanmai—I will make Sohrab "papa".'

Little, foolish girl, Rachel! She thought papa and husband were the same. Seema and Bobby had laughed. But Rachel was on the verge of crying.

That was how she was; pretty but foolish. Papa and Diana Aajji loved her very much. Aajji would copy her and behave like a kid. Ma would get irritated when she saw this—'Old people should teach small children, but look at her spoiling the child by behaving like a child herself. She tells her ghost stories, which will make her timid and meek.'

Faint-hearted Rachel. She saw a ghost in every nook and cranny. Every rustling leaf turned into a thief. As she grew up, that fear added an unknown mystery to her charming face and made her look even prettier. But the things she did remained as silly and childish as before. She couldn't pedal the bicycle forwards: she could only move the wheels in reverse. Seema learnt to ride with a pillion, but Rachel kept pedalling the wrong way. She would be found crying on the chabutra next door, saying that she had lost her home. She would often doze off while brushing her teeth, a finger still in her mouth. She would be given a front bench in class because of Papa's status, but she remained a laggard in studies.

Papa always took his timid daughter's side. Danny made fun of his younger sister.

But Bobby looked after Rachel.

Seema would get annoyed with Rachel when she imitated her. Ma would be irritated by her stupidity and clumsiness. 'Uff! Why didn't you tuck your frock properly? See, there are dirty spots all over! This girl of mine can't even cross a puddle without soiling her dress!'

And yet, this same girl crossed over that huge abyss of

life so easily. Standing on this side of the abyss, Ma and Papa kept calling out to her. But Rachel went away with that same pretty but foolish face of hers.

Papa, Samuel David, Under Secretary. Short-tempered, egotist and religious. Incapable of hearing a word against Judaism. After Rachel died, he would just sit and brood. When Rafu cried to be nursed, he would push the door open and rush down the sixty stairs. Perhaps the somewhat dry and outspoken Samuel David never forgave Rachel till the end. But he kept this fact to himself. He suffered but never mentioned it.

A light shiver crosses Miss Samuel's heart. She remembers Samuel David's last days, when he was losing control over his sternness and emotions. He would call out to Rafu, 'Raafuuu! Come, let's play hide-and-seek.' He would get up unsteadily and search for Bobby. He would curse Danny and Rosie when he saw them around, and get irritated with Ma. He would utter soothing words to Rachel: 'Don't cry, Rachel! Come and sit with me.' He would ask for pieces of meat from his mother, close his ears to the cacophony of Mili and Sarah, and then crouch in fear, even in the absence of Jyotsna Prajapati, chanting the name of David: 'David, David, David.'

Then, the house became completely empty and Seema would sit at his bedside.

Casting aside the thick cloak of sadness, Miss Seema Samuel removes her blanket and looks out of the window. In the far horizon, the signs of light were glimmering. The hilltops peeped inside through the bars of the window.

Get up, Seema, see the new dawn that has broken. Look, the brightness is about to spread out through the fluttering wings among the dense trees. Whenever you open your eyes, you should be awake.

As she slides her feet into the slippers under the bed, who knows how the words of the old song '*De di hamein azadi bina khadag, bina dhal...*' slip out. Yes, Miss Samuel mutters to herself, 'Freedom to increase inflation, corruption, and terrorism, without shield, without armour.'

I smile. *Miss Samuel, hear how your voice trembles! Only I hear your murmurings. Yes, it was all a long time ago—maybe fifty or fifty-two years ago.*

Outside, Raghu is calling everyone out for tea.

Chapter 2

As I walk, my eyes fall on the pathway.

The mountain track slopes. At the next bend, it goes down and then goes up. Wildflowers bloom all around. The green of the mountains looks dull in the last rays of the sun.

In the hushed silence of the mountainside, I move on.

The feeling that he is following me freezes my legs for a split second. I start walking faster but I feel that he is walking almost with me. In that haze of unease, I carry on.

Will you keep quiet like this all the way?

The silence of the lonely pathway seems restless. It's just me and my footfalls. The mist has started enveloping the valleys. The whisper of the winter chill matches step with it. I slip my hands in the cardigan's pockets and walk faster. I see Parisar on the flatland before me, with a red-tiled roof, silent.

Loneliness at this age hurts a lot, he whispers into my ears.

My face flushes with anger—loneliness has been with me all my life. His face dims, and I increase my speed. I think I hear him breathing heavily as he follows me.

Then, it is all quiet. I look around. He is nowhere. I feel my speed slacken; I am a little breathless, too, because of the steep climb. My footsteps shorten. I see the pathway climb up. Just a little more to climb. Then I feel him overtake me and murmur sadly, *Since when have you started walking behind, like Rafu?*

The sorrow on his face is soon replaced by a touch of humour, though the question still hangs. Ignoring it, I walk past. But he shoots another salvo, as though not accepting defeat. *It seems you're tired now, isn't it?*

My head throbs like hammer beats. Something is being crushed inside. Something is waiting to explode at any moment. My mind escapes far away; then, as though tired, it comes back, stands before me and asks, *Are you tired*?

'Maybe,' I murmur, and then I keep to myself.

Before me stands the Parisar gate. Rama Aajji sits on a chair in front of her room and waves at me to come. I sit down breathlessly on the stairs before her and look out at the courtyard. He isn't there anymore.

'Has he left?' asks Rama Aajji with a knowing smile.

I look at her.

'How long did he walk with you?' she asks me again. I am sad.

Holding the reins of its last rays, the sun is about to sink into the valley. I watch the sky turn saffron. Then, slowly, the lighter shades of the sky change into grey. A thin layer of mist now swathes the entire valley.

While watching the slowly receding hills, I remember the half-shut windows of our apartment on the third floor, from where he used to look out and wave goodbye to David and me. His old and frail right hand raised in blessing, his thick, aged lips gently murmuring Psalms. All these have remained etched in my memory. In the colony, when I would turn around to see from the pavement, it would seem that he was smiling. But that may also have been a half-finished gesture of sorrow. How much could one see of the semi-darkness of the third-floor window in the dazzling light of day?

He was Samuel David, my father.

A long time has passed since this incident. It is 2003.

America has browbeaten Iraq into submission. The year-long mourning period of the Gujarat carnage and two years of that earthquake are over. Gujarat welcomed the rainbow dreams of Holi, even if with a heavy heart, because life springs from the cracks and crevices of barren corners, too. I have safely kept the pictures of the Holi celebration from the local newspapers.

I come from Amdavad*.

I sit on a stone bench in the lawn. It is the smaller lawn. On the other side is a bigger, sprawling one. The residents of the campus who had been sitting on the chairs and benches are now leaving. The buds of the parijat flowers have burst open and their scent is spreading.

The campus where I live is surrounded by hills. There is silence, always. I can see residents of my age, some even older, shuffle from one room to another.

Constructed at a distance of two hours from Pune, all stories seem to end up here, in this building. Having crossed sixty-three, I, the third child of my parents, sit on the stone bench that is slowly turning cold and wonder if I, too, will have a long life like my father.

It's getting chilly.

A little brown bird has strayed away from the lengthening shadows of the night and perched at some distance from me. Her long tail rhythmically bobs up and down. Perhaps she hasn't noticed me. A tiny movement of my head scares her, and she flits away and hides in the dense Chandni flower bush behind me. Its leaves rustle in the breeze and touch my neck and shoulders.

---

*The Gujarati pronunciation of the name of the city of Ahmedabad.

'They sting. No, Nanu, Rafu is scared!' A frightened Rafu hid behind Seema. He shivered and cried. He never dared to touch leaves, branches, hanging flowers, or creepers. 'They bite me;they become angry with me and ask, "Why did you touch?"' He was too young—much younger than his age; around six or seven years old, but his mental age was that of a two- or three-year-old.

Back then, they lived in Apartment B-7 on the third floor of Gitanjali Society. They were Papa-Ma, Rafu and Seema's younger brother, David, who was named after his grandfather.

Every evening, Seema would take Rafu to the triangular park at the street corner in the society. Papa often came along. As soon as they reached the park, he would hold Rafu's hand and force him to run faster. But every time, Rafu would stumble and fall and cry, all sprawled out on the ground. Papa would cover his mouth. 'Shut up. You idiot!'

His eyes brimming with big unshed tears, Rafu would look at him helplessly and stammer. His choked voice would swallow the words, and he would lisp, 'No, Nanu! Rafu small. He fall. He hurt.'

Sitting on a green patch and watching this sight, Seema would rush to stop Rafu from crying.

Papa would look at her with disapproval and turn away to walk on the track. Seema knew he would try to fulfil his wish again.

As Seema walked slowly with Rafu, Papa would come grumbling after them, grab his hand and drag him on.

'Come Rafu, let's run. Run!'

Staggered by fear and force, Rafu would sit down. Annoyed, Papa would try to pull him up, 'Get up, veda—silly. Run. We'll go under that pergola and come back.'

Rafu howled, 'Mama, Mamaaa! Nako. No, the leaves will bite me.'

Samuel David shook his shoulder roughly. 'Do leaves ever bite? See, I have crushed them in my hand. Did they bite me?'

Rafu would try to wring his hand free and say, 'Nako, no, Nanu. I want to go to Mama. They will bite.'

Snatching his hand away from Papa's, Seema could hardly hide her anger. 'Why are you so adamant to prove him normal, Papa?' Papa would turn away, his face flushed.

Teary-eyed Rafu would watch him go till he was at a distance, and then, his face radiating with his sweet, crooked smile, say, 'Gele! He's gone!' As he walked with Seema, he would punch the air with his good right hand with great joy. Trying to outrun Seema, he would drag his feet faster, his left hand, bent from the elbow by birth, seeming to outrun him.

Papa must have been in his early sixties at the time. He had retired some four years ago. His anger and resentment over the incident in 1972 or '73 still creep through my bones sometimes and peep out of my old and knotty fingers to ruffle the leaves on this quiet campus.

'Chavte. They bite,' Rafu would say. He couldn't speak Marathi correctly. He used feminine verbs for himself, just as Seema did. He would sound certain words incorrectly, using 'r' for 'd' and the 'l' instead of 'r'. Everyone would laugh, and he laughed too.

'Leaves sting…,' Rafu would say.

For Diana Aajji, age stung. A woman's long and lonely life gnaws at her joys and memories. Shrinking bones open pores through which desires and happiness seep out, only her fading eyesight witnessing her loneliness.

Diana Aajji. She would lie beside Seema at night and mutter in the darkness.

Now, when I think about it, both Rafu and Diana seem

to complement each other—one a mentally challenged child, and the other, my father Mr Samuel David's mother, Diana.

For Rafu, thirty-one-year-old Seema was like his mother. All her worries and concerns revolved around him. Had he not been there in her life, would she have been different or somewhere else? It's difficult to say. Human nature is not only ambiguous because of the innumerable experiences, pressures, thoughts, and samskaras, but it is also mysterious. Often, we choose circumstances and paths that would likely confuse us. It is useless to call it destiny.

It's a different matter that Rafu couldn't stay much longer with Seema in his journey of life. And when he left Seema, he was a young man of twenty-five whose mental capabilities were that of a five-year-old child. He couldn't even wear his pyjamas or trousers properly. While giving him baths, Seema had to make him hold a bar of soap or a mug, or else his hand would roam around his intimate places and play with that thumb-sized body part. Managing his daily routine was a tremendous challenge for Seema, but she kept a straight face and diverted his attention by chatting with him. She probably wanted to take no notice of it because, at her age, a woman's body is youthful and aches for no reason.

❁

Feeling restless, I look up. Sudha Akka was coming towards me. She sits at a little distance from me, lost in thought. Such losing of oneself is not painful. In fact, it soothes like a balm. How vulnerable such lonely people would otherwise look when hurt!

No one knows such lonely and lost people. Loneliness takes away colour, warmth and joy. Empty eyes and the darkness of the deep lake are the last refuge of their bundle of memories.

I pull myself closer to Akka. Curiosity returns to her face and she says, 'What's been cooked today; any idea?'

I check the laughter that has sneaked in on my face and say, 'What else except lauki curry, chapati, khichdi, a dry cauliflower side dish and sweet raita?'

A feeling of disinterest settles on her face. 'This was cooked two days ago. Why can't they give us green peas for a change?'

I gently hold her hand and say, 'Akka, our digestion is not like before. Dinner should be light. Other members also have problems with their teeth. And then, Baba Ramdev's advice is that lauki strengthens the heart.'

She laughs instantly. Then she turns to me and says, 'Is there still something left within to be strengthened?'

When she smiles, the gap created by two missing front teeth reminds me of Rafu when he was seven or eight years old. He had once slipped and lost his two wobbly front teeth.

'Mama! Rafu fell. His teeth!' He howled and pointed at his teeth lying on the ground and cried again, but he was also scared of the fallen teeth.

Seema picked up the loose teeth, hugged him and said, 'Okay, don't you cry now. All kids lose their teeth. Now Rafu will have brand new teeth.'

'But you haven't lost any? Shall I take yours out, Mama?' He clenched his fist to knock out her teeth.

Seema had broken a sweat trying to loosen his fist. Then she was afraid that he might tighten his fist again and suddenly punch her face and knock out her teeth. Even if he couldn't break them, they might have got loose. Nature had been too generous in giving him strength.

Seema distracted his attention by talking to him.

'Kids lose their teeth, beta; big people also lose their teeth, but when they are old.'

'Who is a kid, Mama?' he asked after thinking for a moment.

'One who is younger in age and who doesn't know how to do his own work, like you, Himanshu, Mitali. But Nanu and Nani's lost teeth will never come back.'

'Why?'

'Because they have become old.'

'What is growing old, Mama?'

Seema was in a fix. She didn't know what to say to this special child.

Trying to explain, she said, 'Just as Nani is old, Himanshu's Dada, Sandhya's Nani, the vegetable seller, Baba, who comes in the evening—all these people are old.'

He snuggled close to Seema. Then, he held her shoulder, touched her cheeks, and asked, 'But Mama, how did Nani become old?'

A sharp pain arose within Seema. She didn't have a quick answer. She thought for a while and said slowly, 'Son, Nani has lived for many years, so she is now worn out. This is growing old. See, your shirt is so new. So, a child is like a new shirt, but when its colour fades, you can say it has become old.'

Seema was disturbed when she said this.

'Even Nanabapu is old?' he whispered in her ears.

Seema wanted to say that he wasn't, but then how could she make a distinction between mother and father to this differently abled child? So, drawing a deep breath, she said yes.

'And are you old, Mama?' he smiled.

Seema touched the tiny dimples in his cheeks, 'You naughty boy! Do I look old to you? Veda! Stupid!'

He became a little sad. 'Why does everyone call me veda, Mama?'

Seema was alarmed. She hugged Rafu and said, 'No, dear! My Rafu is very bright, very intelligent. Aren't you, Rafu?'

Rafu clung to Seema's neck for a while. Taking him in her

lap, she said, 'You know, Rafu, your smile looks sweeter after losing your teeth.'

He clapped happily and hung around her neck, and asked, 'Mama, do I now look like you?'

'Yes, my dear! Just like me,' Seema said with a big smile.

'Then why don't you make me wear a sari?' he asked, pretending to be angry.

Seema laughed loudly, 'Are you a girl?'

'Yes, Mama, I am,' he said innocently.

'Silly! Girls have long hair, they make plaits and buns, they wear earrings, their bangles jingle on their hands, they apply kajal to their eyes, and—'

'And they have big bulges on their chest, like yours…isn't it, Mama?' Rafu finished her sentence.

Those curves on her chest! Rachel's beauty had sprung from her well-endowed, shapely body. Charming and attractive but clumsy, she wasn't conscious of her curves at all. Dressed in loose-fitting clothes, Rachel looked all the more alluring. She tried to copy Seema so much that it irritated her.

And Seema? Does she still remember taking down the little mirror hanging on the bathroom wall, inspecting each part of her body and comparing herself to Rachel's beauty? Dim-witted Rachel! How could she ever copy Seema's shrewdness?

If only Danny or Ma didn't have to always correct her manners and threaten her to behave properly. If only she knew that she was very pretty and men grow prickly pears in their eyes for women. Their desires and greed turn into beastly wolves which pounce upon their victims on lonely alleys. Oh, how sharp were Master Jamaal's fangs! If only Rachel knew that caution and cunning is necessary for survival, else the game is over.

If only Rachel could have followed Seema in all these things, Ma wouldn't have cried her heart out.

'What are you thinking, looking at my toothless face?' Sudha Akka, with her sweet, smiling face, stands before me.

I become conscious of her presence. 'No, Akka, I had wandered into the past. And don't worry, even my face will be toothless very soon. Has anyone been able to stop this process?'

'Okay, keep sitting. I feel a little cold.' With that, she wraps herself in her shawl and leaves.

❁

When people become old, they tend to become quieter. They are also lost. Even Ma had become quieter. Gradually, names, places and objects started fading from her memory. She would mistake Seema for Rachel and confuse David with Bobby. She would shrivel in the presence of Danny and Rosie. Was there anything left of her when Danny and Rosie left for America?

Before they left, Danny and Rosie had limited their interaction with other family members. With Papa, they often had heated discussions. Seema looked for a way to keep Rafu occupied else he would rattle the chain bolt on Danny's room and run away. Rosie would come out, shake him, and yell, 'You mad boy!'

Rafu would howl.

This would make Rosie shriek even more.

Danny would try to pacify his wife. Ma would press her ears with her hands and wail, 'Bobby, Bobby, Bobby!'

Papa would bang on the main door.

David would chew his nails nervously as he stood on the balcony.

How could Seema, who found support in this extremely challenged boy, ever forget?

But Seema had forgotten Tahmina. Actually, it was the seventh birthday of Sohrab's sister, Firoza. At home, women were busy cooking dhansaak and patra ni machhi. The entire Parsi Colony had been invited for the occasion.

The evening was consumed by dance and drink. Everyone danced—Papa and Dhanmai, Dhanmai and Danny, Sohrab's Papa as well as Ma, who was dragged to the floor, Jalu, Firoza and Rachel, men from the colony, and Seema, who was taught the dance steps by young men.

'Gori, gori, O banki chhori, kabhi meri gali aaya karo...'

Firoza, Rachel and the other children ran around and enjoyed. Seema's face was flushed and her feet danced. She felt her hot earlobes melt and drip. How she wished the song continued ceaselessly and Sohrab kept looking at her and smiling this way.

Just then, Tahmina's hollering cry was heard: 'Bastards! Don't you know that this mother of yours is hungry, and you're dancing!' Smiles, banter and noise—all were absorbed by the earth. Everyone heard the curses and abuses.

'May you turn to dust, may you be ruined, may your mouth crawl with worms, may your mother die!'

The magic disappeared.

Moments of magic are short-lived and sublime, for their trance suddenly breaks, and then we hesitate at the threshold of hard reality. All colour fades from our lives.

The white Jews, as far as they could remember, had no ancestors who had married outside their community. Rosie, the daughter of a white Jew, spoilt the charm of B-7, Gitanjali Society, much like Tahmina. And though Tahmina could be forgiven, for she had climbed the steps of insanity, Rosie could not be forgiven for destroying the peace and joy of Samuel David's home forever.

Suffering a series of emotional setbacks, Ma, too, had reached the last threshold of a deep abyss.

Chapter 3

'Listen! Today, we will have halwa for the evening tea!' Sudha Akka says as soon as she enters the room. Her face seems to carry the aroma of delicious halwa. Excitedly, she comes quickly and stands before me.

I smile and say okay and share her joy. 'Is it a fast today?'

'No, dear, you know what? Today is Sakhu Tai's birthday. When I got a whiff of semolina being roasted for halwa, I went out quickly and peeped into the kitchen,' Sudha Akka tells me. Akka's dim eyes twinkle with excitement.

'It would have been so good if we had two-three Sakhu Tais, isn't it? Then their birthdays would have come one after the other, and my dear Akka could keep getting her fill of her favourite halwa.' I tease as I motion her to sit with me.

'When Bharat and Shatrughan were kids, I cooked a sweet dish every day, or else they would just not have their food. *He*,' she says, referring to her husband, 'too, had a sweet tooth. Then he passed away, Bharat also went to Canada. How would his wife Nancy ever know what our halwa is? Shatrughan's wife Neerja made delicious halwa—in desi ghee with cashew nuts, raisins, cardamom. But she would tell me, "Your stomach will get upset," and give me only two spoonfuls. The two elder sons had already left home.'

Her toothless face seems to crumble. Her eyes blink back

unshed tears as she absentmindedly rubs her hand on her sari. I see her lips quivering.

To divert her mind from that tense moment, I assured her that when I visited Pune next, I would get her the delicious halwa that my sister-in-law, Dolly, made.

She smiles, 'Who knows, by then, the desire may die!'

Anxious on hearing this, I tell her that desires never die, only their impulse diminishes, making them less intense and thus suppressing our feelings.

'Do you think our feelings could be suppressed?' Akka asks at once.

I didn't have an answer.

'You still have a long way to go to become old like me,' she grins broadly and gets up from the chair.

I can't stop myself, 'You still keep track of age, Akka?'

A strange emotion touches her eyes…as if something had been left behind…as if she craved to grasp something…as if she tried to forget something that she suddenly remembered! She walks slowly to the door and then almost stops, 'Other than these remaining days of life, what is left in this old bag of bones, my dear?'

She stands outside the room for a moment. As she closes the door, she looks at me and asks, 'Do you write about those unfulfilled days when you shut yourself in your room for hours?'

The doors close behind Akka.

I ask myself, did everything remain unfulfilled in my life? Or do desires remain unfulfilled only if there are too many? Is there fault in our concerns…love…feelings? Our attitude hardly matures with time. Do our frustrations, fears, cunning, and selfishness remind us of our inadequacies? Even worse, we women hardly open the doors of our minds to let in the whirlwinds of fresh air, falling leaves, springing sprouts, and sparkling light!

Do the circles of darkness and light that terrify, and are themselves terrified, leave us to linger in sadness?

Sudha Akka never talks about her past. This attitude is quite different from that of men. Men never want their illustrious lives to be forgotten, so they pretend to live in that perfect past and remember: *Then, I was the head of the department and I had great clout at the university...*

Women pretend to forget their family and household, their competence, intelligence, and sacrifice, and justify the insult of being abandoned by their near and dear ones in their heart of hearts and become another Rama Aajji, Sudha Akka, or Ashalata Ghorpade. Some continue to remain like Mrs Chitnis or Madam Marie, who neither forgot their past, nor their damaged dignity, and those who break become Vimla Shinde.

The last call for dinner is over. As I come out of the room, I hear laughter and talking in Vimla's room. Like me, the rest of the inmates are busy with their work and ignore it. Meandering in the past, Vimla plays and laughs with her absent children. She doesn't even know that her children, now parents of grown-up children, will soon admit her into a good mental hospital and finish off their last duty.

Oh, this hourglass of relationships! A dense bottom and a tapering neck. Only a grain of sand falls through it. The importance of relationships is over.

'Where is the free time, Ma, to pile up all that rubbish in my mind? Why don't you accept that your time is over now? You don't have anything to do, nor do you have prayers and religious observances to occupy your time. So you focus all your attention on poor Mamta. The truth is that you could never accept another woman, Ma.'

Mrs Chitnis's only son had said these words out of irritation when she had reproached her daughter-in-law for not remembering to get a Marquez book from her office library for more than a week. 'How do you only forget to bring *my* book, Mamta?'

The very next month, Mrs Chitnis had arrived at Parisar. Mrs Chitnis, though apparently quiet, simmers within.

While returning from the kitchen, I find her door open and see her absorbed in a recorded speech by George Bush on TV. George Bush's warning words create a fine web of echoes. It seems as though he had turned into a spider and was crawling towards Saddam Hussain, who was caught in its web. Beware! A single movement of yours has sent vibrations down the filaments of the web, and the spider will now swathe you into a strong bobbin to eat you up later!

She calls me to her room, 'Why do you want to sleep so early? Come and sit here. It's such a strange scene, Miss Samuel. The world watches this exciting display of terror, pain, helplessness, violence and loot every moment of its life. The oppression of Iraq is not a part of this exciting game at all…it is more about Bush's heroism and the media reports. Just the way the society has become…selfish and indifferent.'

Disturbed, she looks around for the remote and switches the TV off.

'Actually, the present generation has forgotten its naturalness. There's a tough fight to bring in more and more of artificial colour from outside. If they are asked, tell us the colour of love, they will say the mixture of egoism, selfishness, shrewdness and sensation is love. Their colours have no space for empathy, duty and decorum and neither do they want these.

'So, Miss Samuel, when the entire world is shrinking fast, nations, families and homes are bound to shrink! People like us, who live in this world of muddled up fake colours, have been chucked out.'

Mrs Chitnis's eyes, framed in spectacles, stare at the dark screen of the TV for long.

Then, she looks at me and asks in a stable voice, 'I often wonder if dying is that difficult, Miss Samuel?'

I place my hand on her delicate hand and pat it gently before coming out of her room.

My room is next to hers. An earthen pitcher of water is kept next to the railing in the veranda. I drink some water and stand holding the railing for some time. The cool rays of the moon rest on the quiet lawn, and the trees stare unblinkingly.

Parisar is quiet, and I stand in the vacant veranda...

The sudden noise of the night insects makes me conscious, and I return to my room.

The bed is as cool and quiet as the night.

By seven or eight in the evening, silence hovers around Parisar. Silence...crouching inside hearts and stalking outside! In a way, it's good...because no one is left with any courage to perceive the oddities, within or without.

Twenty old women living in twenty rooms, growing older day by day. They close the doors, windows and crevices of their past in the lengthening shadows of the night. Outside, it is dark...inside, there is an empty void.

I turn restlessly in bed. On this side is a white wall. On the whitewashed wall are scrawled in big, bold letters in charcoal—*Pappa, both the school half-pants have worn out on the back. Please get another stitched for me.*

❁

David Reuben's thick sideburns trembled with anger. He came out quickly from the bathroom and hollered as he reached the well in the courtyard.

'Diana! Diana! Where is that bastard son of yours, your darling? That swine has no sense at all. How dare he spoil the white walls by writing on them? Bring my cane; if I don't skin his back, my name is not David Reuben.'

Diana quickly came out from the rear door of the kitchen. Her face had collapsed. Seeing her husband's fuming face, she shrank. The husband took water from the bucket kept at the edge of the well and washed his hands with soap. So enraged was he that he had forgotten to close the tin door of the toilet. As a result, a foul stench had spread around the courtyard in the rising heat. Handing the towel to her husband, Diana quickly went to the other end of the courtyard and locked the door.

Smiling uneasily, she came closer to her husband and whispered, 'Please, speak softly; the boy is a grown-up now.'

David Reuben shouted hoarsely, 'He's grown up, that's why his head is stuffed with shit. You bitch, it's because of you that he's become a foul-tempered beast. How dare he do this!'

Unintelligible words came from Diana's fallen face, 'No, no, David…his pants have actually worn out. I have mended them twice or thrice, but they tear up from the same place.

'He is afraid of you; that's why he wrote on the bathroom wall…just a little while ago. I will get the wall cleaned. I have told you a number of times about this, but at night, you are drunk, so you agree, but by morning you have forgotten everything. Please buy me some khaki cloth.'

'Will the money come from your father? Or your miserly brothers? Only a few months back, I got him half-pants stitched, but does this idiot, who is now in matric, know anything other than frolicking on the slides with young children?

'Where is that bastard, Sam? Must be hiding somewhere at your prompting! After I return in the evening, I will give him a thorough dressing-down.'

Samuel hid behind the door in the dark storeroom, holding his breath. Sam's Pappa, David Reuben, grumbled for some time and then, stamping his feet, went inside the house. After guzzling down an omelette of two eggs and a glass of milk, he instructed Diana to keep two lamps of coconut oil ready for the evening Sabbath prayer. 'Cook chicken, kebabs and apricot pudding for dinner.'

Diana listened to her husband's instructions attentively and handed him his hat, the baton with a golden handle, and pocket watch. David Reuben walked towards the veranda, called out once more for Sam, and climbed down the stairs.

Sam heard the click of the heel and a crisp salute from behind the door; then he heard the rattling of the receding tonga; only then did he peep out of the room.

It was quiet outside. The house seemed relaxed. Ma was busy working. The chicken stewed in a pot on a charcoal stove, releasing a delicious aroma. On the sawdust stove, brinjals were being roasted. It was Friday. Sabbath would begin from sundown. Pappa would place floating cotton wicks in glasses of oil, and then all the family members, with their heads covered, would raise their hands towards the holy light and chant the Hebrew prayer, '*Barukh ata Adonai Eloheinu, melekh ha'olam...*' (Blessed are You, Lord our God, King of the universe...) 'Amen!' Touching each other's hand with their right hand, they would kiss and greet each other, 'Shabbath Shalom!' (Sabbath of peace!)

The aroma of the chicken being cooked tempted Sam. Nuzzling up lovingly against his mother, he demanded a few pieces.

'Let me see how it tastes...otherwise, Pappa will bang his plate at night.'

Diana glared at him, but she couldn't overlook the greed lingering on his face. Serving two pieces of meat in a brass bowl, she said, 'Eat quickly and tell me how it tastes; the girls may come in any moment, and I will have to give them, too.

Don't you know what a tantrum your Pappa throws if he gets lesser than he wants to eat!'

Sitting before his mother and eating, Sam got irritated and said, 'Why don't you buy more then? How little you give Lily and Ruth. On Saturdays, they only get the leftover gravy because it being a Saturday, Pappa won't let you cook, and we get to eat only leftovers from the night before.'

Diana watched Sam eating. With a touch of embarrassment and helplessness, she said, 'Your Pappa has told me to serve the smallest portions of meat and fish to the girls. Don't you know this?' Sam didn't meet her eyes.

Sam will never forget that taste of the meat he had hurriedly gobbled down. He knew that Pappa got the largest share because he was the head of the house, the earning member. When he grew up, he, too, would look after his household and, like Pappa, he would get the largest portion. If he had daughters, he too, would not give them a rich diet because he knew now how girls grew up too fast on such a diet and later indulged in scandalous acts, bringing dishonour to the family.

Miss Seema Samuel remembers Papa's long Jewish nose, which Rachel had disgraced in one quick stroke. She also remembers Tahmina's hanging body.

Seema had even seen her father shoving and pushing Dhanmai. But thirteen-year-old Seema couldn't understand why Papa was so frustrated when Dhamnai, with whom he played badminton every evening, had run away with Ramu before her father had returned after Tahmina's death. And why had he stopped Seema from playing with the colony's boys? 'I will break your legs if you go out. These girls! Nobody knows when they will disgrace us!'

Miss Seema Samuel turns in her bed and smiles.

Girls and honour! Girls disgracing their families!

And boys, upholders of honour.

Papa's respect in the community was enhanced because his son Daniel (Danny) had become a doctor. Now, he sat with pride at the synagogue. As it is, there were not many people in the community of Papa's stature, and he was the first boy from the Jewish community of Amdavad to receive a degree from the Civil Hospital.

An event had been organized to felicitate Danny at the synagogue. Mr Abraham Pezarkar delivered a speech in English, but since there were not many people who understood English, he had to repeat the same thing in Gujarati because the low-class Israyels, and even others, mostly spoke Gujarati.

What the poor people in ordinary clothes understood was that Mr Samuel David's elder son had opened his own clinic at Relief Road.

By the second month, Danny was exhausted. 'Get more felicitations done. I had told you, the less the news spreads in our community the better, but then how could Papa show off his greatness? Now, I have to bear the brunt! Other signboards have the names of doctors such as Rama Jain, Arvind Trivedi, Saras Bhai Desai, and Jyoti Ben Pandya. Mine is the only signboard that stands out with a non-Hindu name—Dr Daniel Samuel. Neither do I have any links with the well-known doctors, nor does Papa know influential people.

'So, hardly anyone turns up at my clinic other than those who arrive with their troop in tow and say, "So, Danny, son, don't you recognize me?" Forget about the fee…they will even demand sample medicines. Imagine, Bade Mian is expecting a grandchild but wants a bottle of power tonic for strength and vitality for himself!

'And Ma, if, by any chance, I tell them discretely to

produce fewer children, they will raise their hands to the sky and say…"It's God's will that he has provided us with working hands. Otherwise, where is the land or property for us?"'

Ma tried to cool him down—'Forget it, son. They are our brethren, after all. The good Lord will make you prosperous… just wait and see; you will succeed. They will say that Danny became so successful! That he was the first boy of the Amdavad Jews who went to America for higher studies.'

Miss Seema Samuel imagines a ladder rising high in the air, the way a snake inflates its hood and rises. Sometimes, the snake quickly bites.

But David, her youngest brother, did not know this. Its poison changed him forever!

❁

I have become restless. I can hear the noise of flapping wings. I can hear a kind of whistling sound. At that moment, the door rattles loudly. 'Tai, sister, please come out fast.' I see Manda.

'Rama Aajji isn't feeling well. When I went to keep a glass of water in her room, I saw she had fallen on the floor. I somehow made her lie on the bed. She is delirious. Come quickly. I am going to call Sister Mary.'

Rama Aajji, with her silver-white braid of hair, is over eighty. She is cheerful and healthy for her age. She is diabetic, for which she takes precautions, and then there is the fenugreek-seed-soaked water and the Diabinil pills. After her bath, Aajji sings bhajan-kirtans before the deity of Vithoba in her room. Then, the rest of her day is filled with laughter and chatting! She has a sweet tooth, and if someone points that out to her, she makes a sour face and says, 'Don't I take pills every day? At this wretched age, as it is, one eats less and then one has to take precautions! I tell you, if one has to die, one should eat and die rather than die hungry. And girls, listen! Our bodies lost their desires with age, and our hearts dried up because of our own near and dear; now, at least don't be after what the tongue desires.'

Mary Varghese and I are over sixty, and Mrs Chitnis is five or six years older than us. But Rama Aajji is 'Aajji' to us all! She would laugh and say, 'How does it matter, dear, if you call me Aajji or Akka? All these are the fickleness of young age, bai! If I couldn't be Aajji or Aai for my own people, at least I am Aajji here.'

Sometimes, she would sigh and say, 'A woman should never live too long. Every coming day gnaws at the remaining joys of her heart and turns them into dust…it's more painful to die pining.'

Rama Aajji is restless. Her palms and soles have gone limp. Mary wraps her in a blanket, but her hands and feet jerk in agitation.

'It seems her blood sugar has gone down. I wish the doctor came sooner,' Mary says.

The doctor comes and takes charge of Aajji. He suggests getting her admitted to a hospital the next morning. 'Let's wait the night,' he says.

During the day, Rama Aajji had kept the puranmasi or full moon night fast, but she sat in the veranda and chatted with everyone. In the afternoon, I had reminded her to rest, 'If you talk too much, your sugar level will go down.' She had taken this very lightly, 'My dear, if I don't talk, I will die suffocated. Don't you worry. I have lived till I was destined to live.'

Sometimes, the cheerful Aajji would become quiet, 'There was so much loneliness in my life after Narayan Rao passed away. I felt like a useless object. I didn't fit in anywhere. I wandered here and there on the pretext of visiting holy places—the temples of Kashi, Mathura-Vrindavan, the doorstep of Tulja Mai, Sai Baba's ashram. I was so tired, you know.

'It is peaceful here. My elder son, Uday, put me here before shifting to Bangalore. Both my son and daughter-in-law are, what do you call that, computer engineers. I think this shall be my last stopover.'

We find Aajji in her room, exhausted and weak, looking wistfully at us. There is indeed a restlessness in the eyes of this quiet and gentle Aajji, but there is no fear which is usually noticed at once in the eyes of the old people. I keep her head in my lap, and Mary rubs the soles of her feet. Manda is scared. Sakhu Tai and the doctor are busy preparing glucose and saline drip. Aajji begins to feel better after the glucose is administered. She looks at the ceiling and slowly closes her eyes. Mary and I slowly get up to leave. The doctor sits on a chair. Closing the door behind us, I turn back and look at Aajji's face. A tiny smile lurks at the corners of her lips.

Gentle and quiet Manda speaks sweetly. She is the youngest in Parisar. She looks happy…but she isn't. After losing her only son in a car accident, the mother-in-law accused her widowed daughter-in-law of his death. High school-pass Manda sold off her jewellery with the help of her brothers and came here. Since then, she has been treating Aajji like her mother and looking after her. Looking at Manda, it seems she had lost everything once again.

We walk on the veranda. When I stop before my room, Mary too stops for a fraction of a second and murmurs, '…It seems as if Aajji's life is seeping out of the soles of her feet! I may be mistaken…but…'

I keep watching Mary's plump figure recede slowly before my eyes. Before entering my room, I turn once again to look at Aajji's room. She is standing there, smiling. I rub my eyes and look again…there is complete solitude. Inside the room, the light is faint.

Seema found Rafu sitting on her bed and waiting for her to come home. His face brightened when he saw her. 'Why are you so late? Why didn't you come earlier? How will Rafu sleep alone, tell me? No one switched the lights on. Small children are afraid, aren't they, Mama?'

Moving him aside, she said, 'How did you know that time passes, my dear? You don't even know the small hand of the clock from the big, and you say…it's late!

'Why didn't you go to sleep? Will you keep waiting for me, my sweetie pie?'

The dimples on his face brimmed with happiness. His smile was as sweet as when he was two…now he was seventeen, and still had that same innocent face…and an unaffected smile.

What else could he do? Smile, talk to himself, run around in the room or inside the house, dragging his feet, go near the balcony's parapet, thump loudly on her back and run away… as if someone was coming to catch him, watch the food being cooked in the kitchen for long, look at the clock a thousand times and ask everyone, 'Is it mealtime? Rafu is hungry.'

Shoving Rafu, who never came out of his own world, she said, 'Go and sleep now. You had a lot of fun, baba.'

He could never sleep immediately. He would push aside Seema's hand and get up, and before the sleepy Seema could stop him, he would run around in the room. In the silence of the night, the sound of his dragging feet irritated Papa, who would be awake, listening to classical music on the radio.

The door of Seema's room opened with a bang.

'Now, go and sleep quickly, silly boy. Why do you have to create a ruckus at this late hour. Sleep.'

Before Rafu could say something, Samuel David yelled at him. 'Shut up and sleep.'

God knows what happened that day. Rafu, who was always so scared of him, raised his healthy right hand to his ears and said, 'Quiet! You, too, shut up! Shall I slap you, idiot?'

There was a pin-drop silence. Papa's eyebrows were knitted in anger. His face distorted with extreme rage as he shook Rafu roughly and fumed, 'Such insolence! How dare you say you'll beat me?' Then he looked at Seema and walked towards the door. Rafu regained his balance and ran after Papa with his dragging feet, pushed him lightly on his back and said, 'Run away, stupid...idiot...veda!'

That day, the door behind which Rafu stood still had to bear the brunt of Pappa's fury and anger.

Sleep had left from the exhausted Rafu's eyes. He stared hard at the ceiling. Then, turning to Seema, he asked, 'Mama! Where is Nani?'

'She died, beta!' Seema answered sadly.

'Who dies, Mama?'

What could Seema say? Then she thought and answered, 'Those who have life in them, like those who eat and drink, laugh and talk, sleep and wake, cry and laugh...are alive. But they will also die someday.'

Seema could only try to answer him. Otherwise, in that dim light of the room, how could she make a child-like mentally challenged boy staring at her with unblinking eyes understand that the moments of joy and sorrow, happiness, terror, and freedom or captivity were all a part of life and living?

Rafu patted Seema and said smilingly, 'Now I know Mama. Like when Nanu laughs loudly or gets angry...it's not like that...dying is smiling slowly and quietly. When Nani wasn't talking loudly and people took her out, she was smiling slowly, quietly...because she had died.'

When Mary and I had left Rama Aajji in her room, we had noticed a tiny smile lingering on the corners of her lips.

Chapter 4

Unlike every day, Rama Aajji didn't wake up at dawn the next day.

'No one wants to leave this place before the final day, please, try to understand this, girls. The sorrow of separation is here, but it doesn't have the cruel coldness of the world from where we have been removed,' Aajji had said. She left, leaving that last day behind.

Manda had informed us in the morning that the way the doctor had put her to the previous night, Aajji was found dead in that same posture. All residents had assembled before her room. Aajji's body waited for her dear ones in vain till late afternoon. We bathed her body and sent her off to the cremation ground.

The day seems lazy. Whenever it is cloudy, the morning in this hilly town becomes moist and dull. Manda has gone to buy vegetables with Sakhu Tai, so that she can control her tears. Mrs Chitnis sits on the veranda stairs and stares into the void. Rama Aajji's belongings have been put in the storeroom, and her room has been washed. For the first time, I see a lock on her room.

Looking at the bundles of Aajji's belongings, I remember many items and household goods in my acquaintances' homes. I remember the ball bearings of Papa's bicycle, letters, greeting cards, doctor's prescriptions, receipts of various stores, lottery tickets—utterly useless but treasured knick-knacks. In some corner of my mind, the two-anna brass coin given to me by Sohrab seems to jingle, and among other letters, *his* first letter to me...'Paro, please don't forget your Deva.'

A cloud of shadow crosses my face.

A couple of suitcases, an old album, a glass and pot of brass or steel, a book of scripture, brass or silver idols of deities, pictures of saints or babas, glasses, chappals, and carefully preserved photographs of dear ones who had been left behind...'he is my elder son...and he is his son, Vikas... Visu never had food without me'...and complete loneliness! These were the belongings of a woman like Rama Aajji, who lived in an old age home.

Rama Aajji would wear that pair of black and somewhat new slippers when she visited the temple close by. She only went there occasionally. She would laugh and say, 'Why would Vithoba want to see my old face daily? He is happy when I go there sometimes. He doesn't wait for anyone. I am also like Vithoba—even I don't wait for anyone. Now look, everyone is happy in their world, so they don't remember me. I also live my days happily, so why should I remember my dear ones?

'This whole business of life is a biological activity, my dear. Other than the human species, which female in this universe remembers her offspring and pines for them? So, whether your own people remember you or don't...why make an issue of this? Why suffer in grief?'

Manda would always retort, 'Aai, how can you say such things? A human being is the highest and the ultimate form into which Homo sapiens evolve. It is the best form—with a developed mind and fathomless heart, and adorned with unique memories. It experiences universal feelings. Women are more emotional in comparison to men, so how can they merely be reproductive organisms?'

Rama Aajji's face would quiver with despair. 'So, despite so many unique qualities, what did you get in the end, my daughter? You wandered at such a young age. You became a burden to your sister-in-law, the "other" woman to your brother-in-law, and trouble for your daughter-in-law. It is better to kill your feelings yourself than to die many deaths thrust upon us by others. Finish.

'When our own tend to forget us, daughter, just become a female and put a full stop to the ever going and eternal tragedy, and free yourself from pains of frustration.'

She would say all this very easily. She left with the same ease.

Ma had to suffer a lot.

Seema can never forget the arrival of Manorama Kaki in her last days.

Although the residents of Gitanjali Society had no concern left for Samuel David's family by that time, people would at times visit them to establish their religious faith. Manorama Kaki had come with the photograph of the religious baba, Gobardas, and a tiny lump of earth.

'Mira Ben, chant "Ram" a thousand times a day and make hundred pills of this mud, and swallow one every day... you will be freed from all your sufferings. Baba's name is miraculous. If you worship him every morning, your life will attain its destination...all worldly desires will leave you.'

Ma had shouted. 'Leave my home, you fraudster!'

Seema had rushed to her. Manorama Kaki was grumbling. 'God damn, no one appreciates this. The old hag may die any day, so I thought to lessen her suffering, but it seems to be a different ball game altogether. Die or live. How does that affect me?'

Rushing out of the home, she grumbled some more, 'These God-damned Christians! They will never learn how to worship. Go to hell!'

Seema had banged the door shut.

Ma had howled.

Was Mama crying only at her own suffering? Papa's discipline and fear, Danny's intolerance and disgust, Bobby's sensitivity and gentleness, Rachel's clumsiness and timidity and David's dilemma and sadness—was Ma swabbed by all these like the wet mud?

Did Ma die her own death? Can anyone live alone? Could Rama Aajji live alone?

Rama Aajji was from Pen town in Konkan, Maharashtra. She knew who the Israyels were. 'Are you a Bene Israel? I know about your people. Before my marriage, at my parents' place, I would visit the homes of these families. I even had some Jewish friends…Aabi, Sheba, Ruby, Yerusha, Lisa… In Pen, they used surnames such as Penkar, Navagaonkar, Aambekar, etc. Now, most of them have left for Israel. Villages after villages became empty.

'After my marriage with Narayan Rao, when I went to Nadiad, I made friends with an Israyel girl…Lily.'

'She was my Atya, my aunt.'

'Oh? So, you are Sam's daughter?'

The secrets Papa wanted to hide were known even to Ma and Diana Aajji. Lily hadn't died of cholera. Aajji, who noticed everything and didn't like to mince her words, had said with hatred, 'Her own father poisoned her.'

Her old shrivelled skin shivered.

One death is that which God sends...it comes without a sound. The other, walks along from young age and all the music of life turns into a storm and howls. The sound of such death never disappears from the universe.

Receding into a moment in the past, Aajji said, 'They say, ankle-length hair brings bad luck. Good that she died. Else, how could she hide her bloated belly.' She took in a deep breath, 'I had heard that Manoj had become deranged and then one day, I heard that he was found dead on the railway track. Who knows if he killed himself or someone...' Aajji closed her eyes, 'What did that damned girl get, after all? Only the haunting darkness of a cold grave.'

When the darkness became too heavy, and members of the family were in deep slumber, Diana would toss and turn. Seema's hand over her Aajji would keep falling down. Seema would wake to find Diana Aajji staring at the darkness with blinking eyes and whispering to someone... 'Why did you come late? Come and sit near me, dear?'

'Why are you sitting? Whom are you calling out?' Seema would ask. Aajji would bring her face near Seema's ears and say, 'Don't you see...It's Lily, I am calling her.'

Seema would sweat with fear. She would look around. Besides the dark, shiny night, there would be the chirping of crickets and Aajji's suppressed whispers... 'Come, no...Come.'

'Now sleep, Aajji,' Seema would make her lie down and say, 'No one will come now.'

Seema still remembered Dhanmai's noiseless howl. Aajji crying was something like that.

After a lot of effort, Tahmina's body had been pulled down from the ventilator, but her head remained bent to one side. Dhanmai's mouth was open, her hands and feet jerked, but no sound came out from her mouth. Seema felt as if Dhanmai's voice, too, had strangulated itself with the same noose.

Something tossed and turned inside young Seema. She stroked Aajji's body with sympathy. In the dim light of the night, she could see her heaving her shrunken breast, her breathing coming in intervals from her toothless face.

On a night like this, Diana had caught hold of Seema and said, 'I couldn't save Lily. She had slowly turned blue. She had held my hand tightly, saying, "Mama, don't leave, don't leave..." She had kept saying this. But did your Azoba hear her crushed voice coming out of her dry lips?

'He sat in the drawing room blind-drunk.

'The howls of her pain had suffocated in the closed room. I couldn't save her. She comes to meet me sometimes. She calls me. She stands afar and laughs. Can you see her?'

Seema knew then that Aajji was no longer alone. Trying to overcome the noise within her, she had gone to the noise of the past and lost herself there.

Miss Samuel looks up. Rama Aajji was telling her, 'Bai, the custom of burying the dead among you people is quite inconvenient. Buried in a six-foot hole, and waiting for the Day of Judgement till you turn into a skeleton. Look at us... here we die...and there we go up in smoke! Who cares for the ash? If someone cares to take it away, fine, else there is wind, water, and light.

'Empty wait in the dark...which means restlessness!'

It's a play of dark and light. There is light in the veranda at campus...and darkness in the room. Rafu was too afraid of the dark. He could not step inside a dark room. He would hold one end of Seema's sari wherever she was. She would get annoyed.

'Let go of my sari. I have switched on the light... Now go

to sleep. You are a big boy now, but you are still afraid. Am I ever afraid?'

Seema had erased the difference between the two of them.

He yelled with laughter. 'You are scared of Nanu.'

Seema looked at him. Did he really understand natural feelings?

Turning her face to him, he asked, 'Mama, is Nanu bad?'

'No beta, don't say like this.'

'Then why was Nani so afraid of Nanu?'

Seema was shocked. Did this mentally challenged teenager know of the turmoil in the house?

Those days, Samuel David would be annoyed without any reason at the smallest pretext. Coupled with Rosie's awful temper, there would be fights in the house almost every day. Danny would always take his wife's side, without even batting an eye, and get irritated at his father. 'Just because you funded my two years of higher education in America doesn't mean that you have enslaved me for life. Haven't I told you that I will return each and every penny of your Provident Fund? I will take care of David's education and will keep him with me. What else do you want?'

'Did I ever mention any fund?' Papa's voice was sharp.

'Then why do you quarrel with Rosie every day?'

'I quarrel with her? Does your ill-mannered wife know how to behave with anyone—young or old? Forget about that; I try to save each penny. I don't take a bus and walk miles, and this daughter of Rockefeller walks out of the house with the light and fan switched on. No one knows when she will go out or come back. She bangs the door shut, and there she goes! She is ready with rude answers.'

Rosie came running, 'Just look at him! He is old but doesn't know how to behave with his daughter-in-law. Am I your Seema or Rachel, who will keep mum? And what of

Rachel? Could you control her? I pleaded with Danny with folded hands to take me out of this hell, but what to say of this obedient son who only thinks of his responsibilities? Shit! What kind of a life is this? Your family is not even worth a penny!'

Samuel David exploded. 'Bitch! Shit on you and your rotten family! You will not rest till you destroy our family.' Lifting his hand in fury, he rushed towards Rosie.

Danny caught his hand right when he was about to strike. 'Enough Papa. Not a word from you now. Go to your room. Don't forget that she's my wife.'

Hearing all the commotion, Ma started grumbling. When the din rose above her grumbling, she started shouting... 'Bobby! See, someone is hitting me. Bobby? Sam....!'

Samuel David returned to his wife. Rosie and Danny went to their room, but Rosie came out a moment later, grumbling in anger. Standing outside Rosie's room, a petrified Rafu urinated in his pyjama.

Rosie grew angrier. 'God, please take me out of this hell.'

Cleaning up the ten-year old boy, Seema, who was now in her early thirties, thought, 'How far is heaven and hell from one another? Is there a dividing line between the two? How ironical it is that one has to look for one's joys among sorrows and miseries!'

Samuel David was argumentative by nature. How could Rosie tolerate Papa, who was in the habit of finding fault with others and asking questions in a row? Seema and Bobby often got stuck in his trap. Seema would keep quiet, leave the room, or, at times, speak harshly. And Bobby?

Sensitive, cheerful, lively, polite and affectionate.

'Oh Papa, you too? Just as the Ramayana and the Mahabharata are Hindu epics, the Bible, according to some scholars, is not a record of actual events.'

Papa would be annoyed, 'Nonsense! The Bible is history. It is a genealogy of our ancestors. There are incidents and tragedies, even information, forecasts and warnings.'

'So what? Even Rama's—who is said to have been born five thousand years—birth chart, date and the exact moment of his birth, horoscope, everything have been determined! The existence of the Pandavas has also been verified by their place of exile, caves and footprints. The purpose of religion is to awaken faith and to destroy evil, to protect ourselves by looking at the precedents, and not to promote bigotry.'

During such debates, Samuel David, desperate to gain the upper hand, would finally say, 'Actually, you are a history student…it's no use arguing with you.'

Bobby would laugh and hug him, 'My poor Papa.'

But Rosie couldn't laugh. She wanted complete control over her husband. A mother-in-law who was drifting towards darkness, an eccentric and short-tempered father-in-law, a spinster sister-in-law, Seema, a mentally challenged teenager like Rafael, and the huge burden of responsibilities of her young brother-in-law, David—they were all trouble for her. She hated this middle-class Gujju family. She had started digging a private tunnel of escape in apartment B-7 of Gitanjali Society.

Seema didn't know that Rosie, with her husband Danny, would soon flee this personal hell created by Samuel David and become a distant memory. Neither did Samuel David.

So, when the house became empty, the retired Under Secretary, Mr Samuel David, started pressurizing his daughter Seema, who was moving towards spinsterhood.

'How long will you postpone it?' he asked when he came to her room one night. Then he looked at her for some time and said, 'There are no unmarried boys of your age available in our community so we can't put on airs.'

'Do you suggest I grab anyone's hand then?'

'Do you know what people say?' he retorted angrily.

'People have the habit of poking their nose in others' affairs. Please forget about them. Don't you know Ma's condition? For the past four-five years, we have only received New Year's cards from Danny, and nothing else. Twenty-eight-year-old David is suffering from a nervous breakdown...And then Rafu?' Seema asked flatly.

'So, what is the way out? Shall we send Rafu to an orphanage...I...mean...to Bombay's Jewish Orphanage? Shouldn't we at least inquire from the Founder?'

Perhaps Samuel David hadn't thought of speaking so plainly. Perhaps when he had said this, he had felt guilty and that's why he had lowered his eyes and his voice had trembled.

But Seema thought of all this later. At that time, his every act seemed hostile. She couldn't tolerate her father anymore. She burst out. 'Don't you feel any pain at all, Papa?'

'Can only pondering over problems solve them? Think carefully. Tell me. What is left for us here now? Even if you don't want to get married. We can at least think of moving to Israel.'

'So, you're only interested in going to Israel...not in my marriage!'

'You have learnt to answer back, you know.'

'Truth is bitter. But, who will sponsor you?'

'There are some relatives. Friends from the Khamasa gate, such as Dandekar and Erulkar, also went last year only. They will also help to some extent.'

'Then, go.'

'How? Unless young people like you and David are with us, the Government there will pay no heed. Things were different earlier. At that time, the nation was being built. Now they need the power of the youth.' Samuel David took in a long breath and lamented, 'I wish Danny was with us!'

'Yes, and that white Israyel girl, Rosie, too.' Seema's voice was sharp.

'Why think about nonsensical things?'

'Yes, like thinking about Rafu.'

Okay, we will take him along. He is Rachel's son; his mother is a Jew, so he is half-Jew.'

'And, what would you write under his father's name?'

Samuel David was quiet.

Seema asked with pain, 'Why is it, Papa, that you loved and understood Rachel the most, and yet you still cannot fully accept her innocent, helpless and imperfect son? Is it that you are being mean to that poor boy as an excuse to punish Rachel!'

'Shut up!' shouted Samuel David. The pigeon sleeping on the window sill fluttered and flew away.

He didn't want to return to that past. His affection and compassion had dried up after Rachel's death, and his old eyes were full of unpleasant memories. He had withdrawn himself.

Seema had seen the insult of hopelessness and contempt on his drooping shoulders.

She saw him leave the room with sadness.

Samuel David pushed the door behind him while leaving the room. The old doors creaked a little, moved to and fro for a while, and then became still, leaving a slice of gap.

A long time ago, Samuel's father David Reuben had similarly pushed the door behind him. Before coming out of the room, he had peeped into the other room from the drawing room. Sam, Lily and Ruth were sleeping. His wife Diana looked like she was sleeping, too. He quietly slipped out into the courtyard to take the stairs to the tiny room on the roof. The after-effect of the foreign liquor in the evening and his favourite dinner had stirred his dormant desire. The firmness of the ripened body of Lakshmi tinkled in his heart. He quietly came up the stairs.

A snatch of a melody…*'ugich ka kantha. ugich ka' (Ovain love)'*…was stuck on the lips of David Reuben, the lover of drama and the Natya Sangeet. With a smile on his lips, he knocked at Lakshmi's door and whispered, 'Open the door, Lakshmi!'

Inside the room, her shallow breathing could be heard. The room was overcast with the gloom of restlessness and fear, the noise of agonizing silence. Lakshmi extinguished the oil lamp with her hand and shrank in a corner. Hiding the many images of hatred and helplessness in her eyes, she kept sitting, her blouse wet with sweat.

Government jailor David Reuben placed his ear on the door only to hear silence coming out of the darkness through the cracks. In a gruff and demanding voice, he blurted, 'Are you opening the door?'

Silence. 'Will you open the door, you bitch?'

'Please go, Baba…I won't open the door today.' It was a trembling voice.

His brows knitted in anger. 'Stop this drama, Lakshmi.'

There was a long silence. The Jailor Sahib's intoxication wore off at once.

'How dare you! The whore of that bloody bastard Keshava and such tantrums! Even the bravest and the boldest whimper before me, and this bitch shows me her temper?'

He shouted, 'You whore, bastard, bitch…if I come in and don't rip off your thighs and feed them to kites and crows, change my name. You bitch, adulteress, no one will come to know who gobbled you up.'

The room was full of sobs, and the smell of mourning

spread in the air. Young, beautiful, widowed Lakshmi wanted to melt into the darkness with her meagre belongings.

But she would not open the door. Instead, she cried for help. 'Mother, please come here fast and help me!'

Lakshmi's cry tore through the midnight and struck Diana's ears. She was fast asleep on the ground floor. As soon as she understood the situation, it seemed like thorny bushes had grown in her eyes. Her voice trembled with anger and embarrassment—

'Has the old man gone mad?'

Slipping out of the room, lest she wake up her sleeping children, she quickly climbed the narrow stairs. The lamp in her hand kept burning, carrying her shame and restlessness. Her heart released a flood of words. 'You devil! Are you readying yourself for your funeral? In this house with grown-up children, this old rascal burns with desire. O, you ill-fated man! Don't you hear the footfalls of the future? Your masters, the British, won't be here for long. Then, the people here will take revenge—have you ever thought of this?'

Puffing and panting, Diana caught hold of her husband's reeling body with her strong hands and dragged him downstairs. His unsteady steps and slurred speech found respite on the bed, and the Jailor Sahib started snoring.

That day, Diana had known that her lustful husband would repeat the act. He would claim his right over Lakshmi. She would feel stifled and stressed and would writhe in agony. Losing the fight against her youthful body, she would one day hang herself with her sari by the ventilator.

The echo of her crushed cry soaked with sobs would vibrate through David Reuben's family for years: 'I had called you Baba (father). Still, you made my life hell. I curse you from my innermost heart that there would be no one to carry your name forward in the coming generation…!'

Lakshmi's cold body was found hanging late in the morning.

David Reuben's eldest son Samuel remembered the dark night when he had tightly shut his eyes and grasped at the strips of the cot and kept awake sweating profusely. Lakshmi's kohl-blackened eyes and the peacock tattoo on her chin were out hunting and seeing him sleeping, smiled. It seemed Ma was standing on his chest. He felt the ebb and flow of the sea in his throat. Hiding his face in the pillow, he repeated his mother's words—

'This old man is getting ready for his own funeral!'

It was morning before Sam could finally sleep.

Chapter 5

I turn on my side. The night lamp on the table is making a circle of light. I keep watching the light. Suddenly, someone steps into that circle. I strain to see. Who? Who is that? Oh! Lakshmi? She laughs inside the circle of light. I call out, 'Lakshmi?' I see her leaving the circle with sad steps and then hear the muffled sounds of her sobs. I am upset. I ask vaguely, 'Lakshmi, why are you crying?' At once, I see her swathed in light. I smile, too. We stand before each other. Her eyes are fixed on me. Then, there is a disturbance—the sound of footsteps. I see Lakshmi trembling with fear. She wants to scream, but no sound comes out of her open mouth. Her beautiful eyes become larger and larger with fear. By the time I can help her, her lovely long neck has rolled over to one side. But she is not Lakshmi anymore; it is Tahmina. I want to howl with fear and disbelief, but I am paralyzed, only my breath comes out in pants.

I wake up, agitated. My heart is pounding; my throat is dry. I drink some water and pick up my watch from the table. It is three at night. I sit for a while, leaning against the wall. Lakshmi's anguish can still be felt in the room.

Would Lakshmi still be horror-stricken after so many years?

And the government Jailor David Reuben? My Azoba, my grandfather…where is he now?

❁

Samuel David's Pappa, Khan Bahadur David Reuben. Jailor Sahib. A beard with sideburns, an awe-inspiring face, small but piercing eyes, a heavyset body, a high forehead, a prominent nose…and a face taut with anger. Subordinates and prisoners were terrified when he crossed their way.

When David Reuben was fourteen or fifteen, he visited his grandfather's ancestral home at Navagaon during the vacation with his Aaba, Reuben, mother, Sheba, two younger sisters, Esther and Yerusha, and their youngest brother, Moses. He might have forgotten most of the incidents of his childhood and teenage days, but he could never forget that evening, when at sundown he had stood amazed, holding his Azoba's hand, before the infinite expanse of the ocean.

During that twilight hour, the sea had discarded her blue attire and had draped around her the first shade of dusty grey. High waves melted as they rushed to the shore. Some had crashed against the rocky shore with full force and left heaps of foamy bubbles. David had watched for long the bubbles break and flow into the waves.

Holding the hand of retired Subedar Isaji Eloji of the Tenth Native Infantry Regiment of the Bombay Army—his Aaza, his grandfather—and standing by the sea shore, David would remember all his life the dreams his grandfather had planted in his mind, and the tragic journey into the past that he and his brother Moses had undertaken, riding on their grandfather's words. The two boys were of completely different temperaments—even then, David had been short-tempered, rude and stubborn, the way he was when he grew up.

That day, as retired Subedar Isaji had fixed his eyes on the distant horizon, something soft had melted in his throat. David had felt as though his Aaza had been speaking from the distant saffron horizon where the sun had descended on the waves of the sea.

Isaji Eloji had told them of their ancestors, the Jews, who had come from a faraway place in the west called Palestine. They had disembarked somewhere here on that shore. The shore must have been terrifying and rocky back then. It was said that their raft had crashed against the upright rocks, and a large number of people had been injured. What else could the survivors have saved except their crushed voices, frightened sobs and suffocated screams? The rest had been swallowed up by the sea with their raft. The ferocious water of the ocean had snatched away their dreams. The storm and rain had made their lives miserable. They were shattered. Only their dear ones remained.

'We will never know the names, addresses, language, or attire of our astounded and miserable ancestors because they had landed somewhere here from that far-off country some two thousand years ago...'

Holding Azoba Isaji's finger and standing at the Navagaon shore, David had watched the approaching sunset. He would always remember the history of his ancestors, which he would narrate, word for word, to his coming generations.

David's father, Reuben, a teacher, was reticent, but his mother was fearless. David enjoyed his grandfather's company the most because he told David stories from the Bible and from around the world that David had no time to read. He didn't like his Aaba's ambiguous attitude towards religion; neither did his mother. In comparison, his Aaza, although not a fanatic, was an expert in religious knowledge.

Every evening, when Azoba Isaji—Isaac—would leave for the prayer hall in Navagaon, he and David would touch the mezuzah placed to the left of the main doorway with their right hands and then kiss their hands. Azoba would place a handkerchief on little Moses's head, lift him and make him kiss the mezuzah, too. He would tell Moses that the Hebrew letter 'Shin' was written on the mezuzah because God's name began with that letter. 'By touching the mezuzah, in a way, we pray or place our trust in the Lord that He will keep us safe through all our comings and goings! David, these signs remind us that we are but displaced people, dispersed from that same great culture.'

The sun had sunk into the water. The sky above had turned dark. David felt Aaza was tired. Isaji lifted the five-year-old Moses, who had been making sand castles, into his arms and walked home. He was quiet on the way. Lost. He wiped his eyes with his shoulder-cloth. David couldn't understand for sure if his eyes had become misty or blurred.

'Where are the survivors?' David asked him as he walked along.

Isaji Eloji smiled with sadness. He held David's hand tight, 'Son, water and people always find their way. They must have taken the path they saw. Such paths are not easy to traverse. There are plenty of hurdles. Our ancestors had to face a lot of suffering. They wore old and worn-out cloths, ate coarse and stale food, made their camps wherever they found a place… that's probably how they survived.'

'Why didn't they study? Had they studied, they wouldn't have had to take up small jobs such as agriculture, carpentry, oil-pressing, etc. In Poona and Bombay, people study, and so they get good jobs. But here, I see that our people have almost no concern with education.'

Isaji stared into his grandson's eyes, 'Our people are very poor. Poor and short-sighted. How could they bear the burden of education when they believed that more children meant more working hands? Those who got educated found good jobs and settled in cities, like your Aaba. His children are successful. The rest suffer from the blows of destiny.'

'I will study and become an officer, Azoba. An officer has power, status and money. I don't want to become a teacher like Aaba.'

Isaji smiled, 'Yes, son, you must become an officer, but don't forget to be human. Don't let the spring of innocence in your heart dry up.' Then, knocking gently on little Moses's head, Azoba asked, 'And what will you become, my little lamb?'

Before Moses could speak, David thumped him on his back and said with a laugh, 'What can this simpleton do, Azoba? Except for tomfoolery or frolicking with a drama company. Hahaha!'

Little Moses's face turned red, and his eyes shone. Lifting his face, he looked at his Aaza and Dada, his elder brother. Then, swinging from Isaji's arms, he said, 'Yes, I will only become Sita or King Harishchandra's queen, Taramati. Can you stop me, Dada? Is dancing bad, Azoba?'

Before Azoba could respond, David kicked Moses lightly on his buttocks and said, 'You good-for-nothing! Girly! You are a bugger!'

Helping Moses up, Isaji questioned, 'David, is working in a drama company really bad? You enjoy watching plays. But you don't like working there?'

David's voice was gruff and annoyed, 'Oh, Azoba, why you don't understand? Is it decent to act in dramas?'

Resting on the raised platform built around the peepal tree in front of his house, Subedar Isaji Eloji sighed and asked his elder grandson, 'Tell me, David, aren't all jobs like slavery? But, you know, an artist is never a slave, never forced by circumstances! Working for art is not slavery, it is devotion; it is the flame of aspiration. He treats his diligence as godliness and gets engrossed in it.'

Isaji was quiet for a while. David very well knew of his Aaza's diligence. He remembered his mother's hushed protest against this very diligence of her father-in-law—'Nonsense! Drama and tamasha at this old age? He's not even bothered about the disgrace that this has brought to our community! What kind of an interest is this?'

David thought that if their mother came to know of this, she would certainly skin Moses alive. 'God damn! You want to become an actor? Was one Narayani not enough for this family?'

David's mother, Sheba, didn't like her father-in-law, Isaji. 'This man is good, but his deeds are a dime a dozen. When his wife died two or three years later, this "gentleman" turned Narayani from the drama company to Nora and married her. The clan's blood was made impure by making the future generations black. If Reuben hadn't been educated and well-off with landed property, my Aaba wouldn't have even come to spit at their doorstep!'

Sometimes, David's father would reply with harsh words of his own, 'Sure, your father shouldn't have come to our doorstep; it would have done you good to be a wife to some carpenter or oil presser…the white Israyels!'

However, David never understood why his Azoba, who had such knowledge of religion and was so committed to it and his brethren, would commit such an act.

Perhaps, Moses had not forgotten the kick on his butt. He

raised his head from Azoba's lap and asked, 'Azoba, Aajji also sang in the drama company, didn't she? Was she a Hindu? Ma told us.'

David gave Moses a tight slap, 'Stupid fool! Why do you have to bring Ma into all this? And after having Tevilah, does anyone remain a Hindu?'

Retired Subedar Isaji Eloji of the Tenth Native Infantry Regiment of the Bombay Army smiled gently, 'Yes, Moses, your Aajji was indeed a Hindu. And yes, she sang very sweetly. Her wish to sing drew her to the drama company. And, David, you listen carefully because Moses won't understand—religion doesn't mean bigotry. When you grow up, you will understand the difference between the two, or perhaps you may not understand and drift along. I may not be alive by then, but remember my words: there is a very fine line between them. So, to know their difference, inner awareness and patience are necessary.'

David would also always remember his Azoba Isaji Eloji's death. It was the first time that he saw someone so close to him pass away, and he had to participate in the rituals of the funeral.

On the bier, his head, which usually lay facing west, was placed in the east, and his feet towards the west. Aaza would always remind Moses as he turned his legs from west to east, 'Our country, Palestine, is in the west. Keeping your feet in that direction is disrespectful.' The Qazi had placed Isaji Eloji's palm on his closed eyelids and said the prayer of Shema.

'This was the only prayer that helped us find our identity,' he had told David as he explained its meaning.

Isaji Eloji was washed and draped in the shishith, a silk shawl knotted at the four corners with silk threads. A corner of Azoba's shishith had been pulled out. Azoba seemed to whisper in David's ears, 'The four corners are symbols of stability. Like Solomon's grand temple at Jerusalem before its destruction, a house is supported by four corners, a place of trust, hope and shelter. But death, who knows what is beyond death!'

Azoba's cassock, handkerchief, turban, cap, shoulder cloth, waist cloth and pillow were by his side. After the rituals, his body was kept in the courtyard. Then, the Qazi asked those assembled there, 'Do you forgive this departed soul for his likely sins?'

'Yes, we do,' a chorus had risen.

David repeated in his mind, 'No, Azoba, I will never forgive you for making our blood impure and for taking part in drama and tamasha.'

At that time, David hardly knew that following his mother's footsteps, he, too, would be so deeply rooted in his caste and religion that his daughter, Lily, would get caught in that trap. She would struggle but would never get free. 'Mama, please don't leave my hand,' she would say. God knows where she disappeared to!

When the Kaddish, the last prayer, was recited after Isaji Eloji's coffin was lowered into a dark pit, David had smiled like Azoba. Not death, but the glory of life and the Lord, His greatness and wish were remembered in the prayer. David knew that Kaddish meant sacred and, like many other words and prayers, it was a word from the Aramaic language in which a large portion of the Bible had been written.

Draped in his shishith and performing the rituals of death, David, one of the men of minyan, hardly knew then that during his last stages of semi-consciousness, when he would wish to speak to his eldest son Samuel, his words would be trapped in his throat, his breathing would be laboured and his body's shadow would walk away. At that time, there wouldn't be ten men in all Nadiad who would willingly form the minyan for his funeral ceremony.

Retired Subedar Isaji Eloji of the Tenth Native Infantry Regiment of the Bombay Army had planted some of his own dreams in the heart of his grandson, David Reuben.

'David, how I wish I could have returned to that distant motherland and my body could have been buried there. But you and your successors should return so that that the two-thousand-year-old sting of displacement can be lessened. We are Israyel, Bene Israel—the descendants of Jacob, who was awarded the name of Israel by the Lord. Who knows where his progeny, with their broken dreams, with their sufferings and neglect, are buried and in what parts of the world!

Like his mother, David would always remain sore about his blood having been adulterated, especially when he saw his younger brother Moses with his longish Hindu face and features, always occupied with animals of all kinds—dogs, cats, parrots mynahs, squirrels, rabbits, etc.

'He has gone exactly after his grandmother,' David's Ma would remark.

When he was young, everyone at school thought David was a Christian; when he grew up, they thought he was a Hindu-Jew! When young, he would not pick a fight with others, but as he grew older, David realized that half-Jewish families like his were looked down upon in his own community. In the synagogue, while people admired his youth, health and smartness, they also had a tiny smirk etched on their lips. He felt awful when he couldn't visit the Red Temple in the cantonment in Poona because they were 'black'. Only pure Baghdadi Jews and British and white Jews were allowed inside.

Standing alone in a corner, Khan Bahadur David Reuben would often wonder about what might have enticed someone with so much faith in God as his Azoba to marry a Hindu woman and disgrace the whole clan!

Hindu! Huh!

When he was drunk, Government Jailor David Reuben would swear at his Hindu friends and subordinates—'Hindus, you scoundrels!'

'You stay with the Hindus, adopt their customs, dress and food habits, take their girls as mistresses, turn a Hindu girl into an Israyel by giving her Tevilah and produce children with her. Then, in a moment, you say, Huh, these bastard Hindus!'

Fuming with anger and hatred, Samuel David's mother, Diana, would yell at her blind-drunk husband and swear at him, gesticulating wildly with her hands. 'Why do you screw up your nose, David? Don't forget that you, too, are half-Hindu!'

A sozzled David Reuben would roar in anger, 'Shut up, you bitch!'

Seema had seen the pain behind her Aajji's deeply wrinkled face.

'I had never liked this stubborn, angry, and debauched son of Uncle Reuben, but no 'white' Israyel was willing to give their son to Aaba. Although, how does it matter whether I was willing or not? I couldn't even save Lily and Ruth.'

Seema remembered her Aajji's blinking eyes and toothless face.

Sitting in her room, Miss Seema Samuel can see the night approaching the dawn. When he was getting old, Khan Bahadur David Reuben would be mortified to see his wife Diana talking to her dead daughters in the silent room. He would drink even more. Then, he would stand before his hallucinating wife with folded hands and beg, 'Please forgive me, Lily!'

Diana would laugh.

Rachel had gone away first. Ma had been unable to bear the shock of her and Bobby's deaths. Raphael, the grandson Samuel David could never truly forgive and whom he had tried to get rid of in any way possible, Seema's father would call out to that same grandson during his last days. He would talk to Rafu even though he was not there.

Then, in apartment B-7 on the third floor of Gitanjali Society, there was Seema. There was her father, Samuel David, in a state of being and not being, and there was David, Seema's younger brother. Named after his Azoba, he was a very sensitive, impulsive man of a nervous temperament.

Chapter 6

I can see her walking up from afar. The slightly bent, thin, and tall woman, walking on the meandering road with her hands tucked in her cardigan pockets. In this old age home, Parisar, everyone calls her Miss Samuel.

We can't see her when she walks down the slope. But four minutes later, we will see her again, climbing up the slope, as the rays of the setting sun try to enter her eyes. Then, she will place her thin, long, veiny hands over her ageing eyes to prevent the intruding rays. Although it is impossible to see things from so far off, I know that her lips will be murmuring something at that time. She has a habit of talking to herself.

Miss Samuel, Seema, is generally reticent. She never offers any advice or suggestions unless sought. Yet, I always notice that people often become quite close to her.

What should be the meaning of closeness? Is it a corner in our hearts from where, through narrow lanes, intimate feelings of pain, hurt, love, regret, frustration, and sin emerge, only to submerge into a larger expanse? Or, is it that if someone touches the silent strings of our heart, they vibrate? Or is it just the pleasure of going with the flow?

She used to say, 'You know, Sarah, innumerable glowworms hide in the tiny dark space of our heart. As they fly, they suddenly light up brightly, then, as suddenly as before, they grow dark and there is a fine ray of light, and sometimes, a howling silence. These are the unreachable corners of light and darkness, movement and stillness, winning and losing, a repertoire of many conflicting words.'

This is what she would tell me when we were alone.

My father loved Seema very much. She was his younger sister, but they were more like close friends. But their friendship lasted till their youth. After that, my father was no longer with her. I have heard her speaking to my father. She even speaks to her father. Her father was Samuel David, and mine was Bobby, Mikhail Samuel.

She is my Atya, my paternal aunt.

I know a lot about her. Though I do not know 'many things' about her.

There may or may not be those many things about her. For that matter, we can hardly claim that we know everything about even our own selves.

It's a scientific fact that Earth remains steady due to the gravitational pull of the moon when it rotates on its axis at an angle. But sadly, we have no moon to keep us steady, and perhaps because of this, our thoughts and feelings are not stable. The moment we are unhinged, we collapse and scatter, who knows where to. But even if we forget about gravity or axes, we can still say that since man is a complex being and exists in many dimensions, he appears confused and incomplete. So, everyone tests and scrutinizes him from their own perspective! That is why his final truth or falsehood is always debatable.

She never married.

It is said that she had some love affairs.

She had difficulty getting married because of Rafu.

But after Rafu passed away, she was all alone in her advancing age.

The family agrees that she is a woman of liberal ideas.

But that is far from the truth.

The truth is that contrary to her liberal thoughts, she never lived her life in freedom. They say that Vaibhav Saxena, one of Seema's love affairs, had got tired of this frustrated woman with liberal thinking. Seema Aunty herself had shared this with me.

When I heard this, I realized that a life of paradoxes is not only extremely hard but impossible. Half the world is caught up in its vicious cycle.

Like those Russian nesting dolls, there is always a woman within a woman, and within her is another woman, and inside the very last shell is a woman who doesn't want to be a woman. She is naked, natural, like an escaped drop of a lively rhythm. She wants to be the free-flowing wind, but that never happens. Trapped within the darkness of her lonely, suffocating heart, she accepts restlessness as her natural rhythm. As a result, the unreal game of hide-and-seek begins. She seeks, she runs, and she hides!

More women are affected by psychological problems than men, and I meet them every day because I am a psychiatrist.

My friend, Dr Sunanda Nadkarni tells me that I am happy because I am unmarried and because I am not a Hindu. 'In our religion, a woman's competence is the last thing to be considered. First, her feminine qualities are tested to determine if she would prove to be a cultured, obedient and gentle woman; only then can she be a good wife and mother. My husband is also a doctor, but he will always be considered more intelligent, more powerful, and will earn more than I do.'

I laugh at this and tell her that it didn't make much of a difference whether a woman was Hindu or non-Hindu, because it was not God but nature that endowed every woman with a uterus and vagina so that she had to endure motherhood and wifehood all her life, willingly or unwillingly, and continue being exploited! 'And, the institution of marriage is in itself too complex and problematic,' I add. 'Hinduism is a vast and multi-faceted faith; it lets in diversity and plurality within its fold, and it is liberal, but in all Semitic religions, the authority of God and religious leader is supreme.'

Sunanda and my elder sister, Mili both are highly educated, independent and intelligent women, but even then, there is barely any difference between them. Both stand on sharp edges of the cliff—but they neither jump off nor retreat. They just shut their eyes when they look into the depth of the valley and let time pass. Such women generally depend on others for their decisions. That support could also be the society.

Take my mother. She would always worry about me getting married and settling in life so that I would be socially acceptable. She would often stare at me and then walk around the house dejected.

One day, I finally asked her, 'Do you want to say something, Mama?' She said she felt ridiculed in the community because of me.

I wasn't angry, though it pained me to hear the same old words that she had learnt by rote now also inscribed over her values.

I said, 'Mama, society exists because of me. Merely following community norms won't make me faultless and perfect. How could you forget Seema? And Rachel? It is not in my nature to live in suffocation, Mama.'

'Then, why don't you get married to Abeer? Am I stopping you from doing that?'

She was tearful. As it is, she cries easily. Blowing her nose, she said, 'Did I even stop Mili?'

'Tell me, did Mili get what she wanted out of marriage?' I asked her instantly.

Mili had felt suffocated. Before her marriage, she had suffered when she tried to convince my mother, and after marriage, she stood on an edge, answerable to all—her mother, community and society. Mili, my elder sister, who married a Hindu.

I had told her that the community's response didn't matter, and that first, she should decide what she wanted to tell herself. She understood what I had said. It was for good. And time moved on.

In the beginning, my mother cried a lot for Mili. Even for me. With a lot of patience, I tried to convince her with reason. 'Listen Mama,' I used to tell her. 'Till I know I am at fault, I will be deaf to others' opinions. If I try to listen what this or that person has to say, or pay attention to the cacophony, I will certainly lose my mental peace. Let me live as I want.'

Now, my mother doesn't interfere. She looks happy.

Seema believes that happiness cannot be implanted from the outside. I was emotionally attached to and influenced by Seema, but the irony was that she could never follow her thoughts and views in her own life. And the guilt and regret of this seems to have added one more line to her old, wrinkled face.

She couldn't deal with anything: the few people close to her, her decisions, and even her responsibilities.

She could certainly not deal with her father.

Her father, Mr Samuel David, retired Under Secretary. Also, my father Bobby's father.

Our family had inherited this silence from Samuel David, who couldn't rebel against his Pappa. He would grumble, but he never had the courage to go against him. As a result, when Mr Samuel David grew up, he became bitter, self-centred, and an opportunist.

When left alone, he became frustrated.

Samuel David's Pappa was David Ruben. He was a jailor during British rule. Unlike the sluggish and ridiculous '*angrez kay zamaney ka jailor*' with a Hitler-like moustache whom Asrani played in the famous Hindi film *Sholay*, David Reuben was a powerful, domineering, and arrogant man with a handlebar moustache. That was my great-grandfather, Khan Bahadur David Ruben!

I have only seen him in photographs, but my grandfather had told me that when he became angry, he would go completely out of control. When he waved his leather belt in the air and yelled at his youngest daughter, the delicate and sickly Ruth would often pee her pants in fear, but never dared to cry.

His son Samuel was the father of five children—three sons and two daughters—Danny, Bobby, Seema, Rachel and David.

My great-grandpa's name was David, and my younger paternal uncle was also named David. This is how the Jewish community named its children. The grandfather's name would pass to the eldest or youngest grandchild. Thus, if Daniel Uncle, my father, or David Uncle had had a male child, chances were that he, too, would have been named Samuel. This ensured the continuation of the family line. A feeble and somewhat ironic attempt to keep alive one's name on this earth, even though we Jews didn't believe in rebirth.

But this never happened. The son who could have continued the family name was never born. Most women kept giving birth to girls one after the other in the hope of a male child, even though every educated woman knows that it is not in her hands to conceive a male child. Still, in India, women are easily oppressed, humiliated and degraded.

My father never gave much thought to having a male child. But my mother? She had said that when I was conceived, she had hoped for a male child so that the family could be 'complete'. She had admitted that she was disappointed when I was born. She had been all the more disappointed when she realized that her desire for a male child would never be fulfilled because she had refused to remarry. My mother had accepted that the family line had come to an end. The names that had been circulating in the family stopped there.

But my Nanu kept his hope alive till the very last moment.

We called our grandfather Nanu. My Nanu! Although he was my Azoba, my paternal grandfather, but since Rafu called him Nanu (maternal grandfather), and Milcah (Mili) and I were younger than him, and all of us had grown up together, we, too, started calling him Nanu. Mama had told me that our real Nanu had passed away a long time ago, when she was just twenty, in an accident.

After David Uncle married Jyotsna Prajapati, Nanu wanted David to have a son with her because Danny Uncle was childless and my father had left this world. Jyotsna Prajapati was eight years younger than David Uncle, and she had had no child from her previous marriage. Yet, she remained indifferent towards David Uncle. So, David Uncle did not have a child who could be named Samuel and my grandfather never found peace. He must have left in great pain, physical and mental.

The Jews, known as the Bene Israel in South India, had begun their journey from Palestine. Theirs had been a long, arduous and tragic journey. My great-great-great-grandfather Isaji had seen this journey in his imagination, which arose from the sea waves at Navagaon. Over time, his grandson had sowed the seeds of this story in the consciousness of the next generation.

My father, Bobby, did not have much faith in the world of imagination. He was a student of history who believed in verifying the facts of the past historical events. After researching on this minority Jewish community, he had written a long article for a local English daily.

Seema keeps a copy of his essay in her drawer. I have read this article.

Seema Aunty had told me that Bobby died before he could see his own article published.

So, does it tell a completely different story?

Man's life is a flow of stories like Aesop's fables. The way a writer, or a ghost, or a protagonist raises questions in these stories, our life, too, interrogates us. But life ends without providing an answer or solution to those questions.

Like life had deserted my father, Bobby.

Like Danny Uncle had left for America, leaving everything unsettled here.

Like my grandmother, who asked the same question again and again.

Like Rafu, who had gone away, leaving Seema alone.

Stories often remain incomplete; the teller never returns. Sometimes, if he does, by then, the script of life is over.

When Danny Uncle returned from America, our Gitanjali Society flat had already been sold, Seema lived in Parisar, David Uncle had gone missing years ago, and Rosie Aunty, whom we had once seen as beautiful and young, had turned into a schizophrenic old hag. Danny Uncle had stayed in a five-star hotel and then flown back to America. The loose ends of the stories fluttered aimlessly.

Will these stories ever come together through our efforts?

Mama says, 'Sarah, you're as inquisitive as your father. I am never at peace.'

My mother is a very simple woman. I don't like to say things to her which might hurt her or unnecessarily make her think. I believe that thinking should be eliminated from those people's lives who never plan to follow their thoughts to any concrete base. Such people look startled, shocked and frightened, like a child caught in a crowd. My mother, Dolly Mikhail, is like that child. Her real name is Hannah. Woody Allen has a famous movie titled *Hannah and her Sisters*. The film's story has a perfect yet strange mix of love, sex, attraction, revulsion and the worthlessness of life. That shadow-like figure of worthlessness is my mother. So, I try to ensure that she is not disturbed. She wanders like a shadow in the house, outside her own existence.

I never got an opportunity to address my father Bobby as Papa. I only saw him in photographs in the family album and guessed what he might have been like. He and Danny Uncle were married on the same day in 1966, in Pune's Rasta Peth Synagogue.

Danny Uncle's wife, Rachel (Rosie) was from Mumbai while my mother was from Pune. Rosie Aunty was a White Israyel. Since Jews determine a child's lineage from their mother, if the woman is 'white'—from a pure bloodline—her children were also considered 'white' or pure. My mother was a 'black' Israyel.

Rosie Aunty was very proud of her white Israyel lineage and treated all the other family members as worthless and inferior creatures. After Rafu was born, and my father Bobby's demise had affected my grandmother's mental balance, Rosie Aunty successfully severed Danny Uncle's umbilical ties and guided him on to the only path that mattered—towards America. Mama remembers when Nanu had returned after seeing the two off. He had switched on a light in the dark house and said, 'God himself has said in the Bible that because Woman is created out of Man, a man shall leave his father and mother and be united with his wife. Then what is so strange about Danny's behaviour?'

Mother also tells me that gradually, Nanu's pension and

Seema's salary weren't enough for the growing needs of the family—granny's medical expenses, the frequent visits to the doctor for Rafu, and the psychiatrist's fee for David's depression. Because my mother did not know Gujarati and was a Jew, it was very difficult for her to get a job in a private or missionary school. After Papa's death, Mama returned to Pune with the two of us. Even though Nanu opposed it, Seema supported Mama throughout. 'The natural development of the girls will be hindered by your constant interference, bickering, stinginess and pressure,' she had made it very clear to Nanu. 'Let Dolly be free.'

Mama and I had tried to convince Seema to stay with us, but she always found some excuse. She would say, 'Sarah, it's time for me to shed my skin. I have reached the last stage of my life. Let me live the way I want to, my child.'

If you didn't pay attention, you wouldn't understand what Seema meant. And if you ever told her this, she would smile. Sometimes, she would say, 'Sarah, there isn't much difference between understanding and misunderstanding. Something that makes sense to someone may not make any sense to another. How will the world continue if this did not happen?'

Whenever I think of my father, I feel like Seema had a point.

Javed Qureshi was my father's close friend. They had been friends since their school and college days. Both had worked in the same company. So, when the company declared itself bankrupt, both became penniless. Javed Qureshi wore a pant-shirt and a tie like my father.

The incident goes back thirty-five years. That day, a mob had surrounded them. Things were going very wrong.

Javed Qureshi's selfish desire to live made him leap higher than my father.

The desire to live!

The joy of escaping!

The feeling that only he was human enough to be saved.

Javed Qureshi had pleaded with his palms together. 'I am a Hindu. My name is Vijay. Vijay Patel.'

And so, Vijay Patel, spared by the mob, fled.

And my father? 'Take off your trousers!' they must have screamed at him. Then, they had probably removed Mikhail Samuel's trousers themselves.

Then what?

Mikhail's meek plea—'I am a Jew'—must have gone unheard or was perhaps lost in the hysterical frenzy of the mob. Vijay Patel found the joy of escaping, but Mama lost her mind. And my grandmother never stopped asking the same question—'Sam, but my Bobby was Israyel, wasn't he?'

They say Javed Qureshi could not enjoy the bliss of surviving for long. He fell into the circle of sense and senselessness. One day, he lay down on a railway track.

'Pain can be personal, but not happiness,' Seema had said sadly. 'Happiness has roots, Sarah, which draw nourishment from the sorrowful past and, therefore, when happiness moves forward, it also drags its past. Perhaps that's why, deep within happiness, there is always the shadow of sorrow, which disturbs us.'

Mili believed that man can attain true happiness only by praying to God. I often argue with her. I tell her that accepting the presence of God in one way or another proves our incompleteness and fear and, therefore, the happiness received from a supernatural power like God may just be a feeling; it is not real. She gets irritated. She has become very irritable these days. In her sad times, she often thought that God, along with the whole world, had also cheated her. Mili had never been like this before.

When Nanu was nine or ten years old, he had extracted five

rupees from his mother, without the knowledge of his short-tempered jailor father, to buy an effective mosquito repellent advertised in the newspaper. In those days, five rupees was a big sum, but after much negotiation, his mother surrendered to his wish out of love for her son. A few days later, the postman delivered a parcel—special equipment to be used as mosquito repellent. There were five beautiful boxes packed inside each other. The last box was tied with a red ribbon. When Nanu opened it, he found two flat stones in a shiny packet. With the stones came a printed letter which read:

Catch the mosquitoes, put them on one stone and crush it with the other.

And the mosquito's game will be over.

Perhaps ten-year-old Samuel David hadn't felt this cheating so intensely. But for Mili, a thirty-eight-year-old woman who feels that her husband has cheated her, such small betrayals too might have stung quite sharply.

I tell her, 'If you are in doubt, you will always remain undecided. Either allow yourself to be cheated completely or just face it headlong. The fire of resistance simmers only for a very short period, and, surprisingly, the tenderness of emotion is felt the most during this time. Then, even tenderness evaporates like vapour, Mili.'

Mili is very emotional and, like my mother, cannot see clearly. She gets carried away easily. That is when you forget that you can swim. Sometimes, when she feels very lost, Mili says that God had perhaps chosen a difficult life for her.

At times, her statements make me uncomfortable. I tell her that she has turned God into a perfect, handy peg to hang her dirty linen on. Hang all your burdens! One should learn how to give up one's worries from Mili.

In times like this, my mother mediates. Mother and Mili believe that the first duty of a true Israyel is to treat

God as everything and trust Him completely. But I say that this universe is the result of an intense and long struggle. God has no role in it. Mother gets offended by this. To prove me wrong, Mili likes to narrate the story of the great Rabbi Maimonides.

In the eleventh century, the greatest Jewish philosopher and religious leader, Maimonides, was busy working on a complex book when an atheist scholar came to meet him. When the scholar saw the excellent book, he was curious about the writer. Maimonides told him that the book simply got written when the ink from the ink pot before him spilt over plain papers. The visitor was annoyed and argued that he was no fool and knew that only an intelligent and learned person could write such a book. The religious leader smiled and said that just as a capable artist is needed to create an excellent work, an all-powerful creator would certainly be needed to create such a huge, magnificent and beautiful universe.

Even Nanu would argue with my father. Seema had told me that once Nanu had almost fought with my father about Darwin's Theory of Evolution. 'Even if we accept your Darwin's theory of evolution, who created the first cell or the first unit of life that pulsated on this earth?'

Mother always becomes very emotional when narrating such stories about my father. She says that there was no similarity in our natures, but because she sees a shadow of my father in me, she loves me very much. Both Mili and my mother fear that something untoward might happen to me because I hold such irreverent ideas about God.

I worry when I hear such things. Is there any merit left in these so-called meaningful words—good or bad, sin or reward—in this world? If they still held meaning, why would words like selfishness, aggression, cunning, cruelty and shamelessness get so much attention? Why would George W.

Bush know the story of 'The Lion and the Lamb'* by heart? Why did radicals like Bal Thackeray and his sons, the Bajrang Dal with its godmen and women, or even religious leaders who encourage fanaticism become important? The heartbreaking scenes splashed on the front page of *Frontline Magazine*—an ill-clad child trembling in bitter cold outside a cave on the Afghanistan plateau, a Bihari victimized by the fire of casteism in Maharashtra, hundreds of people travelling on the roof of a train, or Palestinians running in panic with their dead or injured children in their arms—are these just figments of the media's imagination?

This is sequential deception. God, fate, sin or virtue do not liberate, they only restrict. But Milcah and our mother felt that I was just being a deviant, and thought they could cure me with their love and affection. Despite the vagueness in their own thoughts, they want to intervene in my desire to see things clearly. And I am not ready for this.

When seen this way, most people are hardly able to make sense of anything that is undefined. Life is nothing but a bridge for them; its only purpose is to help them reach the other side. Unfortunately, midway, the hurdles come to uproot them. Like Mili, uprooted from her natural rhythms.

She inherited Rachel's sweet voice. She was intelligent like Papa but emotional like my mother. She wrote poetry. She cleared the Sangeet Visharad degree in music, and since

---

*The story of the Lion and the Lamb is referenced in the *Book of Isaiah* in the Old Testament. Its symbolism is used both in Christianity and Judaism to represent the Messianic Age. It is a story of peace that predicts that all beings will live in hope and harmony in the Messianic Age: 'The wolf shall live with the lamb, the leopard shall lie down with the kid, the calf and the lion and the fatling together, and a little child shall lead them.' (Isaiah 11:6-9)

In Christian connotation, the 'Lamb' and the 'Lion' also stand for 'Christ sacrificed' and 'Christ resurrected' respectively.

she sang so beautifully, she would often sing on Ganesh Chaturthi and in programmes at the synagogue. But, despite her mellifluous voice, Mili's Jewish heritage always interfered with her training. To a Hindu guru, Mili was from an inferior caste, and to the Muslim teacher, she was just one of the fanatics who brought about the downfall of Palestine!

Mili had many failings. She accepted defeat easily; she was not a fighter like me, a trait I inherited from our father. And she had no patience at all. So, it was quite natural for her to be depressed. Mili always felt that the whole world conspired against her. She thought she had finally conquered the world by marrying Srikant. But she couldn't accept Srikant's growing religious fervour and fondness for rituals.

Mili stands on the bridge, perplexed.

My great-grandmother Diana, too, couldn't cross the bridge. She collapsed midway. After her daughters Lily and Ruth died untimely deaths, Diana lost her sanity—first because of the tragedy of her daughters and then, the terror of her husband.

It seemed like a tradition in our family—someone or the other would eventually lose their sanity and become unhinged. We never got any news of Nanu's younger uncle, Moses. Isaji's father, Eloji or Elijah, too, had become a monk. And right before my eyes, David Uncle was gone!

In our family, people were either too hot-tempered or they were eccentric. The latter often tried to flee from noise and crowd. However, nobody knows if they ever found freedom from this turmoil, because none of them returned to tell their story.

My father, Mikhail Samuel, would say that insanity and madness are not synonymous. Insanity can be hereditary, but when one loses control of oneself, then he is unhinged. Insanity is like a static, sad circle of depression.

People say that Eloji lost his mind after his wife and daughter were raped and killed by a British soldier. Some say that he was misled by a sadhu. Others say that he was put in jail on the charge of theft. There are different versions of the story and so many of them. But it is true that his photograph is not in our family album. And even Isaji never said anything about his father to his dear grandson, David.

You must be wondering what strange names these are. The truth is, after our ancestors first set foot in the Konkan region of Maharashtra, they discarded their feeling of displacement, hoping to make this land their new home. As the Hindu population was in the majority, it was safer to imitate the Hindu names and mingle with their culture. So, Isaac became Isaji and Elijah became Eloji. Similarly, we have names like Abaji, Ramaji and Hasaji. That's how they survived!

My father's friend Javed Qureshi had become Vijay Patel and survived.

Seema had once asked, 'Sarah, which names can protect our right to live with dignity in this country, which is daily moving towards a frenzy of fanaticism?'

I added—'Yes, and a woman's honour is always put at stake in such a situation. She has to face humiliation everywhere, whether she falls for someone or she falls in someone's hands and gets violated.'

Perhaps, even David Uncle didn't have the means to live honourably. He would often be depressed. Even then, how could an educated man who had lost his job multiple times sit idle, especially when he had a cunning and cautious wife like Jyotsna Prajapati, a hooligan brother-in-law, Mayank, and an ill-natured mother-in-law who was always sick.

All of them had gradually entered Samuel David's house.

Have you seen a snail? It is a boneless, fleshy, and sluggish creature. It builds a shell around itself to protect its soft body.

The shell is like a home. But the truly clever creature is the crab. It cleverly displaces the snail from its shell and then makes the shell its own home and enjoys its life in the water.

Jyotsna Prajapati's family was like a crab. They had grabbed flat B-7 at Gitanjali Society. Pretty Jyotsna had cornered Seema. In place of the lamps meant for Friday evening's Sabbath prayer, the photo of a Hindu deity, Santoshi Mata, was placed. The three members of the Prajapati family started holding devotional singing every Friday. A huge image of another Hindu goddess—Sharada Mata—adorned with haldi, kumkum and a sandalwood garland, her feet in golden anklets, was placed in our drawing room. The main door was engraved with the words 'Jai Mata Di' in red.

The women of the housing society embraced Jyotsna Prajapati wholeheartedly. 'Now this house looks like a true Hindu home!' they would say. 'How could these Muslims have ever occupied it?'

All this was before the 2002 Godhra riots in Gujarat. Yet, this story is not just one like it or another, nor will retelling it to infinity matter, because stories never end. Each story gives birth to another story, just as a cell divides into two, four and then into multiple cells.

Sometimes, a story and a cell may become distorted. When such a cell multiplies, it becomes a malignant tumour. Samuel David's home had become malignant.

Seema was chucked out, and we lost David Uncle forever in this vast world.

The new inhabitants sold the house at a huge profit. Danny Uncle and Rosie Aunty stayed in a five-star hotel for a while, and then left.

For Seema Samuel, Amdavad was now a forgotten past.

There is only a thin line between the past and the present. Whoever dives into the past and surfaces on the banks of the future survives; for those who can't, it is dark and deep there. My aunt's childhood friend Ameena couldn't come out of the deep, dark waters of the past.

Every present may not dive deep into the past and create history. Sometimes, the present burns and crackles on the edge of a crater, like volcanic lava, and, instead of sinking into its depths, asks several questions from life, holds it responsible. It is then that the collapse of people like Ameena disturbs us.

Who could have saved her?

I push my thoughts back and look up. Seema stands at the gate. Seeing me there unexpectedly, joy and surprise light up her sunken face.

'Seema!' My hand tries reaching out to her.

Chapter 7

Rama Aajji's room was cleaned and mopped. Incense sticks were lit. Later, it was whitewashed. It was then that we knew someone was shifting into her room. It would be inhabited soon. Rama Aajji would hover around the room for some time and then fade from everybody's memories.

The frustration, unemployment, hooliganism and apathy caused by the fast culture of multiplexes, malls and multinationals, and the race to become millionaires and billionaires has hardly left time for the older generation. For the old people, huddling together and laughing loudly in parks, sitting quietly in the corners, or on chabutras outside the houses, finishing useless domestic chores, scurrying around homes like scared rats, the younger generation has discovered an excellent shelter—the old age home. Vacancies are available according to your status. Come and place your household objects worth forgetting here!

Parisar is a shelter for single women like me and for the older members of well-to-do families. There is no bickering and slandering, no theft, filth or disorder, like in other old age homes. But, even here, as in the other old age homes, a colour is familiar: the permanent colour of sadness!

A long time ago, Mrs Chitnis had asked me, 'I am sure you know the literal meaning of the word Parisar. How appropriate it is: the vacant space around the house or place, the neighbourhood, a circumstance, or even death!'

Mrs Chitnis comes and stands by me. She looks upset with Rama Aajji's whitewashed room. 'It seems death is the only solution to all restlessness and chaos. Still, I don't know why a strange anxiety overcomes me. But why? When I think about this, I am confused. I am not certain about anything. Is it a yearning for life, the sorrow of leaving this beautiful world? Or, is it like Yudhishthira's reply to Yaksha's third question, the desire to live forever? Who knows?'

'It is only you overthinking,' I say with a simple smile. 'The more simply and naturally life is spent, the more peaceful and painless it is. Else, would the hustle and bustle of life let us breathe?'

She stares into the void for a long time before saying, 'Perhaps!'

The raw fragrance of the freshly-mowed lawn has permeated the environment. Holding her hand, I walk towards it. By the time we reach the lawns, she has got over her melancholy. As she sits, she asks, 'Who's coming into Rama Aajji's room?'

She hesitates a little before continuing, 'You are right, Miss Samuel. It is all right to be serious and philosophical about life, but one cannot live that way. In fact, it will leave you in a haze of sadness, and you will start losing yourself.'

Around seventy years old, Mrs Chitnis is thin, tall, and slightly bent, with sparse white hair and a high forehead. She wears a pair of metal-framed glasses, a round watch on her right hand, and a silence, trapped in the shadow of experience, crisscrossing her face. That's her. Whenever a thunderstorm rages within the half-shut doors of her heart or the hot wind lashes against it, in panic, she opens one of the windows, a skylight, or a faraway outlet. Then, you may peep inside her—otherwise, there is that same hushed silence. Mrs Chitnis. Doctorate in Economics, foreign-returned.

'Some Muslim woman from Amdavad.'

I look at Rama Aaji's room. 'Sakhu Tai was telling me that she is coming from my city. Honestly, I am delighted.' I say laughing.

She also smiles, 'You were right. Only when we move on naturally can we break the stillness of time. Otherwise, we who have arrived here, leaving behind our dear ones, remember those who leave this place forever with sadness and eagerly await the arrival of newcomers.'

Mary Varghese comes closer and says, 'So what? Now, this is our family. Whatever has been left behind was another life. Then she winks at me as usual, 'Oh! Sorry! I keep forgetting that I don't have a previous life or an afterlife, yaar.'

Mrs Chitnis and I are both silent. Our quietness stings Mary. 'O, come on! Say something! Okay, let me tell you a joke. A mouse and an elephant were in love. One day, the mouse cried and whispered in the elephant's ear. Suddenly, the elephant fainted and collapsed with a thud. Now, tell me what exactly the mouse said. Come on, tell me!'

Neither of us speaks at first. Finally, for Mary's sake, I say, 'I don't know.' When neither of us says anything else, she is a little disappointed. Still, continuing in the humorous vein, she says 'Yaar, it was the most popular dialogue of Hindi cinema, "I am going to be the mother of your child!"'

Our faces are expressionless. Mary stares at us in confusion. Maybe misery or inferiority or perhaps bitter melancholy swims across her dark, pockmarked face. And yet, wading through it, she fakes a giggle, 'Oh dear, were you born an old woman? Laugh, let your lungs breathe, let emotions show on your face. This is your time to eat, dance and be merry!'

A smile returns to my face. Suddenly, seeing me, she is sad, and her face dims. 'Yaar! I am not as educated, as you all. I came from a small place to fend for myself and became old, slogging all my life in hospitals. Who else was with me except the ward boys, nannies, sweepers and other nurses? Doctors are lords. Patients are Gods. So, with the rest of my companions, I talked in this way, joked and laughed or showed off. After all, what does Matron Mary Varghese know of profound knowledge and intelligent debate? She has only learned to laugh things away. Otherwise, how could this pockmarked and hunchbacked female have fought the beauty of this world?'

She becomes silent. The two of us don't feel it right to say anything, so we remain quiet, too. 'I am going to tune in to the radio,' Mary says before getting up and leaving. Mrs Chitnis and I sit, staring at her stout, retreating body.

Mary Varghese says that men desire a beautiful face, besides a beautiful body. 'There was nothing in me except female flesh and lustrous hair. That man-eater! I remained unaware of the cheating of love for quite some time! Miss Samuel, it was nothing but the exploitation of my body and shattered heart. I came to my senses. I extracted my price. Still, the fact remains that there was always a tiny, fluttering hope that, perhaps, he understood me! But hardly. In this bare world of glaring lights, they only saw the monstrosity of the ever-increasing hunch on my ageing body and the scars of pox marks on my aged face than the depth of my big black eyes or my lustrous, long, curly hair. Being an ugly woman is a curse. You will never understand, Miss Samuel.'

Sarah doesn't agree with Mary. She says that it's all make-believe. The vanity of good-looking people or the distress and anguish of the ugly—all this is bullshit.

I don't believe this. I think neither good looks nor ugliness are chosen. Each is received according to the laws of nature, although, sometimes, tragedies or accidents may add to it. I believe Mary did not use her body to achieve her goal because she knew pretty well that she was not blessed with beauty. But the body is not a ladder but a foundation, Seema. As with men, the body is equally gratifying and alluring for women and important, too. But a woman is afraid to accept this fact. Sexual relations are an individual's primitive need, a necessity which is quite apparent on this earth.

'Didn't you ever feel it, Seema?' Sarah had audaciously asked her.

❁

Abdul Zaidi had grabbed Seema while she was fleeing on the running track and pulled her towards him.

'Run slowly, girl!'

Abdul, an eleventh-grader, had embraced a seventh-grader, Seema. The children who were going to participate in the competition were called early in the morning for PT practice. Sir was late that day. The other children were either late or beginning to assemble.

Seema almost hid inside Abdul Zaidi's firm embrace. She would remember Abdul's fine line of moustache, heavy breathing, quivering lips and breathless syllables. Seema would also remember the touch of Abdul's soft, lean palms on her blossoming breasts, which had sent a shiver, almost like a ripple, down her body. The leaf was pulsating in the first drizzle of the rainclouds—and the universe had stopped!

Hurriedly, Seema freed herself from the embrace of the most intelligent and attractive boy in the school. That day, Seema registered nothing and forgot everything. She didn't realize when she was scolded by the PT teacher for taking longer than the scheduled time in every round of the race.

She forgot to say 'yes, sir' to the roll call in the class. She even forgot to play on returning home!

Miss Seema Samuel still remembers how, at the age of thirteen, she had tossed and turned the whole night. It was only when she had hugged the sleeping Rachel that she could finally sleep. Something trembled in Miss Samuel's aged body. A shadow of a faded memory stirred and drifted away. Perhaps it was a suppressed sigh, a reaction towards the changing geography of the body, who knows!

❁

Mrs Chitnis notices me smiling tenderly.

'What were you thinking?'

'Nothing,' I say, shaking my head.

She is silent again. She is not intrusive. She calls needless meddling 'digdaah', an intrusion.

Sarah's question still hangs in the air, like a bat hanging upside-down, watching the incoherent shapes of the reflections formed by the shadows of my half-finished memories and Mrs Chitnis's silence.

I grope for words.

'Our childhood is a magic box, Mrs Chitnis. Every time you open it, something new pops up. A pigeon, a handkerchief, a ring, an egg, a hen, a banana, an apple, an orange, a bead necklace, a mouth-shut monkey, a pack of cards, a smiling clown, a red ribbon, and sometimes, a djinn! We are afraid. We want to escape, but our eyes, our minds, are hypnotized. It's important to watch the whole show.'

In the front row, Seema, wearing her hair in two braids, listened attentively to Trivedi Sir teaching Wordsworth's poem. While explaining to the class, the teacher looked at his favourite student. 'Now, take out your notebooks and write down the word-meanings. Let me see what have you understood,' said Trivedi Sir.

Quickly opening her notebook, Seema flipped through the pages to get to the next blank sheet when a crumpled letter went whirling towards Trivedi Sir's table and landed there.

Seema almost froze. Trivedi Sir noticed her pale, drained face, trembling hands and teary eyes. He opened the letter:

'My dear, the queen of my heart, how many letters have I written to you but you never come? If you don't come today, you know what will happen, don't you? Don't ask me later who writes those dirty things about you on the bathroom walls! I even know your brother Danny. Shall I tell him about that playground incident?

Meet me in the same lane; the one I had mentioned earlier. My dear birdie, my lips are hungry. Do you understand?

Your admirer.'

While the whole class was busy writing, Trivedi Sir quietly came near Seema and wrote in her notebook, *'Bahaar aav…* come outside.'

Seema went out silently. Sir was standing near the tower, at a distance from the class. She sobbed as soon as she reached him. Sir held her gently and comforted her affectionately, like a father, 'Don't cry, my child. Do you know that miscreant? Have you also written to him?'

After a while, Seema's trembling voice became steady. Meanwhile, Surendra Shah, Doctor Kailash Shah's spoilt brat, and Seema's classmate, a backbencher, the seventeen-year moron, came out thrice of the classroom with an excuse to spit. Calm and composed, Trivedi Sir noticed this and sent Seema back to class.

In the evening, when school was over, Seema saw Surendra walking out with a limp as discreetly as possible so she wouldn't notice. Then, he didn't come to school for a week, and when he did, Seema saw him go into a different section, Section C.

Did the first djinn, which had emerged at the age of thirteen, go back to hide in the magic box again?

She hadn't known then that djinns can change shape.

❁

Before her, Mrs Chitnis sits with her head on her knees, caressing blades of grass. Her forlorn posture makes her look like a lonely, lost girl.

The waning sight of sparkling rays filtering through the foliage and creating and dissolving images, a growing chill in the blowing wind, the slowly melting light on the distant hills, the silence of Parisar, and two old women sitting in the lawn in the dim light of sunset.

This moment, ready to hide in the pages of time, will end now, and the page will turn over.

Game over.

Mary Varghese's favourite statement is 'game over!'

'Yaar, what to say; they were too small, my two brothers, when my father died. Arre, it was the same—country liquor. He was a daily wager, working in the fields. He had three favourite pastimes: drinking, thrashing my mother and his children for making his life hell, and producing more children every year.

'I was around a year and a half old when he flung me to the floor, yelling at my mother for bringing me milk. It must be my father's terror which erupted as a hunch on my back.

The three middle ones died of illness and poverty. The twins survived because he passed away before they could.

'Ma would shell coconuts and sell them in the market. I helped Shetty's wife. In return, Shetty paid for my school fees and clothes. I walked three miles to school every day. Sushila Madam would praise my beautiful handwriting and intelligence.

'In the meantime, my brothers grew up, and Shetty's domestic chores, too, increased. It would be night when I reached home, but my brothers' education was also important. Then what? I had just completed high school when I had to leave home.'

All of a sudden, Mary Varghese's eyes grew moist. 'Have you suffered the youth of a poor girl? A worn-out petticoat, a blouse and a scrap of cloth tugged and pulled continuously to cover the breasts like the shade of a roof. The nails of her toes scrape this accursed earth, always, and her embarrassed eyes are lowered and blind to the flames of the sun! In a scuffle, I slipped out of Shetty's grasp and fell on a stone. My one-and-a-half yards of cloth cover was caught in his grip. Look at this scar under my hair.

'Father Peter helped me get admission at the Kochi nursing school. I raised my brothers, washed their knickers and shit. I sent money orders for their studies from my stipend money so that they could achieve something.'

Then?

Then the game was over.

'They became big men. Went to Saudi. Amassed gold. Got a two-storey house constructed over our tiny hovel. Brought wives. And gave a room and a kitchen to my mother and me in the outhouse!

'One comes to know that the game's over, Miss Samuel, when our bones start decaying.'

One day, Mary had said this with sadness. It seemed she had pushed aside a sob and said, 'Yaar! Now, the game of life ought to be over, too. Look, the flesh has started leaving the bones. The way rats desert a sinking ship. Hair, teeth, bones, skin, honour, desires, dreams, all want to run away.'

She gazes at me for some time and then laughs loudly. Winking mischievously at me, she asks, 'My dear girl! Why do you feel sad? This is our time to enjoy.'

Mary's earlier remarks are getting muddled within me. Mrs Chitnis says, 'Perhaps Mary looks at beauty, love, and sexual relations as separate strands, although these do not exist in straight lines but are entwined, like the chromosomes in our DNA. But there was only hollowness in my life. The pull of attraction never concretized itself into a passion that matures as true love. Madhav Rao was near, but not close! Happiness was served in a premeditated manner. The body became a playground where the game began at the blow of the whistle and, once exhausted, lay breathless, mechanically.

'One didn't have to go far to look for the causes. The daughter of a millionaire father, Sonal Patel, was in the same University department as him. Older than Madhav by seven years, she was beautiful, bright and intelligent. Madhav couldn't resist her. By marrying me, a poor farmer's son had removed the obstacles from his way and by coming closer to her, he made his future bright.

'One may intrude only till the threshold of a home, Miss Samuel. Forcing your entry beyond this is digdaah or encroachment. It is violence. All directions in the sky look red and fiery even after sunset. But to transgress the courtyard of the red sunset is inauspicious.

'I wanted to avoid this sinful episode, so, as soon as my contract with the University abroad was over, I left with my son, concerned about his tender mind and the adverse social conditions. But in due course, when he created his own world, they complemented each other, and *I* was considered the digdaah. Then I was thrown out and came here.'

She gets up at once and leaves me sitting there, quickly climbs up the stairs to her room, closes the door and disappears. I stare at her image dissolving in the air.

Shanta Chitnis had perhaps enveloped herself in the cloak of her high-middle-class values. Perhaps the bubble of mistrust had expanded and burst. She stood all alone.

Dr Shanta Chitnis likes walking into the dim light of the sunset. Both glorified and weighed down by her own knowledge, she had missed out on the practical tips of life. When this daughter of a Saraswat brahmin father fell in love, she knew she had done something extraordinary, but she couldn't rise above her tradition-bound nature. She broke but couldn't change herself.

And Papa? Could he change himself? Could he rise above his father, David Reuben, in matters of women? Under Secretary Samuel David hadn't listened to Bobby and Seema and had married off dim-witted, foolish and two-and-a-half month pregnant Rachel to a forty-two-year-old alcoholic widower and junior engineer Joel Garson, who lived in a small village in Maharashtra, two nights' train journey away.

Someone whispers softly in the emptiness of my heart: 'I like Sohrab so much. When I grow up, I will marry him.'

Foolish Rachel. She never grew up and went away as she was, leaving behind imperfect Rafu.

I climb the stairs to the veranda. Sitting at the door of the kitchen, Sakhu Tai is helping Rasayan chop the vegetables.

A very old Marathi song floats in the air—'*Ja muli ja dilya gjari tu sukhi raha.*' (Go, daughter, go, may you find happiness in your other home.)

Could Rachel, who was six years younger than me, find any happiness in that other home?

Chapter 8

She arrives in Parisar like a shadow and generally remains quiet. This new occupant of Rama Aajji's room is Ameena—Ameenaben Iqbal Rizvi. She must be the same age as me. Our chatterbox, Mary, has tried to strike up a conversation, but her silence is forbidding. She spends entire days confined to her room. Often, dinner is sent to her room, and if at all she is seen in the dining room, she is lost in thought, completely aloof and detached. Ameena is her own world.

I often find her sitting alone on the staircase late into the night, staring at the sky. In the silent, cold nights, the lights flicker in a few homes on the hills like fireflies. As I sit on the stairs on my side of the veranda, I see her lost in the depths of solitude.

It is a dark night. The stars are clear and bright on the hills, while the distant hills, enveloped in darkness, seem like a huddle of huge, mysterious creatures. I feel as if I have become disembodied and am floating in the air. Trees, roads, lamp-posts, houses, marketplace, temples, hills, twinkling stars, silent, fluttering wind, and Ameena, who sits like a statue. I step closer to her.

I don't know why, but suddenly, one of Meerabai's couplets from my grade eight textbook slips through my lips:

'*Junu to thayun re dewal junu to thayun*

Maaro hanslo naano ne dewal junu to thayun'

(The temple is now old, but the swan is still young.)

As soon she hears this, she grabs my hand, '*Gujarati jaano cho*?' (Do you know Gujarati?)

'Yes, I belong to Amdavad.'

For a long time, silence stands between us. Lifting her head from her knees, Ameena says, 'C.P. Shah used to teach Gujarati literature. When he taught us poems, the layers of meaning opened up. But at our age, our minds could not absorb the meaning; they merely brushed us and went by. Our mind would fly, who knows into what wildernesses, yet we were not afraid. That was the thrill and excitement.'

To explain the next few lines, Sir asked my friend to stand up—'What does the poet want to convey here?'

'*Aa re kaya to hansa dolwane laagi re,*

Padi gaya daant maahyalun rekhoon to rahyun.'

(This body has become old, teeth have fallen, and now only the hollow shell of this body remains.)

While she explained the meaning to Sir, I drew the face of an old woman and her toothy grin in her notebook.

'Ameena Hussain?' I cry out with joy of recognition.

'Seema Samuel?' She hugs me.

My mind flies far away. It races, leaps across forty-five… forty-seven years, and stands before the school gate, holding a bundle of books in its hand.

'Why didn't you come yesterday?' Seema complained.

'Arre, Baba had caught me, so Ammi told me not to go to school.'

'How did Baba come so early?'

'Yaar, I had stolen and eaten a lot of tamarinds; maybe that's why.'

'I come to school every day whether Baba catches me or not.'

'Why will it affect you? You are as thin as a skeleton. You won't know that Baba pounces on and catches hold of a strong girl like me. It's only on the fifth day that I could finally pour water over my head and have a nice bath,' she said, rolling her eyes.

Then she quickly took out her arithmetic notebook and handed it to Seema, 'Now, come on, do my homework fast or else that lame Shrotriya Sir will pull my ears and make me stand.'

Then she looked around and whispered in Seema's ear, 'How I hate that cripple, Seema!'

'But why?'

'You know, when the whole class is busy solving problems, that rascal comes and stands next to me, pretending to take a pencil, rubber or a pen from my desk, and touches me…here.'

Her face had flushed, and so had Seema's.

'Next time, sit on my left side,' Seema said with love and concern.

Ameena Hussain, who had once sat on my left, was no longer bold and strong. I can hardly recognize this Ameena with her silver-streaked hair, sunken cheeks, and dull eyes.

I sneak a look at her, sitting there as dark as night. She looks like a picture of trauma itself. In the twinkling darkness of the night, she lifts her arms, cries 'Allah', collapses in my lap like an injured bird, and bursts into tears.

'I can bear everyone's death but not my surviving, Seema! O, Allah! Why do I have to suffer this hell, day after day?'

I have no idea how much time passed by. Only the slow rhythm of our breathing can be heard once the chirping of the night insects stops. The stars slowly begin to move closer to us. I spread my hands to hold the stars in my fists.

'There are no stars, only darkness. Look, even your fists are empty,' she is speaking faster, in case she forgets what she will say next.

'You know, Seema, I can't sleep at night. I couldn't save anyone. Abba, Iqbal, my two grown-up sons, daughter-in-law, my daughter Ghazal and granddaughter Sana. I only kept watching myself live.'

'Did either of us ever look like a Jew or a Muslim?' Ameena asks. 'Despite being a lecturer of political science, I could hardly tell them that no culture in this country is complete and absolute, and no race or religion is pure. We all share our five thousand years of heritage. That we are mere bubbles in the flow, not the stream itself; but alas I couldn't tell them, Seema. They destroyed this five-thousand-year-old stream in just fifty minutes. All that was left were the naked, exposed bodies of Sana, Ghazal and Ayesha, and the broken bodies of the men.

'I wore a Gujarati-style sari, and this Ameena spoke Gujarati, so she was pushed out of the crowd which had shouted, "*Gujarati ben chhe, emne jawaado*" and survived.' (She is Gujarati...let her go.)

I don't know why, but the receding darkness becomes heavy and sinks, drowning us both.

Time has stopped. The night is still. Our minds and hearts are stunned into silence. I wish someone would wake us. I wish the pendulum would move. It is such a weightless-but-sinking feeling. When she suddenly shivers, I suffocate. I try to calm her, but she jerks my hand away, like a stranger's hand. She withdraws within herself. Her voice seems to emerge from deep inside her: 'Do you know what I see? That all my dear ones are standing around me. They point at me and laugh. Their laughter terrifies me. When I wake up soaked in sweat, I realize it's dark. A blackout. In the dream and beyond. Have I become joke?'

The day has broken. The stars have dimmed. The fluttering of birds' wings blends with the distant sound of the blowing of a temple conch-shell. In just a few minutes, the night will disappear behind the hills. I hold her hand and help her get up on her feet, 'Go and sleep Ameena; you'll feel better.'

As if in a trance, she gets up, climbs the stairs and goes to her room. Watching her silent, shadowy figure blurring, I feel like she's a walking ghost.

I slowly climb the stairs and reach my room, which sprawls under a dreary light. Forsaken. I don't know how, but I realize for the first time that this room will look exactly like this in my absence, spread out desolately.

When people live, their presence makes a difference, but when they die, it hardly matters. Life goes on. The pushing and jostling crowd doesn't let anyone stop. Ameena has come a long way, but she probably wants to go back. This is dangerous. There is a risk of losing balance when running against the flow.

Ameena's silence, her monologues, her strange disbalance, scares me. She is afraid to come out into the open air. Spinning round in the inner recesses of her mind, has Ameena taken to my mother's ways?

Ameena wants to forget that circling, violent mob and its echoes. She wants all of it to become an illusion, something that didn't happen. But illusions are meant to be broken, and when they collapse, man crumbles without a whimper.

For two hundred and fifty years, the structure of Wali Dakni's grave had been in a state of delusion. It took pride in being an auliya, a saint, a part of our syncretic culture. It was the delusion of a tarred road under the inky darkness of night—when the yellow, dried leaves of autumn rattled on that paved road, and blew away the delusion.

I think of the doors of the abandoned room that Ameena had pushed open in her moment of forgetfulness. It was good that I kept quiet because she was empty to the core of her inner self. In such a situation, the hollowness of my words would have only hurt her.

In the end, we are all so lonely.

It is said that the first man in the universe was troubled by his loneliness. He saw the sun, the moon and stars, animals and birds, and tried to enjoy nature. Still, he was lonely. He wanted to speak. He wanted to express himself. Then, one fine day, he climbed onto a hilltop and shouted from atop, 'I…I am…'

His voice echoed and he got scared of the sound of his own echo.

Those who come out of loneliness try to surround themselves with a horde of sound. Sometimes, this noise is snatched away from them, but often, they themselves get tired of this noise. Thus, this vicious cycle of this primordial game of the universe goes on.

Ameena was my friend since grade eight. Her father had been transferred to Amdavad. He was the section in-charge in the Income Tax Department. She got admitted in the middle of the session to the Nootan High School at Navrangpura, which was closer to her father's office. A tall, healthy and pretty daughter of educated parents, Ameena was full of life and quite mercurial. She often said to me, 'Do you know the meaning of your name, Seema?'

'Yes.' I would reply. 'River of quicksilver.'

'But you aren't like that, Seema. You are so quiet.'

'So what!' I would exclaim, miffed. 'I am as bright as quicksilver.'

'Yes, dear, I know you are very bright. But you should also cover yourself like our Muslim women, otherwise—haven't you seen those boys of senior classes, Kishore and Manu? Even our respected Sir…'

'Enough! Will you keep quiet for two minutes? How can you talk all the time? It seems like an Englishman coined the word the chatterbox after you.'

'Let the rascal say what he wants, who cares, but, honestly, I really love chatting and gossiping. I don't know how people, especially some people, can remain so quiet. I would suffocate and die!'

She was the same Ameena—my frightened, quiet and scared friend with grey hair, a flat, sunken face and a flabby body. The tides of her silence gushed through her eyes and, hugging me, she had said, 'Everyone is lost, but at least I have found you Seema. O Allah! Thank God I found you at last!'

No matter how serious the subject being taught in the class was, Ameena, silly girl, would draw pictures and scribble jokes in my notebook and, clearing her throat, would pass it to me—

Let Khatri Sir go to hell! Let's go out and eat berries.

Look at Anupam Shah…he is watching you and me and not paying attention to Sir.

Look at that pigeon. It's cooing with its puffed-up chest.

It seems 'baba' is about to catch me.

Last night, Ammi and Abbu had a big fight. Do your parents also fight?

Why didn't you make two plaits today? You look like a doshi, an old hag.

Ameena has forgotten everything. She stares at the blackness of night, day after day, without blinking. She cannot forget that encircling mob, those echoes, that restlessness, and the utter futility.

'Not everyone's death but my living, is what I see.'

Was anything left in Ameena?

How many people who have suddenly experienced depression, trauma and the darkness of hopelessness could save themselves?

Could B-7, Gitanjali Society, survive after Rachel and Bobby's deaths?

Isn't it necessary to have more inner strength than outer support to survive? Perhaps that's why Ma crumbled in the same corner where she had stood in a state of emotional disquiet.

'I'll come back soon, Ma,' Bobby had said as he kissed the mezuzah and left. Ma had seen him leaving from the balcony.

That same day, a riot had broken out in the city. Bobby never returned home. Ma kept repeating the Psalm from the *Book of Genesis*, 'The Lord is my Shepherd and I shall not want. Yea, though I walk through the valley of the shadow of death, I will fear no evil: for thou art with me; thy rod and thy staff, they comfort me. The Lord is my shepherd...my shepherd... my shepherd...The helper and friend who was our comfort with his strength and fearlessness had left our green pastures.'

The strong howling winds had destroyed my mother's peace of mind. After coming out of three days of unconsciousness, Ma had caught hold of Papa and asked in her broken voice, 'But, our Bobby was an Israyel, wasn't he, Samuel?'

Memory plays strange games. The flow of nostalgia doesn't follow a set pattern. Hanging on to the edges of some special places, colours, circumstances, people, time periods or snatches of sentences, it plunges into another time and spreads over the present, like a poisonous vine. The making and the unmaking of the collages of memory cannot be checked by the past.

❁

Diana's face is frozen within the window frame on the third floor of apartment B-7 of Gitanjali Society. So is Rafu's face, fixed and frozen in the dim light of that room. This entire episode had already been scripted. How could it be stopped?

When Danny didn't return from America, when Bobby met an untimely death, when Hannah (Dolly) and her daughters settled down in Pune, when mother passed away, leaving Seema with Rafu, Mr Samuel David became emotionally dependent on his high-strung son, David.

He took to doing small chores for David to keep himself occupied. But this unsettled David more. David's hesitations, his lack of confidence, his doubts, grew, but Papa always thought he was right.

David, I have put your breakfast on the table.

I have sent your clothes to the laundry.

I have taken out your clothes for the interview.

I have cleaned your scooter, too.

I have written both the applications for the jobs; just sign them.

David...

David...

David...

David shouted at Papa, who held his shoes in his hands. 'I don't want to go for any damn interview. Will you let me sit quietly for a moment?'

Without having his breakfast and stomping in his slippers,

he came downstairs. Papa quickly went to the window, stretched out his right hand and prayed for his son's wellbeing.

Seema had silently watched this scene as she served breakfast to Rafu. She heard Papa muttering to himself, 'Perhaps he was getting late for the interview. That's why he was angry.'

Disturbed and upset, Samuel David paced up and down the room.

Rafu stared at him for a long time. Then, he got up and stood in his grandfather's way. He touched Samuel David and said, 'Nanu! David was angry with you, no? Haha, hehe... He scolded you.'

Samuel David walked away, trying to ignore Rafu, but Rafu tagged along, dragging himself. Flinging his twisted left arm forward, he touched his grandfather again and repeated the same thing, 'David was...'

But before Seema could stop Rafu, Papa turned and slapped him hard with the same hand that he raised for David's wellbeing. Rafu's highly challenged mind collapsed before the crazy behaviour of this normal, sane person.

He fell flat on his face, too shocked to even cry.

By the time Seema picked and hugged him, Papa had already climbed down the sixty stairs. Seema saw from the window as he walked towards David, who sat quietly on his scooter at a distance, under a tree.

In order to survive, one must understand that along with inner strength, in any human relationship, space is equally important. However, even though he was their father, this fact was lost on Samuel David.

The issues that Seema, Bobby and David had wanted to ignore or forget, he brought up over and over again:

David, why didn't you object when they said you were unfit for accounts work?

David, did Danny say anything about taking you to the US?

David, has your friend Kavita Taneja left you?

David, why don't you consult a psychiatrist?

Samuel David thought he was concerned for his children's anxieties, for their future. Perhaps, he never understood the futility of his intrusion. By encroaching into their space, he wanted them to accept him completely. As a result, he became more distant from them, lonelier. He struggled within, but refused to change. He was so, very lonely.

Even Mrs Chitnis looks very lonely. Perhaps she never had the time to think about this. Life is not only about thinking about oneself, it's also about opening your hearts to others, even if they move far away from your reach. The warmth and spark of their presence remains in some corner of our hearts, even in their absence. Amidst the gloom of melancholy, this void opens up like a safe cocoon and assures us of our existence. Otherwise, what is the meaning of this long life?

Did Samuel David's long life hold any meaning? None, except silent anticipation and incoherent ramblings.

Was the silence of Parisar also mute, incoherent rambling?

Was there any meaning to Ameena Iqbal Rizvi's incoherent ramblings?

Chapter 9

Samuel David remembered that helpless evening when he had felt very weak, sitting alone in the balcony of his third-floor apartment, watching the evening emerge from behind the clouds.

His balcony faced the other balconies of the neighbouring apartments, each displaying the same middle-class life. Freshly washed clothes fluttered on clotheslines. Housewives were busy doing chores. The children of the colony were playing cricket on the grounds.

He hadn't retired yet, and dreams still twinkled in the eyes of his family members. The siblings behaved like siblings, and waited for each other for the Friday Shabbat prayer.

David was young. Once, while he played cricket, Samuel David watched his son batting fabulously from his balcony. Akram, who bowled, was annoyed to see David's innings rising. The well-built Akram hurled a bouncer, aiming at David's head. By the time Samuel could warn David, David had fallen flat on the ground. When he reached the grounds, climbing down the sixty stairs from his apartment, a scuffle had started. Akram was sitting over David's chest.

'You katua, you cut-up bastard! Ach-thoo!'

David had spat on his face.

Two tight slaps landed on his cheek. 'Say that again, you

son of a dog!' Akram's face was flushed with anger.

The rest of the boys of the colony were enjoying this free-for-all show, while Samuel David tried to control Akram. David slipped out of Akram's grip, clawed at his face and kicked him in his belly. Akram's father, who had returned home, ran up to save Akram and slapped David, who had by then already been pulled away by Samuel. David fell on the ground and howled with pain.

'You bastard, you son of a bloodsucker, how dare you hold him and not let go!'

A stunned Samuel stared at his son's dusty body and the red face of Akram's father. By then, a few Muslim men had huddled around Akram's father, Muhammad Ansari, and whispered amongst themselves. From the verandas in the colony, Gujarati gentlemen and ladies looked on and enjoyed the drama.

Akram's father had found quite some support. Arrogantly, thrusting his chest out, he put his hand on Samuel's shoulder and said, 'Samuel Bhai, it's better to stay grounded in reality. It doesn't affect us, huzoor, there are millions of us in this city who will stand with us. Just measure yourself up against us. As long as fights and storms are kept in check, things are peaceful.'

Samuel David remembered that day with bitterness. He also remembered the ruckus David had created. He had cried and fallen down again and again, asking him why he, too, hadn't slapped Akram instead of dragging him home. More than that, he hadn't even said a word to Akram's father! He was a coward. He was not his father!

'I will crack the skull of that bastard katua. I will scratch out that bastard's eyes! I will never keep my mouth shut like you.'

Samuel David had laughed at David's howling and said, 'Jews, too, are katua.'

'So, what! No one knows about it!' David had said as he cried.

Samuel felt a stab in his chest. David's statement, though uttered years ago, pierced through his heart. Alas! If only one could turn the clock back. Alas! If only people knew that even Jews were katua, Bobby would be alive.

He sighed and looked down from his balcony. People were returning from their work, the way birds return home. No one returns to this house when the sun sets. It's been around ten years since Danny and Rosie left for the US. Bobby and Rachel will never return. Miriam is quite ill these days. Seema has taken the fifteen-year-old challenged boy, Rafu, for a walk in the park. And David, who had once challenged to crack the skull of Akram, was slowly becoming a nervous wreck!

He came in and looked around his flat. It was old, with cracked plaster, without any paint or polish. A lifeless home. Like him, who was on the wrong side of seventy. Sparse grey hair on the skull, grey stubble, sunken cheeks and droopy lips! Taut face, sunken eyes and a bent figure. He grinned suddenly. Now, I look exactly like my mother! One finds traces of some ancestor or the other at different stages of one's life. Ma, Pappa, grandmother or great-grandmother, who knows whose genes the body, this bag of flesh and bones, hides within itself. He had hardly anticipated his future before this.

Sitting on a bench with his two little sisters at the small Godhra railway station, when twelve-year-old Sam had watched the arrival and departure of trains, he never anticipated that one day, tossed around in life, he would lose his children and will be lonely and sad, in this empty flat on the third floor as the dusk fell!

In the balcony of C-7, the house right in front, a newly-married couple came out with arms around each other, but sobered up after seeing Uncle Sam. Vijay let go of Gita's hand and asked, 'Hello, Kaka. Are you alone?'

Samuel ignored his query and asked him instead, 'How come you are home early today? You usually come late at night.'

'We'll go out to see a film tonight, Kaka. It is showing at the Relief Talkies.' He looked at Samuel for a split second before shooting another question, 'Kaka, when is Danny Bhai coming home?'

Vijay's question pierced through Samuel and disturbed him. He knew that most of the residents of the colony had seen how Danny had fought bitterly with everyone and left home, never to return. But who can check the human desire to attack the other at the slightest opportunity?

Seeing Samuel's crestfallen face, Vijay felt a bit embarrassed. Trying to make amends, he added, 'I asked because Kaki has been unwell these days.'

Samuel knew that sometimes, people asked such irrelevant, probing questions because their terms with the colony now were only that of hello-how-are-you? His family no longer belonged to 'our people' anymore, since they were believed to be Christian or Muslim.

Samuel had settled in this colony of Navrangpura before he retired. Miriam had got fed up of setting up homes in government-allotted houses. Quite often, when Samuel would get transferred, he had to go alone, because it would be a problem getting the children admitted to new schools and colleges mid-session. Moreover, expenses went haywire, trying to manage the burden of two households and the education of children on a regular, fixed salary.

Sam had been in search of a permanent, low-cost home in Amdavad. One cannot dream of luxury on a hard-earned salary, so the search led to an affordable housing society on the outskirts of Amdavad, which was expanding in a big way. In far-flung areas such as Navrangpura, Sarkhej, Gulbai Tekri,

Vastrapur, Mani Nagar, St Xavier's College, the big dreams of small people were taking shape. A similar dream had taken root in the Gitanjali Society, behind Commerce College. Sam had come to know of this.

But he had a couple of problems.

Could their limited resources bear this burden?

Second, would they get a place among the Jains, Brahmins, Baniya, Patels, and Shahs?

Samuel David remembered walking for miles together under his black umbrella in the fiery heat of Amdavad. With every visit to the construction sites, his tired feet recovered, the hidden enthusiasm reared its head, and the dream of a home came alive.

'I want to register my name for this housing society.'

'Samuel Bhai! What on earth are you saying? Do you think we can dump our religion into a trash pit for your sake? Arre bhai, however hard you try to make us believe you, have you ever heard of a cat in a Jain family that won't eat rats?'

Embarrassed, Samuel returned home, tired, 'Miriam, no success even today.'

Miriam was irritated, 'Why do you have to go and tell them the name of your community? Just mention your surname, and you won't have any problem. Once the advance is accepted, we will get our allotment, and the rest can be seen later. As it is, eating meat or fish is next to impossible because the prices have shot up. We can have them quietly during the festivals. We can tell them that we are vegetarian.'

He laughed. He thought, *I wish I could also change my name from Samuel to Shyam.*

'Do you think they are fools, Miriam? Is it as simple as eating served food and pushing off quickly?'

Miriam's voice was sad. 'What to do, then? Your retirement is only a few years away. Our budget is tight. Danny has completed his medical studies, but the other children are only halfway through their education. How long can we move from one house to another?'

Samuel David had never thought it would be so problematic to get a house because of his religion. He remembered the large and open homes of his childhood days at Godhra, Baroda, Surat, and Bharuch. Wherever Pappa was transferred, they got to live in huge bungalows, from which the Jail was not too far away.

Even during his own career, Samuel David didn't have to struggle much. But he hadn't anticipated that such a thing would ever happen in his late years, when retirement was near. He had felt the ground slipping beneath his feet. He felt suspended in air.

After every 'house-search campaign', he would return home and tell Miriam, 'You know, Miriam, Mira Ben to your neighbours, I used your tactics today. I went to Navrangpura's Mangalam Society and told them that I wanted to register. They were very happy and asked my name. With all the dignity of a government official and faking a happy smile, I gave them my surname and asked them to take down my initials. The man took down my Marathi surname immediately and then said, "Saheb, *puru naam shu chhe*?" (What is your full name?) I tried hard to keep a straight face and said, "Samuel David, Under Secretary."

'Suddenly his pen stopped. "*Isai chho*?" (Are you a Christian?)

'"No, a Jew."

'"What? Which caste is this? I haven't heard of it before! Jew?"

'Then he struck off my name. His face was even more expressionless and duller than mine. He told me that he had made a mistake, that he remembered just now that the advance for all the flats had already been deposited and that all the flat owners were pure Hindus.'

Sam looked at the figure of Moses on the brass plate on the wall on the west. He stood with two stone tablets carrying the Ten Commandments of the Lord. Standing on the Sinai Mountain, engulfed in the mystical haze of the dark clouds, Moses had led six lakhs Jews from Egypt to God's Promised Land behind the burning bushes, but in that hoary past, Samuel David lost his own moorings.

Sam sat, quiet and gloomy, staring at the copper plate of Moses, and remembered what a struggle it had been to get hold of this house. Contractor Manekshaw had given him the address of this housing society. 'Residents are from different religious backgrounds and it won't be too tight on our pocket also.' An advance of ten thousand rupees had to be paid initially, and the balance would be adjusted within fifteen years. The matter was settled.

Samuel David and his family settled here five or six years before his retirement. Flat number seven on the third floor of the Block B in Gitanjali Society was allotted to him. He himself had picked up the allotment slip. It was only later that he got to know that all flats numbered 'seven' and 'eight' of all the blocks were given to non-Hindu families. Under a planned conspiracy!

'Yaar, these are reserved flats!' Manekshaw had laughingly told him one day. 'The way reserved seats are kept aside for backward communities in government jobs.'

Samuel David shifted to Gitanjali Society in 1962-63. At that time, he had no idea that very soon, he would understand the actual meanings of secularism, friendship and brotherhood.

When they came to live in the colony, all the members of the family were excited. The thought of having a home of their own, familiar neighbours, shared joys, sorrows and concerns made them happy. Gradually, with much anguish, each one of them realized that sorrows only affected the minority families and the majority community had separated itself from their concerns: 'We hardly know your customs and traditions!'

In the beginning, Samuel would visit the neighbours with his family on Holi and Diwali. But no one visited them in return. 'Mira Ben, *tamaare tyan aa tahewaron na thae etla na avya.*' (We didn't come because you don't celebrate these festivals.)

'So what? We also light earthen lamps, buy or make sweets, just that we don't worship.' Miriam would say.

'That's the difference between us…please don't mind.'

'Doesn't matter. Please visit us on our festivals.'

But before Miriam could complete the sentence they would say, 'We hardly know about them.'

Samuel got up and switched on the light. He felt his heart choke. He remembered the way their enthusiasm and energy had disappeared slowly. Then, tying balloons and buying the colours of gulal had become mere formality. The bond of human relationship had rusted and creaked.

The first link to rot was that of Danny. Danny never tolerated any rude comment or bad word against himself or his religion and fought against it.

'Yaar, you are such a fool,' he had scolded Vijay, who was then doing his bachelors. 'How could you reach B.A. if you know nothing about the Jews? Do you think you will mug up for the exam and conquer the world?'

Vijay was embarrassed. 'How could we know, Danny Bhai? We have never heard of such a community! And then the people in the colony said that…'

'What the hell did they say?' Danny had yelled.

'That you are Maharashtrian Christians because you speak Marathi and your women dress up like them!'

'Is that so!' Danny looked at Vijay with disgust. 'Ask those people if they also treat Parsis as Gujarati Muslims because they only wear Gujarati clothes and speak Gujarati? Their names also resemble those of Iranian Muslims, and yes, they even eat meat and fish!'

'Oh, no, Danny Bhai! We know about the Parsis from our history books, but...'

'So, do you think that history books are the last word on knowledge?'

Danny had been annoyed, 'The other day, that recently-turned-electrical-engineer Rakesh was also trying to show off his knowledge. He asked me, and I told him that our places of worship have a formless god and we read from our sacred books, and he asked at once if I prayed in a mosque.

'Don't you Hindus ever hesitate to remark in a split second and give a biased and off-hand opinion about someone else's religion?'

Danny had inherited his grandfather's sharp temper. Had David Reuben been alive, he would have been happy to see that there was at least someone in the family who refused to tolerate a bad word against their religion. Unlike Danny, he had had to laugh away other's shallow comments and ignorance because, usually, he was the only Jew around, wherever he lived.

As he sat in his drawing room, Sam felt forlorn. With whatever little he could save, he had sent this eldest son to the US for higher studies, hoping that Danny would return and to take over the responsibilities of the household. Samuel had believed that Danny, who was like a god to David, would send his younger brother abroad to study engineering. He had hoped that when time came, Danny would take his parents to Israel to touch the holy soil. But now?

'But what do I have now?' Samuel lamented. 'This ageing body, or the dark shadows appearing slowly, why does everything seem to stop? Why are my eyes dim? If my body is made up of this earth, why doesn't it long to mingle with this soil? Why is there a strong craving for a country I have never seen? Can it be the strong pull of those two-thousand-year-old roots? "We will return one day…" Our ancestors believed this when they left their country. But they could never return. Is it our genes or the ghosts of our ancestors buried in the alien soil of different countries that cling to me? Why is there so much restlessness in me?'

Sam sat quietly in the house. The house had a low ceiling, small rooms, a narrow veranda, and a staircase of sixty narrow steps. Where were those majestic homes with big rooms, a huge courtyard and numerous doors and windows? There were no shady trees, no chirping of the birds. Earlier, at sunset, people would leave their homes cheerfully to meet and inquire about each other's wellbeing. But now, people were locked up inside their small houses with closed doors, without knowing each other. Outside, there was only silence.

He felt a strange emptiness and murmured, 'Miriam lies in that utterly desolate corner, but I know that place will also be in ruins soon! How strange it is that our belongings fill the house, yet it seems empty and echoes, and I am at a secluded place.'

He remembered young Sam sitting with his two sisters at the small station of Godhra. Never could he imagine then that the same Godhra would be a witness to such a heinous crime, which would be recorded in history. A terrifying racist dance of death will take birth. The dust storm will choke the minority community with terror.

That day, he remembered his unhappy present and his calm and peaceful childhood days.

Pappa and Godhra.

His Pappa liked Godhra, although he had made up his

mind to settle in Amdavad after his retirement. He was an honest and loyal servant of the British government. Most of his friends were Parsi, Christian or Muslim. Khan Bahadur Sir David Reuben had status and power. As he remembered his father and his terrible anger and authoritarian nature, he smiled bitterly.

There were risings against the British throughout the country. Sam was excited, but Pappa detested it like anything. He shouted at him every day and warned, 'It's only because of the British that we have good jobs, prestige and power. Otherwise, the game of casteism and nepotism would have continued. Not one of them will have any concern for you. Remember, you won't get involved with all this.'

Despite the fear, anger and warnings, enthusiasm simmered within Sam. The bloodbath at Jallianwala Bagh was horrifying. Bapu's Satyagraha, his speeches, and the meetings of the important leaders of India sent waves of adrenaline through his veins, but there was no getting away from Pappa's hawkish eye. He knew Pappa rummaged through his things in his absence. Despite this, Sam would secretly visit Kishore Bhai with Natwar, Dinesh, and Prakash.

He gradually realized that Kishore Bhai trusted others completely, whereas he was always apprehensive about Sam. So, he was only allotted some random work or ran errands. He shared this thought with his friends, and it reached Kishore Bhai's ears.

One evening, he stopped Sam. 'You want to do some responsible and important work, don't you?

Sam was taken aback but said boldly, 'Yes.'

'Okay,' Kishore Bhai murmured. 'I will give you the most important and the bravest work. Will you do it?'

Samuel remembered this incident from his childhood. He had got goose pimples to know that he was worthy of important work. A surge of excitement ran through his veins! He felt he stood tall and could touch the sky. Suddenly, the words poured into his ears like molten lead, 'If you can bring your father's revolver and cartridge, I will know that you can be trusted.'

Sam felt his face drain and imagined his head rolling on the floor. No one was allowed to go anywhere near Pappa's table, not even Mama. Once, when he was about seven, he had picked up Pappa's pistol out of curiosity, and Pappa thrashed him without stopping, even when Mama held Pappa's feet, weeping, to forgive him! Sam's hand was swollen for three to four days, and Mama had to tie turmeric and lime bandages daily.

Did Kishore Bhai not like him coming, or perhaps he wanted to attack a British sympathizer? Sam thought.

For days, Sam was sad and lost in his thoughts. He realized that even his friends kept him at bay. Whenever he joined them, they changed the topic and talked about lighter things as if he were a spy!

Even at his age, he knew his father had nothing to fall back upon except his job. No ancestral property, no kindness and concern of his relatives, and no relations with the high and the mighty.

How could he destroy everything for his own passion?

Samuel David drew in a long breath and smiled. Kishore Bhai had wanted to turn him into a Shikhandi, a pawn in his game. But he gave up the passion and the enthusiasm of his dream.

A whiff of regret moaned within him. He consoled himself and murmured, 'Pappa was right. Although it was because of Pappa's dictatorial rule that he had to take up the job of a head clerk, and what did he get in life? The struggle he had to face in his job! In every moment of his life, there was fear, insecurity and anxiety for the future till he became old! No well-wisher, no co-religionists, and no influential relatives. 'All my life, I got shunted from one town to another like a goods train, got the increments that were due, and on the last day of my service, I was garlanded with marigold flowers in the presence of fifteen staff members and returned home with a box of sweets. I was now retired.'

A long sigh escaped Samuel.

Miriam called from inside, in a trembling, broken voice, 'Sam…Sam!!'

Samuel went in. Miriam looked like a corpse. Her eyes had sunken into shells, her drained face lifeless, her lips parched, her arms and legs were like thin reeds, and a thick cloud of sorrow hovered over her face. This cloud will not rain; it will disappear and leave a desert behind.

He touched the frail arm of his wife, who lay with her eyes closed, 'Miriam…Miriam. Did you call me? Do you want anything?'

Miriam's voice seemed to emerge from the bottom of a deep well. Her closed eyelids fluttered. She tried to recognize Sam through half-opened eyes. She seemed to be emerging from another world. Then, she held Sam's hand the way she had earlier and asked, 'Our Bobby was an Israyel, wasn't he?' She seemed to float and then disappeared into her dark void.

Samuel David's throat was choked with emotion. He continued to caress his sick wife's forehead. He wondered who would believe that this bag of bones who had lost her mind was once a proud and beautiful woman, holding a degree in English literature? She had taken on a lonely path from where neither he nor her surviving children could bring her back.

'I wish our remains could be buried in Jerusalem as Danny had promised us!'

'If Bobby were alive, he would have laughed,' Sam thought

sorrowfully. He would have said, 'What's this, Papa! The soil, whether of India or Jerusalem, is the same. Both have the same germs that will lick our bodies into skeletons. For us, this soil is familiar, fragrant, and has been our own for the last two thousand years. Why are you partial towards the soil of Israel? I would rather be buried in this soil.'

Bobby was buried where he wanted—in that same soil of Amdavad, in the Jewish cemetery near Dilli Darwaza. He lies alone beside Rachel's grave, even before his mother and father died. He carries with him the fragrance of this very soil.

Bobby. Mikhail Samuel.
Birth: 1938. Death: 1972.
Second son of Samuel David and Miriam.
Husband of Hannah.
Father of Milcah and Sarah.

Every year, Samuel David and his eldest daughter visit Bobby's grave on his death anniversary and read the words in black engraved on the white stone. The caretaker's goats quickly climb the grave and munch the roses they placed there. Bobby's eyes smile. '*You don't like my questioning the infinite mercy of the Lord, isn't it, Papa?*'

Staring at the dull whiteness of the ceiling, Sam smiled gloomily. 'How patient I had to be at his logical questions! And Danny! He was always annoyed with him, and the conversation would end in a fight.'

When Bobby visited his friends on Diwali and participated in their puja or celebrated the Ganesh festival, Danny would get furious.

Danny would growl, 'Why do you go to worship stones idols like the Hindus? This is a sin for us. Don't you know what the Lord said to Moses, "I am what I am?" For us, it's only worshipping the formless God.'

The more Danny got irritated, the more Seema was

perturbed. But Bobby remained resolute. He did not give up reason and historical evidence, 'When Abraham left the Ur town of Iraq, the people who followed him were all idol worshippers. Till Moses gave the two stone tablets with the Ten Commandments to the Jews and convinced them to follow monotheism, every tribe of the Jews had their own deity.

'Danny, is it right to get angry with Vijay, Rakesh or with anyone else the way you do? What if you find someone like me who argues that the birthplace of the Semitic race was Arabia, and one of its branches was known as Jew? Does anyone know the actual history of the period when the Israyel settled in India and lived in the darkness of anonymity for a thousand years? It's not right to establish the superiority of one's own religion and self-esteem by treating other religions as inferior.'

Samuel remembered reflecting on Bobby's argument for a long time. Then, he told Bobby one day that he firmly believed that the Bible was not only a book of Jewish history but also an honest, truthful and unalloyed representation of the culture, development, civilization and tradition of their religion.

Bobby's comforting yet candid words whispered in his ears: 'There is no religion in the world, Papa, which is purely based on its own codes of conduct, customs, experiences, cultures or memories. During the various periods of history, different traditions, cultures, and faiths arrived and left, leading to a mutual exchange of folk cultures. In such a situation, which soil and which body could remain pure? Or, for that matter, even religion. The forgiving soil embraces all with the same love and warmth.'

Samuel remembered a favourite statement of Bobby, who was a postgraduate in ancient history, 'This fish is too slippery to be caught so easily, Papa!'

With a broken heart, he murmured to himself, 'He got trapped in the circle of life and death!'

A strong wind blew past: 'My dear Papa, our Judaic faith has no such circle.'

Startled, Samuel David looked around. There was nothing except for the dull evening! He jerked his head lightly and muttered in that lonely surrounding, 'Yes, we don't believe in rebirth, my son. Even so, I wish that we are reborn and that I become your father again! I cannot lift my hand to heaven and proclaim like Job that whatever you did to me was because of some reason!'

In anguish, he walked up and down and continued to speak:

'And surely the mountain falling cometh to nought,
and the rock is removed out of his place.
The waters wear the stones:
thou washest away the things which grow out of the dust of the earth;
and thou destroyest the hope of man.
Thou prevailest forever against him, and he passeth:
*thou changest his countenance, and sendest him away.'**

Tired of walking, Sam sank to the floor in the middle of the room.

An old image came to his grieving heart. Pappa had sat exactly like this in the middle of the room, shattered and lost, after returning from Dr Shah's home. In his entire life, Sam had never seen his father so disheartened.

Pappa had committed a mistake by visiting his friend Dr Shah, the government jail doctor. He had gone to convince him not to resign from his government job on Gandhiji's call. But Doctor Uncle had attacked government jailor David Reuben instead.

'David Bhai, throw away the brass and silver honorific

*Job, 14:18-20

awards of Sir, Khan and Rai Bahadur offered by the British as charity. Spit on their mercy, the power and prestige that your job brings, and stand with the masses of this country. Protest against their every intent, belief, action and atrocity. Be a man, or the people of this country will call you their agent. Be brave and fight the circumstances. Stand with us and be our strength.'

Sam remembered his father's angry face.

Badly hurt, he had attacked Dr Shah in anger: 'Did you ever, at any point in time, think about us? We have lived with you for thousands of years, but did anyone ever extend a helping hand, even a faint consolation or a hint of concern? Did anyone ever want to know about our joys and sorrows, our festivals, religion or customs?

'We were pushed into the slot of "mlechchha" or "pardesi". Did we ever have meals together or become a part of your prayers and worship or marriage ceremonies? Tell me, have you ever experienced the uncertainties of the future, the fear that minorities face, their alienation and isolation from the rest of the people? Or have you felt ashamed of your own timidity, wariness, opportunism or self-centredness, like us? Have you ever dreamt of having a home, higher education, a decent job, and sharing your joys and sorrows with society for generations? Tell me!

'If we stand with you, will you give us all those things we have struggled to achieve since the last two thousand years? Has it ever occurred to you that once the power is in your hands, you will also use us like the British?

'We are exploited by both. At least we know the British attitude, but it is only dark on the other side, Dr Shah!'

Samuel remembered. Pappa had stopped before he left and said, 'I am not even sure if I die tomorrow, you will stand by my family at the funeral or not! And, you know, if this happens, there are only three families of Jews here, and even they don't have the stipulated ten adult men essential for the funeral. There is no cemetery for us in this town, so my body will be taken to the Jewish cemetery in Amdavad or buried in the Muslim graveyard at their mercy till the Day of Judgment!

'The silence of the minorities, their hesitancies and sorrow, are nowhere in your consciousness. So, Dr Shah, goodbye.'

Samuel was soaked in sweat even in the chill of the December of Amdavad. He pulled himself up from the floor and switched on the fan. When he shivered with cold, he switched it off. Then he sat on the chair.

When Pappa passed away, the days were as cold, he thought.

Mother's telegram had arrived. Pappa was unconscious in a lonely room of the Police Hospital. Sam had sat by his bedside for two days. On Friday afternoon, David Reuben's soul left his body. Just before leaving, he had opened his eyes and tried to say something, but the stroke had been too powerful. High blood pressure resulted in haemorrhaging in the brain. The blood accumulated there. Pappa could only produce an indistinct sound. That's all.

'Pappa, Pappa!' Sam had called out. Mother continued to stare at him.

David Reuben had left.

Shabbat had begun in the evening. There was no time to go to Amdavad for the burial.

Pappa rests in the Muslim graveyard.

Sir David Reuben (1882-1937)
Rest in Peace.

Would Pappa's soul be at peace in a Muslim graveyard? He, who was such a staunch Jew, who remembered whatever his grandfather Isaji Eloji had taught him—his advice, sayings, and all the subtle nuances of religious rituals—would he be happy in the Sheol, the abode of the dead?

Samuel David got up abruptly from his chair and reached for the tablet of Moses with trembling steps. He held the tablet firmly, and closing his eyes tight, he muttered from deep within, 'O Lord! Grant me a decent death.'

Chapter 10

Manda calls from outside, 'Didi! Only you are left for breakfast. Please come fast. The poha will get cold.'

I nod, but I don't want to leave my room. My eyes are sore, my head is heavy, and I am feverish. It's eleven o'clock. The morning session of the *Vividh Bharti* programme on the All India Radio is over. The transistor whirrs. I turn off the transistor kept on the shelf.

Silence sprawls in the room. The morning inches towards the afternoon. The evening will follow. Then the night will arrive hand in hand with the evening. Another day of light and darkness will be over. And so will end the three hundred and sixty-five days of a year. But, born 4.6 billion years ago, Earth is not tired yet.

❁

Diana Aajji, who had crossed seventy, looked older than the 4.6-billion-year-old Earth. She was tired. Lying next to Seema, with her eyes fixed on the ceiling, she would mutter, 'I have become a living corpse since Lily and Ruth died. For three days, that girl was locked up in the room where we stored coal. Then, a glass of milk came. She had turned blue-black. She was buried quickly in the darkness of night.'

She turned to one side, then to another. She sat up and then lay down again.

'Go to sleep, Aajji,' Seema said.

Diana looked at Seema as if from some other world.

'Come on, let me press your feet,' Seema said, making her lie down. But Aajji held her hand tight and placed it on her chest, stomach, eyes, murmuring, 'My dear, everything seems to be falling apart. How many of us will you look after?'

There was a lump in Seema's throat. Silently, she gently stroked her grandmother until she thought she was asleep, then covered her with a quilt and lay next to her. But, opening her eyes, Aajji smiled with pain, 'I am tired, my dear, very tired. I don't know for how long I have been living, and I continue to live—like this earth—but now, I am tired.'

Bobby had never known what helplessness was. He always found a spot of hope in the overcast sky of hopelessness and derived energy from it to remain happy.

Seema taught in a college run by a trust, and Bobby was promoted to assistant manager in a well-known paper company. He would laugh and say, 'You know, Ma, I use my knowledge of ancient history to explain the quality of the reams of paper and carbon paper and the efficiency of typewriters so that big clients are impressed and make a deal with my company! I tell them if such inventions had taken place long before, our government wouldn't have to spend crores of money on excavations to know our history because we would have complete records on paper! That amount could be utilized in eradicating poverty and in developmental activities.'

Bobby's mother would be annoyed, 'Never make fun of your job. Thank God you have your share of happiness—a job, a wife and two lovely daughters. Look at Rosie. She is like bubbling hot lava. A seed will only sprout in the earth when it is calm, tender and moist. And poor Rafu! He has no mother, no father, and no sense.'

Miriam remained quiet for a long time and held Rafu, who hung around her in her lap, and kissed him. But Rafu blinked his eyes and sat aloof. After a while, he touched her hand and said, 'Nani! *Mee jau*?' (Can I go?) Miriam dried her eyes with her sari.

Bobby gently stroked her grey hair to help her collect herself. She sighed and said, 'God knows why He gave all sorrows to my Rachel?'

'It's a misfortune, Ma, only misfortune.'

'Immaturity, lack of courage and fear went against her. Rachel got trapped like a fish who happened to pass by just as a fisherman threw his net in the water. In such a situation, there is no role of fate. It is sheer coincidence. The business of this world runs because of an abundance of such coincidences. God did not create this world in six days.'

Ma was sad and sat up. She opened a newspaper to read, but her eyes were stuck on one page for hours. Bobby took the newspaper from her hand. Keeping his hand on her shoulder, he hummed Mubarak Begum's famous ghazal, '*Wo na aaenge palat kar, unhein lakh hum bulayein.*' (Those who have left will never return, however hard we try.)

'*Unhein lakh hum bulayein*' still rings in my mind. Bobby's humming, his standing at the balcony when the days were bleak, his smile—like a patch of sunlight, like butterflies mid-air, like the flow of fountains and the springs of joy. He painted the dance of the birds and called out to the slumber with the sound of music. These are like circles of memories. One comes after another. From the smaller to the bigger.

Then, what happens?

Then, the song stops. All the music, the magic, the joy, all the sound comes to a halt. The rest of the people freeze in their places!

Ameena stares at me with her vacant eyes and says in an emotionless voice, 'There is no churning within me, Seema.'

Startled, I look around. There's silence everywhere.

'My feelings have died.' Ameena had told me one night. 'All the noise of the world cannot fill my ears. It stands out reluctantly. The suffocating silence unnerves and annoys me. I get up suddenly in the middle of the night and feel someone laughing and whispering into my ears: "So, are you still alive?"'

Ameena's eyes are like stones. I rub my palms in restlessness. The fever is rising steadily. My eyes burn. My head is tired of spinning. Oh! The remaining people of B-7!

The story of the people who are alive! Which human DNA has lasted for ten lakh years of evolution among a living people who are frighteningly lonely and sad even though surrounded by people? Separated from the people who left this world, why can't they accept the flow around them easily? Why?

Why can't the mind accept reality, or does it want to live in illusions? But the result is the same—you are dragged away in the flow of life's ups and downs like small stones. The rest of the people of Samuel David's family had just flowed with the flow.

❀

By the 1970s, Bobby's company had started laying off employees. The company's owner, who lived in Bangalore, wanted to wind up his paper business and start manufacturing ball bearings. With hollow words of inconvenience, mismanagement and apology, the salary started coming late. Later, only half the salary came, then even that half started coming in late and partially. In the end, the company declared itself bankrupt and shut shop. The news about starting a ball bearing company was a lie. The clever employees seized the remaining goods and furniture. Bobby was left with nothing.

'Now Bobby can take all of you to Israel,' Danny had raised this issue sheepishly at dinner time.

Before Danny could say a word, Papa had snapped at Danny, 'Why—won't you come along?'

'What?' Danny tried to hedge the query. Then, a little embarrassed, he looked at his wife, lowered his head and replied, 'Yes, yes, we will also come.'

'Seema and I will not go at all.' Bobby said firmly and then looked at Seema.

That night at dinner, Samuel David didn't know that none of them, except Danny and Rosie—who cleverly concealed the fact from them—would go anywhere and even they, giving the false promise of taking the responsibility for David's education, would settle, not in Israel but in the US.

This matter was not discussed further. Bobby was in search of a job and Samuel David wanted to kill two birds with one stone.

'We wandered for centuries and suffered tragedies and insults. Did it mean that our longing for the homeland, which has lain suppressed within us all this while, dies? Now, it's our right to return to the land which is ours. The land of our ancestors has been returned to us with dignity. Son, even migrant birds return home; we are human beings.'

Bobby smiled as usual, 'No other animal except man thinks only of himself. Animals only need a place to make their nest or den. And as far as Palestine (Canaan) is concerned, it was, according to the Bible, given by God. Otherwise, a branch of the Semitic tribe called Canaanites lived there around the beginning of the third millennium BC.'

'Okay, I agree. But even if I agree to everything you say, is there a possibility of a decent job, healthcare, security and shelter for the elderly, and a better future in this country?' Samuel asked, looking into Bobby's eyes.

The brightness of trust and patience reflected on Bobby's face, 'Why not? All our rights are safeguarded here.'

But, it never happened. Even in those days, it was hard for Bobby to get a job. Wherever he went, he only got false promises. Heat, dust, sweat and exhaustion did not change Bobby's resolve. He never wavered. But he was shocked when he had to constantly face people whose questions were in a language he failed to understand.

'What is your name?'

'Mikhail Samuel.'

'Which caste?'

'Jew, Israyel.'

'Sorry, we don't have any vacancy now.'

'Do you have any technical training?'

'No.'

'Well, your knowledge of ancient history is hardly needed for machines. Excuse me, but you are already above age for a new job.'

'These Jews-shews, do they live in Amdavad at all?'

'Yes, we do. We even have our own temple.'

'Okay, okay. You are small in number. Then, it's all right. You won't be able to create problems!'

'Brother, cut the crap. Why are you wasting our time? We give jobs only to the Hindus.'

'Sir, does work have any religion?'

'Yes, it has. In case of a riot, even one of our people can overpower ten Muslims.'

It was harder this time for Bobby. This was flouting the rules of the game. Earlier, whenever he returned home unsuccessful after an interview, he would laugh and say, 'It's a part of life!' But now, he was sad.

He smiled and told his interviewers that it was their misconception that the strange land of Israel was theirs. 'My country is this. I am just like you. I was born of the same soil and water.'

They laughed. He was successful at the interview, but he was disqualified for the job. 'Even if you are Indian, you do not belong here. Like other minorities, you are exploiting our country and resources. Your loyalties will always be towards your homeland. Please go back to your country, to your own soil, so that some needy Hindu brethren may get a job here.'

Any contribution to our society and culture?

Why don't you accept Hinduism?

Are you involved with any group or in any underground activities?

Which political party promotes you?

No one had time to listen to Bobby's arguments and logic. Interviews and rejections became commonplace. If he ever found a job, it was only for lower posts, where the salary was meagre. He accepted any job he could get—a salesman, clerk, even a translator (English to Gujarati and vice versa). For his masters, he was a needy and jobless young man, so they would extract the maximum work out of him without compensating him properly—his salary was often delayed.

Then, Bobby joined a private English medium school as a history teacher. Because his daughter Sarah was very young, his wife Dolly had decided to help Bobby after a year or so. The salary was modest, but it was a regular job, and there was dignity.

And then, one day, after school hours, the world crashed as Bobby was returning home after taking a couple of tuitions.

He never returned home.

Papa tried to assure Dolly and Ma of Bobby's return. Ma continued to chant Psalm 121 of The Bible:

'I will lift mine eyes unto the mountains:
from whence shall my help come?
My help cometh from the Lord,
who made heaven and earth...'

Perhaps God had gone to sleep.

Since then, Ma remained awake, even in her sleep.

According to the *Book of Genesis* in the Old Testament, the father of the Jewish clan was Abraham, the first ancestor. God and Abraham had entered into a covenant that He would multiply Abraham's descendants only if, in return, Abraham circumcised each male infant eight days after his birth as a sign of God's command and will.

Circumcision was the mark of God's command—the Ot Brit.

Following that ancient promise, the circumcision of Samuel David's second son Mikhail was performed on the eighth day after his birth.

Did that barbarous, fanatical and violent mob hear, amidst its frenzy, the faint appeal of a young Jewish man explaining who a Jew was?

❁

I see Manda coming to my room with a plate of batata-poha.

Chapter 11

Mary Varghese is overjoyed. Twenty years ago, she had invested in a fixed deposit scheme in a bank, which was giving her a good return. It is 25 December. Mary has brought a big cake. She has even got sweets, chocolates, savoury snacks, and colourful balloons, shimmery ribbons, sparkling stars, and a lantern to decorate the common room.

Sakhu Tai laughs, 'Mary, it looks like a child's birthday!'

Mary exclaims, 'Aren't we kids, too, Sakhu Tai? We are the masters of our own free will. We have no past or future. It is now or never. So, eat, drink, and be merry. Who knows if there's a tomorrow? We may croak any moment!'

Mary winks at Mrs Chitnis and smacks my back, 'Am I right?'

Mrs Chitnis is a little embarrassed and looks far away.

We have hardly ever seen Mary unhappy. 'Why be sad? Enjoy whatever you have by the grace of God. Who knows, even this could be taken away! At my age, I have neither courage nor desire left, so be content and enjoy life, girls.'

Mary sometimes behaves like Rama Aajji used to do. She has two unique habits—to wink while talking and to smack the person sitting next to her. Whenever she is excited, her hand rises quickly, and the person standing next to her shifts uncomfortably. Then, she laughs and says, 'Are you as delicate as a piece of cloth that a little smacking will hurt you? Come on, be a man!' She talks recklessly with everyone. Her habits have become her nature.

Once, she said light-heartedly, 'Yaar, what can I do? If I didn't speak strictly and harshly with the lower staff at the hospitals, they wouldn't be intimidated. Initially, there was a big problem with language. By the time I learnt Marathi and Hindi grammar, it was time to colour my hair. It's all right, yaar!'

In the beginning, some members were shocked and even angry with her, but when they realized that her intention was not to insult or humiliate anyone; it was just her rough language, they became calm. Mrs Chitnis had once fallen into this trap and became very agitated, but when she realized that Mary's heart was pure, she was appeased.

Whenever Mary is in the dining hall, she has a good laugh—'Eat, eat well, ladies. Sakhu Tai has asked for fruit salad in cream today. Don't worry about upset stomachs; I'll give you medicines, but today, you must gorge like you won't get food for a whole week, or you will regret it!'

Mary Varghese sings a new film song as she puts up the balloons—'*O re piya, ye diya na bujhne diya...*' (O Love, I did not let the flame of the lamp die). Her voice is off-key and cracked but resonates with deep feelings. I smile at her. She stops singing and snaps at me, 'Am I singing badly?'

'Not at all, Mary,' I say.

'Then why did you smile? Because I don't have a sweet voice like you?'

I am taken aback. Patting her, I say, 'Just like that, dear.'

'Miss Samuel, I know I won't be able to sing your favourite song in my voice, but any song of my choice that I can sing is sweet to me. Okay?'

'I get it, meri Ma! Please spare me! Everyone makes mistakes.'

Her tight face relaxes a little. She sinks onto the sofa with a balloon in her hand. I can sense her struggling with a sad feeling. Taking a deep breath, she says that she came to Parisar to live, to talk, to laugh the way she wanted: 'So that the tongue isn't stopped from speaking to a fellow being, so that there is someone who will wipe away the tears that well up in my eyes, or if I did not get up in the morning, somebody would pat me and say, "Wake up, Mary, it's already morning."'

She gently places her hand on mine. 'Do you know, at home—not this one—the one I thought was mine while working with my sisters-in-law and helping them in their chores, I used to hum as a habit. Then I noticed that whenever I hummed, they would look at each other, make faces, and make excuses so that I stop singing: "Didi, serve the food first, slice the salad, then you can sing." One day, it reached the limit. The younger sister-in-law said, "I cannot make head or tail of your words. This jumbled-up words and tuneless singing, is it what you call a song?"

'At first, I was stunned, but then I yelled at them. "I'll do whatever I want with the words, or sing the way I like. Am I pinching anything from your father? Even if my words are meaningless and my voice is croaky, how does it matter to you? Do you think I am Lata Mangeshkar or Asha Bhosle? I sing for own my happiness, not to please you. Understood?"

'Hearing this, the elder one rushed in angrily and said, "Sing or bray—do it in your own room! Why are you bent on damaging our eardrums? We'll have to tolerate this woman all our life. Uff!"'

Mary pauses and looks at me. Then she says, 'So, Miss Samuel, now tell me—are you a "Miss", separated from the creature called husband, or like me, unmarried and a spinster forever: "Miss" Mary Varghese?'

Taking the strings of balloons from her hand, I get up

quickly and tell her that we would analyze the meaning of 'Miss' at leisure, but first, we should decorate the hall.

'I have been at Poona's Sassoon Hospital for the last ten years. I am sure you know that it was built by your Jewish community of Sassoons?'

I reply, 'Yes. And there were other buildings, too, built by them.'

'So, Pune's river Mula-Mutha gave me comfort. I often went and sat on the river bank. People there keep to themselves and don't poke their noses in others' private matters. *Puneri manus*, Pune's people, respect mutual relations and are grounded in their culture.

'Only the sea could nowhere be seen. One had to go to Bombay to see it, but only to find it crowded with shops! You know, there is a strong pull in the ocean. It is immense, endless, and the leaping waves fascinate you, just like your first love! You just feel like drowning in it, but then, only lifeless bodies float on the water!'

Mary has gone to another place as she talked to me. It seems like she was looking right through me.

Then, suddenly, she returns, smiles and begins to sing, '*Aaja bhanwar, sooni dagar, soona hai ghar aa jaa…na sataa…*' (Come, O beloved, the path is lonely, the home is lonely, too, don't torment me.) She pauses momentarily, coming to me, '*Idhar to sare ud gaye…*(All of mine have flown away.) How are things on your side?'

Before she says more, I change the topic, 'You know, Mary, this song is based on Raga Vrindavani Saarang and sung by Lata Mangeshkar.'

She guffaws, 'O you silly, your ragas make no sense to someone with neither a lovely voice nor a beautiful body.'

Suddenly, Mary is serious. 'I have somehow managed to live a long, lonely life filled with discordant notes, but now it seems too difficult, Miss Samuel.'

'Why do you say this?' I ask at once.

She gives me no answer and pretends to be occupied with the decoration. I look at her carefully. Her face is clouded with mixed feelings of anxiety, stress and sorrow. I don't know why, but I am worried for Mary, although I find no logical reason.

Feeling my gaze on her face, Mary laughs sadly and says something completely out of place, 'Miss Samuel, I will not croak so easily!'

She resumes humming and is busy again.

Mrs Chitnis comes to take the bright paper lanterns. She laughs and says, 'Mary, the way you hum these film songs reminds me of my baba (father), who would sing songs from Marathi dramas. Once every week, the troupe would assemble. The melody of the harmonium, the tabla, the violin, and the songs would be all over. I used to sing as a child, but just like you, my songs became off-tune, and the music got lost somewhere!'

The atmosphere has become sombre. I didn't wish to see everyone's happiness fading away so easily, so I quickly added, 'You know Mrs Chitnis, even my Papa was very fond of music. He remembered old songs but forgot the words of new popular songs. And after every classical song, he would quiz us: "Tell me what raga is this?" Ma and Rachel had a good knowledge of the ragas. Because of her melodious voice, as a child, Rachel had cleared three levels of the classical music examinations. So, she would quickly answer, "Papa, it's Bhairvi, or Pahadi or Vihaag, Darbari Kanda, Vibhaas..." Do you remember that song '*Shaam dhale, gagan tale, ham kitne ekaki.*' (When evening sets in the sky, it's so lonely) from the film *Utsav*? It's based on Raga Vibhaas. It was Papa's favourite song. But when the singers were no more, the source of songs, too, dried up.'

I grow quiet. Seeing this, Mary comes to me and says, 'Yaar, I am hale and hearty. Let my afflictions go to hell!'

Everyone laughs—even Ameena.

Ameena's smile brightens us all. When she looks a little embarrassed, I tell others, 'Do you know what Ameena did when she sang as a child?'

'Yes, do tell us'—Mary and Tara Nigam say in chorus.

'In school, when we were shown old films at night, this naughty girl hardly watched them; instead, she would fling pebbles at the boys to the rhythm of the songs! And when Sir was annoyed by her mischief, he would shoo us out, and even as she left, she would sing a parody of some film song! And she was crazy for tamarind, berry, gooseberry and pani ke batashe, those crisp balls of tangy water. She would often scribble in her notebook and pass it on to me: "Let's go out to drink water. We will get some gooseberries from there", "Yaar, Desai sir has bored us to death", "It's raining outside, it will be great fun to get wet", "Just look at Savita, she has dozed off!" I would be scared of the teacher, but she was extremely cool.'

Everyone looks at Ameena. There is no sign of joy on her face. I approach her and lift her face and say, 'Now, please, smile.'

With a hint of a smile, she turns back and stands in a distant corner, like a statue.

Ameena reminds me of Rachel. The situations are hardly different, the circumstances seem similar, and the joys and sorrows that emerge from them also appear similar. Just as Ameena stands stunned like a statue, Rachel, too, had stood the same way in the drawing room at B-7 that day.

'Whose sin did you try to thrust on me?' he had looked offensively at Samuel David.

That was Joel Garson—Rachel's husband, junior engineer, an alcoholic, bigamist and untamed bull, who had inflicted some unimaginable tortures on Rachel—the son-in-law of Mr Samuel David, who stayed a two-night journey from Amdavad and to whom Mr Samuel David had married his silly daughter, even though his son Bobby and daughter Seema had protested.

'Keep this ravaged field of yours with yourself. I have trampled it enough. Now, there's nothing left!' He had smiled through tobacco-stained teeth.

Before Samuel David could say anything, Joel was out of the house. Rachel had stood there like a statue.

When such characters of bone and flesh go against time, strange events happen on this earth.

But the great astronomer Russ Lederman says that the universe is exactly the opposite. Nothing ever happens there. Our idea of time is based on events. The time span between two incidents is called a period. The concept of time is meaningless in the unconscious world of the universe.

How can we ever be the universe? How can we, the most intelligent creatures of the animate Earth, born out of the subliminal universe, forget the events created out of time? If someone were to wipe away the days and nights created out of a time period of our lives, wouldn't we, like Yami, mourn for ages?

But some people plunge into the unconscious universe, escaping beyond the hold of the animate earth, and then, all the concepts, knowledge and support are left behind!

'Why do you look so confused?' Mary comes closer to me and asks. I smile. Wrapping my arms lovingly around her waist, I say, 'This is how I look. Even the wrinkles have deepened with age!'

'You will have to make your arms longer to hold my "roomy" waist!' Mary chuckles.

We all smile. The atmosphere becomes lighter. Mrs Chitnis is now chats with Mary, and the collective chatter of Tara Nigam, Sudha Akka, Manda, Sakhu Tai, and others echoes in the room. Only Ameena stands in the far corner like an image.

I leave everyone and go to her. 'Come dear, why do you stand here alone?' I ask her.

Her face is emotionless. She throws the colourful ribbons and balloons in her hand. 'Is it the twenty-fifth today?' she asks with a flat face and devastated eyes.

'Yes, why? The new year will be here after six days, Ameena,' I say with a smile. Holding her hand, I try to bring her forward, but she snatches her hand away. In a thick and hoarse voice, Ameena says, 'This is enough! Let not time move any further!'

Ameena turns abruptly and walks quickly out of the room. Everyone watches her leave so suddenly. I follow her and see her dragging herself into her room.

Rama Aajji stands smiling at the door: 'You silly girl, 28 February will come again. How many times will you save yourself?'

Ameena disappears into her room, walking through the shadow of Rama Aajji.

Chapter 12

I stare at the white, overarched ceiling every day.

An empire of whiteness spreads from one end to the other. Walls, ceiling, bedsheets, and whatever remains of the spring of life!

But the luminous darkness in the room is quite like the forgetful, slipped memories. Some are visible in this dark; some want to hide, and some are defiant and question. Life is like this. It tempts and attracts, full of anxiety and suffering, painful and soothing, sympathetic, rebellious or embarrassed; it seeks solitude.

If you stare continuously at the ceiling as you lie down, it seems it is sliding down slowly, quietly. The heart sinks, the pulse quickens, and something wrenches within. Moments and events spent in the garden of memories have become lifeless, like fragments of a meteor that had once surrounded the present like a burning ball of fire.

The air churned out of the fan collides with the walls, buzzes and rushes back to the fan. The whirs and buzz ring in my ears. I turn in my bed. The gentle curve of the moon peeps behind the window bars and smiles at me.

But why? I ask.

I find that the smile of the moon is the same as Tahmina's grin whenever she saw a man. Papa continues to stare at her. I keep my eyes open to get used to the darkness and see Papa prying something from the window pane and flinging it at Tahmina. Just then, Champa, the Rabari woman, comes down the stairs after finishing her chores, and Papa pulls her to himself. Papa's old fingers slip into her breasts. She giggles, and Papa takes something from his pocket and gives it to her. She winks at him.

No, this is Mary. I am surprised, then suddenly find Joel Garson moving towards me. His hands tear off my clothes; he looks at my body, at my swollen belly, and laughs loudly. After taking one last drag on his cigarette, he rubs its red-hot tip on my thighs. I struggle to shout, but my mouth is clamped by his rough, strong hand.

O God! God! I push away his hand and yell.

He howls with laughter. The tip of the stub stuck between his lips burns like an ember. Just then, my heart stops beating.

I shriek in delight: *Oh! I am dead!*

I get up with a start and sit on the bed. It's still dark outside the window, and the moon has left the window frame. By now, my heartbeat has become normal. I get up and hold the bar of the window as if hypnotized. My mind wanders off in search of comfort.

❁

Outside, Bhatt Sir was taking his Sanskrit class. In the girls' rows, Seema and Ameena sat together on the second bench. Sir was translating a couplet (sloka) of the Sringar Rasa from Kalidasa's play, *Shakuntala*, and explaining it to the class. Seema looked down, avoiding looking at Sir. Bhatt Sir was so young and handsome.

Ameena nudged Seema, 'Listen, listen, this couplet is meant for you and me.'

Seema whispered and motioned her to keep quiet. Ameena quickly opened the last page of her notebook and scribbled something:

Which one is your Dushyant? Mine is the one on the first bench, the first from the wall!

Seema pinched her thigh, and Ameena cried out, 'Oh!'

Disturbed by the commotion, Bhatt Sir asked them to stand up. 'What's the matter? Don't you want to study?'

'Sir, sir, it was a mouse,' Ameena stammered.

Seema thought Bhatt Sir felt bad to expel Seema and Ameena from the class.

Outside the classroom, both the girls laughed and giggled. Seema shows Ameena her dear Dushyant digging for gold in his nose!

Ameena pretends to be serious and pointed to Mayank, 'Yes, but look, one of your Dushyants is scratching his thigh and the other is teaching the class!'

That same Ameena stands like a lifeless statue now. I wonder how flesh-and-blood people slowly peel off layers of their sensitivities over time and, one day, silently turn into spectres, shadows. Shadows don't howl; they don't weep. They don't even show the blisters made by burnt cigarette butts on their thighs, they don't display dried scratch marks and blue-black spots on their belly and breasts. They don't degrade their minds with rotting filthy thoughts, or they don't fly a glow-worm of joy. They don't yearn for desires; they don't crave for tender-green mangoes. No hurt of insult, no cry of grief, no tenderness of touch, no joy, no sorrow, neither day nor night! Shadows just shiver. The shadows that take birth in brightness mingle with darkness.

Dr Saroj Shah had just stared at the apparition on the operation table. She could only ask, 'Who did this to you, my girl?'

All possibilities of life, even a spark, were finished in that unconscious shadow. In that shivering, wintry midnight, Dr Saroj Shah had shaken the profusely sweating apparition and said, 'Shout! Girl, shout! Let your suffering find a way to come out.'

This girl, who couldn't even cross a tiny ditch of water, who often lost her way home even though it was just next door, who could only pedal a cycle on its stand in reverse, this stupid, simple Rachel had only shivered.

Then? The barrage of pain burst open. It flowed over the table, on the floor, and in the room—drowning all implements, doctors' and nurses' uniforms, bedsheets, pillow covers, gowns, aprons, curtains, and machines. The pain became a deluge. The whole universe was flooded.

An infant with an oversized head swam through this deluge of pain and reached the shore.

Then, the deluge of pain hugged Rachel very gently and got absorbed into the earth.

However hard Ma, Bobby and Seema tried to dig out the pain, it had reached the innermost core of the nether world and dried up.

It was only later that the naked infant got attention. 'Make the baby cry. At least this infant should cry.'

Hanging upside down from Dr Saroj Shah's hand, the baby let out a lusty cry and opened his eyes. She had then placed this deformed infant with a twisted left hand and a weak right leg in Seema's hand.

'That's all. I could only save this one, my girl.'

❁

We who survive in the faded photographs, do we ever get some relief? The scene in Ameena's mind is still not over, so she waits for its return.

'I feel everyone will come back some day because I never saw them going away.' When Ameena said this, I felt a strange insanity in her voice. Her eyes were like deserts. On such occasions, she pressed her palms together.

I offer her some water. When she becomes a little composed, I say, 'The present is often traumatic. It's natural to be sad, Ameena, but dead people never come back.'

'But if they don't come back, why do I feel your Rama Aajji standing at the door and smiling at me strangely whenever I run to my room in great anguish?

'There is an impenetrable wall of death and life between Rama Aajji and me. But between me and my dear ones, it was just the difference of attire and a red bindi on my forehead.

'Since that day, I have never worn a Gujarati-style sari. Ammi used to wear it. My mother-in-law also wore it. We spoke Gujarati at home. Even Ghazal used to put on a tiny bindi. But that day, only I had this sign of life on my forehead. A sign which I have never been able to wipe off.

'Who was wiped off, whose existence was devastated, who knows, Seema?

'I, Ameena Iqbal Rizvi, A woman of Medhani Nagar in Chamanpura, was alive with her family till 27 February. But on the evening of the twenty-eighth, I had put on a Gujarati-style sari and a red bindi, and was thrown outside her colony for dead.

'I could not enter the mob; my dear ones could not escape from it. But I find your Rama Aajji laughing at me. Tell me, why?

'Standing outside the violent circle of the mob, I felt I had turned into an anchor sinking into the deepest part of the nether world. Are we all like anchors?'

Outside, it is the first glow of morning. A gentle wind is blowing away the curtains on the windows. My wandering, distressed mind tosses and turns restlessly. In a dilemma, I push my chair, get up and open the door.

I see Bobby standing at the door. He smiles. 'Silly, if you don't move on, the universe around you will also come to a halt. Don't let your mind and heart pause, lest the game of life ends.'

'Whom are you staring at, Miss Samuel?' Mary says as she enters my room. 'Aren't you coming along for yoga?'

'Yes, sure.' And I gently touch the paused time.

Chapter 13

'Brothers and sisters!'

Mary stands on the veranda. It was the time before evening set in. The sun isn't scorching hot. We sat on the lawn under the dappled shade of the flowering Ashok and Amaltas trees. Then, we notice Mary.

She comes down the stairs to meet us. She has a saffron-coloured glossy leaflet in her hand. As she comes closer, she raises the leaflet and says, 'Sisters and brothers!' Then, correcting herself, she says again, 'Brothers!'

Before we understand what is happening, Mary touches Mrs Chitnis' shoulder and says, 'Sorry, sorry. Not brothers—sisters.' When I look at her, she winks at me and says, 'Although I doubt even this way of addressing.'

But when Mrs Chitnis frowns, and I keep quiet, she is offended. She sits and says, 'Okay, listen, all of you. This is a very important and interesting leaflet! What an effective language, but so phoney!'

Tara Nigam reaches out to take the leaflet, 'You, Mary, will take hours to read it; give it to me, I will read it quickly.'

Mary quickly takes it away and says, 'Okay, I will read now. Listen.'

The voting for the fourteenth Lok Sabha elections has begun. Please don't forget to vote for electing the local representative from your city Pune.

I am overwhelmed by your love and affection. Whenever you elect an MP from our party, you shower your love on me. And this has been increasing day by day.

Friends, your love has filled us with enthusiasm. In the last election, the great city of Pune had elected the MP from our party and made me the Prime Minister. How can I forget this?

I am indebted to your love, but I don't wish to repay your debt. I am grateful to you but won't express my gratitude because then the informality of our relationship will be destroyed, and I don't encourage that.

I believe and trust that you will elect the MP from our party and strengthen our hands. Vote for Lotus because we are always with you, at every step. We not only promise but also intend to fulfil all our promises. Your participation is important to form a stable government by electing a strong leader. Let us unite to fulfil the dream of a 'Shining India'.

Jai Maharashtra.

Jai Hind.

There is silence for a while. Mrs Chitnis makes a face and says, 'Every party claims a better agenda than the other. One has to put a stamp on an elephant, lotus, hand, bicycle, key, lantern, watch and whatnot. In return, twenty-four hours of electricity and water, jobs, good cultivation, a happy childhood, education, health, a secure life, justice and a bright future are promised. With all good intent.'

'Yes, Mrs Chitnis is right,' Tara Nigam smiles sarcastically. 'We see samples of their honesty, integrity and faithfulness on TV every day through sting operations.'

'And yes, do you know what their hitting each other with shoes and sandals teaches us?' Mary asks, with her eyes dancing in mischief. 'It means, boys, give each other such a good hiding that the other forgets the name of all seven generations. This is also a good way to "shine" your shoes, isn't it?'

Mary quickly gets up and plops herself between Ameena and Mrs Chitnis. Punching Ameena on her thigh, she says, 'Damn it, do their faces show any sign of remorse? They look so convincing, relaxed and innocent when they speak before the media!'

Manda, who was sitting, quietly adds, 'You're right, Mary. They have swallowed their shame, so they look straight-faced.'

Soon, we are lost in stories. Talking about everything from elections, politics, leaders to problems, inflation, insecurity, to the tales of the mad rush of life. No one realizes that Ameena sits through all of this without a word.

When she sees Ameena, Rati Bharucha says that it is good that Ameena is not in Kanta Apte's room because some members were busy praising the present ruling party, the BJP there. 'Then I had said that the ruling party and communal groups are hand in glove. What can one say about the riots that recur so frequently? Why is the principle of equality of all religion in our Constitution ignored?

'On this, Vasudha More, Prabha Devtale and Chandra Patil were annoyed. They told me that even when the Parsis arrived in India, they never faced any untoward incidents. Why do such incidents happen only to Muslims and Christians? They believed that Muslims and Christians were destructive nuisance and their intentions were evil.

'Who knows what is in store for us if we live till then!'

Rati Bharucha takes a deep breath. But Ameena, who was sitting through all this quietly, shakes her head strangely. Then, she trembles, and her breathing becomes shallow.

A hissing sound comes from her nose, and when it grows louder, it catches our attention. But she seems completely oblivious!

I press my hand to hers and ask, 'Are you okay, Ameena?'

Oh, what a mocking smile she gives me!

We all look at each other. Mrs Chitnis waves Mary aside and moves closer to Ameena. She touches her on the shoulder and holds her with love, 'Forget it, Ameena. Sometimes, you have to see and suffer nightmares with eyes open, but you can't let your life be one long dream, can you?'

Ameena stares at Mrs Chitnis wide-eyed, although she hardly sees her; there is no sign of recognition in her eyes!

Then she suddenly kneels to pray, spreading her shawl, seeking mercy and looking up at the sky. Her eyes seem to flash. In a broken, husky voice, she mutters, 'O Allah! Give us justice. Give us peace. We, the shattered, the lifeless widows, the women, the mothers of Amdavad, beg of you for mercy.

'If you could not bear good Hajra's distress and infant Ismael's tears and created the source for Zamzam, the holy water in the rocky desert, let the tears of wretched people like us move you.

'O Allah! Have mercy on us. Have mercy on us. Let not the oppressive forces win. Our own people, who died like dogs without a shroud or coffin, will ask us on the Day of Judgment what we did to restore their faith and honour.

'O God, you are virtuous. Your name is blessed. Your honour is great, and no one is worth worshipping except you. Accept our prayers.

'Grant us peace. Grant us peace. Grant us…'

Stunned, we watch Ameena as she continues to bow in prayer. A strange rumbling sound comes from her throat. I am worried. When I shake her, she collapses on the floor and becomes unconscious.

Mary sprinkles water on her face and calls out, 'Ameena! Ameena!'

It seems Ameena has come out of a grave. I can see her

pale complexion, vacant eyes and deep lines of sorrow on her face!

Why did Ameena's eyes become the eyes of Rachel who lay in the operation theatre?

And why did I see Rachel's eyes turning into dead Tahmina's eyes?

Can images mingle beyond the boundaries of time?

Ameena takes long to recover. I help her stand and say, 'You are tired; go to your room and rest.'

As she sits on her bed and looks out of her window, she says, 'In the scriptures, there is a reference to a demon called Dhundhu, the son of the demon Madhu. When he exhales, fire and smoke come out with his breath—the Earth trembles. My Amdavad had turned into smoke and dust! Seema, if such a Dhundhu came again, they will turn the light and joys of others into smoke and hellfire! It is dark all around.'

I stare at Ameena for a few moments. She lies exhausted on the bed. Then I close the door and walk out to the lawn.

It is quiet outside. They are waiting for me. There is concern, not curiosity, on their faces.

'Ameena's sleeping,' I tell them.

Who knows how many images, voices, and fragments of time collide within me! Everything seems muddled. All images are broken, scattered and unclear; my own and others. We hardly live for ourselves! We discover ourselves through others, whether living, dying or being in doubt!

Mrs Chitnis, too, seems to be in a similar predicament. She says, 'Ameena has left her world behind, so she looks unstable.'

Tragedy reflects on Rati Bharucha's face. She speaks slowly and forcefully, using appropriate words. She is reserved and serious. 'I've been witness to such horrifying incidents before,' she says quietly.

She looks up at the trees for a long time as if trying to

collect her nerves. There is a strange chill in her voice, which surprises me. She suddenly says, 'The noise of swords, staffs, spears, the steady shots of kerosene-soaked burning flames, the terrible sound of burning houses, blood spraying out of falling bodies, the stench of burning human bodies, and among all this, the manic, lustful cries of men violating female bodies! And in this whole game, the silence of the frightened and terrified, the hiding and escaping hearts. After all this, how can one live in this world?'

The sixty-eight-year-old retired principal of St Mary's School becomes quiet. She had left Bharuch. She had once told me, 'Miss Samuel, not a single home in the Muslim colony was spared. I was terrified. My religion had made me fearful and my advancing age had failed me. So, I came here to Parisar.'

Everyone is quiet and lost. But how can Mary keep quiet? She stirs, murmurs, then quickly says, 'Girls, I place my hand on Congress' hand symbol.'

The gloom and hopelessness of the moment are suddenly interrupted.

'Whom will you vote for, Miss Samuel?' She slaps my thigh with her bulky hand.

I nurse my aching thigh. When I look at her, she smiles, winks at me and says, 'My dear, this was the slap of Matron Mary!'

We all smile.

'Just wait and watch. The results of the Fourteenth Lok Sabha election will be astounding. Just phenomenal. Like me! Honestly!'

'Are you dreaming, girl? Shining India will look so bright that all the grime will be hidden beneath. Don't you know this, Mary?' Mrs Chitnis smiles at me.

As always, Mary raises her hand to slap but lowers it at the last minute and says, 'It's not a dream Mrs Chitnis, it's a prophecy. Whatever this female predicts now shall come true.'

We see Ameena climbing down the stairs. She comes briskly towards us and stops. Mary does not give us a moment to be anxious. She slaps Ameena affectionately and says, 'Yaar, look, the total numbers of my birth year, month, and the day make the number five. The number five has always been lucky for me.'

Putting on an air of seriousness, Mary continues, 'Born on 5 May 1940, Mary Varghese had grown a hump in her fifth year; my worthless drunkard father died when I was fourteen. The same year, I became a woman from a girl. At the age of twenty-three, I realized that I was in love and that too with the head of my department, Dr Raje. I became Sister-in-Charge at the age of thirty-two and the Sister-Matron at forty-one. And the last one came during my fiftieth year, when my body became free from the menstrual cycle.

'Now the total of all these numbers comes to five! So, children, that's why I tell you that the result of this election will be as I predict.'

When no one speaks, she suddenly grows quiet. But she can't be silent for long. She pulls Ameena and me up by our hands: 'Let's go and see that *Baghban* movie in the only cinema hall we have. And yes, this treat for all of us will be on me because, despite all the shine and glitter, I can see the sign of the "hand" shining over our tricolour. Cent-per-cent!'

When we disperse to our rooms, her clear voice rings out, 'Lovely ladies, dress up fast, or we'll miss half the film.'

This is Mary Varghese. She is bold and brash, laughs and jokes all the time; she is too ready to make friends. She shares the dark, bitter chapters of her life with all, without any reserve and without being sentimental or self-conscious. She is forever ready to help others; she talks roughly, winks and slaps on the thigh or back, and fights with Sakhu Tai or the owner,

Mrs Rane, for her rights. Even then, there are some things which she tries to conceal. In her oblivious moments, I have seen her restless, sad and brooding. But, when she is with us, she is transformed completely—she becomes the same old winking, laughing, boisterous Mary.

When I am with her and listening to her nonsense chatter at her growing age, I often wonder why it sounds phoney? What is nibbling within her, or is there something that scares her?

But why?

Is this why, outwardly, she always looks jovial?

Who knows?

Then, as I think, a sharp pain fills my heart. Woman! As she grows older, she starts ignoring her natural instincts, as if thinking about her actions and emotions is shameful! The walls of the home, balcony, doorstep, courtyard, porch, windows—all seem to whisper:

Look at this old hag, she is singing;

Look at her age and her coyness;

One foot in the grave, but her appetite is still enormous;

Keep yourself busy in prayers and worship, Amma; or death won't come easily.

Yaar, these old people, why do they have to live so long?

Our eyes, ears, minds, and hearts, are full of such talk.

❁

Seema would hardly understand what Diana meant when she talked to herself. Seema wouldn't have grown old until eternity—till the sun and moon gleamed in the sky, till the gentle touch of the wind made her shiver, and the rain made the innermost core of her heart wet, till the butterflies of happiness flitted about and the magic of dreams and sleep continued! So, how could she know what Diana's monologue meant or realize that time discolours old age.

'Have you seen a tiny round brass pot dented on all sides? I know my age not through joy but through the blows of sorrow. But you won't understand, my girl!'

'Why? What Aajji?' Seema had asked, turning her Aajji's toothless face towards her.

'Fear. Fear, my dear.'

How could she save her spontaneity, her individuality? Old age forecasts humiliation if one is not famous or honoured. But how many get to experience such old age?

The rest…

Samuel David never admitted he was old. Even at that stage of life, when his limbs became feeble, and he had almost given up, he never thought he was old. He saw his mother passing away, Rachel, Bobby, Rafu, everyone was dying, but he didn't want to die. With his healthy heart, kidney, digestive system, and liver, he expected something new during meals every day; he watched new films on the TV and did everything on time.

By then, Jyotsna and her family had already made their entry. Samuel David could never tolerate Jyotsna and her people. In the beginning, he would grumble about them to David, but David himself was moving away from the family. When Samuel David saw timidity and meekness in his dearest son, as always, he would fly into a temper. He pushed everyone out and declared that he would remarry.

David looked at his spinster sister Seema and left quietly. This was the first time that David had disappeared for ten days.

Samuel David was perhaps scared after this incident. He tried to justify to Seema that after Rafu's death, she was often away from home for days for college work or with friends.

The Prajapati family might try to take advantage of this. If he married a divorcee or a widow for help and company, this problem could be solved without effort.

Astonished, Seema looked at her father.

After this, he was her father only in name; just a biological father to her. She felt a great void between them, so she maintained a distance from him. She also felt that if her father died the next day, she wouldn't even feel anything. Perhaps human bonding ends up like this. And this is how silence plants itself in the most crowded corners and creates aloofness.

The train rushes onward. Trees and plants, poles, homes, animals, birds sitting on wires, earth, sky, railway tracks, villages, towns, city lights, and the scarecrow standing alone in the field are all left behind. Sometimes, even the memories of relationships, incidents, and affection are left behind. The train leaves the station, our relationships, too, wave goodbye and turn their backs.

The pain of the broken and scattered pieces may have troubled like a splinter in the flesh. Seema realized it very late that the schizophrenic Rosie was manipulating and pressurizing Danny. She mistook their phone calls, which had suddenly become frequent and regular, as signs of affection and closeness, but it was all a selfish game.

And, even at home, the stage for a clever game was already set. There was no sign of David, who often got trapped in the game. Samuel David became bedridden. Seema retired from her job. A male nurse came to clean and wash her father; he changed his clothes, cleaned the catheter, removed the bag of urine full of blood and pus, and massaged his aching bones. But the grief had sunk deeper into his body. Grief seemed to have frozen in Samuel David's room. But even in the twilight of pain, he waited for a miracle. 'I don't want to die,' he would say, seeking Seema's approval. 'It is said in the twenty-eighth verse of the *Book of Psalms* that God can show miracles to the dead. Shouldn't I ask the Lord that if I am not there, who will sing his praises?'

'There is no God,' Seema's voice was flat.

'What?' Samuel David stared at her with disbelief.

'There is death, depression, desire, curiosity, but there is no supernatural power.'

'Even at your age, you don't want to change?'

'Did you ever change?'

'I am always right.'

'Even I am right.'

'You are still as obstinate as ever. Even Danny slowed down with age. He has changed. His roots tug at him, but you seem to be at war with your roots. Why are you bent on pulling them out? It's only because we have held on to our values, religion, God and faith that we can undertake such a long journey. Otherwise, who are we?'

'We are worthless. Leave aside a few; the lives of the rest are sheer mockery.'

'Even relations?'

'Yes.'

Samuel David was quiet. Seema could never tell him that Danny, whom he believed was changing and returning to his roots, was actually planning with his wife, Rosie, to get a share in his will. They were not concerned at all about David's absence, their father's ill health, or his aging sister's hard work and responsibility. They only wanted to be informed when his father took his last breath because 'you know, Seema, in our religion, we should have only vegetarian food during the seven days of mourning!'

On the outskirts of the small town where they lived, Danny was flying a kite. Seema held the reel in her hand. For a minute,

Danny let Bobby hold the kite-string, feeling the honour of being a big brother.

When Danny looked up at the sky, Rachel came to him timidly and touched the string gently and shyly. The children of peasants and labourers living on the outskirts eagerly watched the masters' children flying their kite, clapping cheerfully.

Suddenly, a strong wind lurched the kite wildly. When the wind circled higher, the kite became one with the sky. Then?

Then, the string in the reel was over. The string's end was not fixed to the reel, so the kite was lost in the sky. The fine thread of relationship, too, slipped from Seema's hand, danced in the air and disappeared.

A month and four days later, Danny called up, 'How is Papa?'

'He's no more. The period of mourning is also over.'

'Okay.'

Hearing Danny's flat, emotionless voice, Seema replaced the receiver. The kite had gone beyond the limits of the sky.

❁

As I dry myself with a towel, I look at my reflection. I try to remember Danny's face. The mirror has fogged with vapour. When I try removing the layer of haze with a finger, it turns into drops of water and slides down the glass. I see my face, too, slide down with them.

'David!' I whisper as I see his face emerging out of the mist…

A scared David squatted on the bathroom floor after Jyotsna had slapped him. During the silence that had followed the thunderous fight, Seema searched for David and opened the half-shut door of the bathroom to find her ten-year-younger brother standing before the mirror, lost in himself.

Just as she would hold Rafu, her hand reached out to David and touched him. David was as cold as ice and wet. When she tried to hold him, he stumbled and collapsed on his back on the floor. The water tap hit his forehead, and his left arm was slung over it.

Her heart raced with fear as she had called out to Jyotsna, but there was only silence. After a while, Jyotsna came and stood at the door of the bathroom with her hands on her waist in anger.

Seema was distressed to see David's blue face; his eyes rolled back. With her trembling hands, she sprinkled water on his face, shook him, and shouted his name in her broken voice, 'David! David!'

Jyotsna laughed.

As Seema turned around, Jyotsna raised her finger in a vulgar gesture and said, 'Bastard, bhench—, the whole family is so melodramatic.'

Seema watched in stunned silence as Jyotsna Prajapati left, swinging her hips.

And then?

At that time, the house hadn't been sold. The 2002 riots hadn't taken place either. Then, David would sometimes be seen at home, strolling aimlessly. Then, Jyotsna had started cornering Seema. During the evenings, all the nouveau riche young females of Gitanjali Society would visit 'Jyotsna Ben' for some fun gossip. Then, four times a week, aunts and relatives would chant kirtans to purify the apartment. Then, Seema had to wait hours to finish her daily chores. Then, since familiarity bred contempt, Professor Prafulla Patel, Seema's confidante during most times of need, had started taking Seema for granted. Then, Seema had become a stranger in her own home.

Then?

Then, after much manipulation, the property papers of the apartment fell into Jyotsna's hands, and Miss Seema Samuel, a woman of the smallest minority community of Jews, was defeated by the Prajapati family's conspiracies, threats, deceit, bribery, tactics, fraud and nepotism. In this way, Jyotsna Prajapati, David's wife, became the legal heir to his apartment despite Seema's attempts to stop it.

During those days, Seema would see David walking around the house night after night.

Then, one morning, the main door to the house was found open.

The members of Gitanjali Society who were like her or older distanced themselves from this incident; the younger lot supported Jyotsna. Even the Jewish community of the town kept quiet.

Then, one day, Parvati Patel, the seventy-year-old wife of the Society's secretary, Mr Vinod Patel, accosted Seema in the Society compound, 'We shouldn't have allotted a house to you Muslims. It was a big mistake, and we are now paying for it. Now forget your claim over this house and let poor Jyotsna live in peace.'

Miss Seema Samuel's consciousness had frozen.

Efforts were made to search for David. But no one came for support—neither the people of the colony nor their friends and acquaintances. Seema shared her problems with the community, expecting help from them. But in the entire human history, it has never happened that, at some point in time, a community dissociates its ideology and attitudes from its milieu. So, why should the minority Jews invite undue attention of the majority community by meddling in the matters of an aged woman like Seema? Armed with verbal sympathies and tall promises, Seema returned home slowly.

The days became longer and nights arrived late, and even the duration of the nights seemed longer. Seema learnt to tolerate Jyotsna and her family members coming to their place at odd hours. Then, for many days, Seema saw some unknown men along with Jyotsna. Then, one day Jyotsna packed her things and left. That same night, the doorbell of B-7 rang. Seema got up from sleep and opened the door.

It wasn't Jyotsna but a rude male voice: 'Why don't you vacate the house, Ma-ji?'

Stunned, Seema watched them. Then a second gruff voice echoed in the house, 'This will now be the party office.'

'What? Why?' was all Seema could utter.

By then, a dozen boys had entered and were all over the house. They began displacing everything. Seema knew none of them. They laughed.

'—This old woman asks why?' Their laughter echoed against the walls. '—O Ma-ji! This house is not yours anymore. The owner has sold it off to another party now. Understood?'

Miss Seema Samuel had never before known the disconnect between speech, vision, hearing and mind, all at the same time. A grey film arose before her eyes and she almost fainted. Her mind wandered.

'By when will you vacate the house? Tell us quickly. Or we will throw you out along with your bundles.'

Miss Seema Samuel stared at the men, who were easily old enough to be her sons, speaking so harshly with her. One of the boys, with spectacles, pulled off Seema's glasses, winked, and told the other, 'Yaar, at her age, old hags can always fall and get hurt. They can even die, can't they?'

Seema stood stunned in a blast of laughter. But she regained her composure after some time.

Seema turned and went to the balcony. In the dim moonlight, she saw many shadows around her, staring at her.

By the end of the twentieth century, Gandhiji's two monkeys had opened their eyes and ears in revolt. But the third still sat with its mouth shut.

Who knows for how long she stood in dark under their gaze. Gradually, other balconies vanished in thin air and a vacant, silent desert was spread all around.

Miss Seema Samuel found that she was trying to dig her bare feet in the sand, but a sandstorm was stopping her way, and she was gradually getting immersed in the sand dunes. As she continued getting buried in the sand, she heard a dirge rising within her. Seema started crying. Hot tears rolled down her face and dried up. She felt as if she wanted to howl like a primaeval beast because she was as forlorn as him, a howl that pierced through the earth, the sky and the universe. But though she tried with all her might, Seema's howl stuck in her throat.

Did Seema stand there eternally?

Slowly, she went in. The house was open, lonely and silent.

When Miss Samuel left for Parisar, she was reminded of her first day at B-7, Gitanjali Society. Samuel David had first placed the mezuzah over the front door. All seven members of his family had kissed the mezuzah before entering the house.

When she left for Parisar, Seema handed over the keys to the secretary of the Society and looked up at the sold B-7 apartment one last time. She felt Papa, Ma, Rachel and Rafu standing there silently, watching her leave. She raised her hand in goodbye.

Dusk fell and the sound of the footsteps on the pavement could be heard. The waiting auto-rickshaw whirred once more.

Gitanjali Society slowly receded from Seema's view before disappearing completely.

❁

'How long will you take to get ready, Miss Samuel?' I hear Mary's booming voice. She bangs the bathroom door. 'Everyone else is in the auto-rickshaw. Come quickly.'

Sitting in an auto-rickshaw with Mary and Ameena, I leave to see a blockbuster of the superstar of this century.

Chapter 14

Last night, Sakhu Tai's pet parrot, Mitthu, died.

He was in Parisar for the last four or five years. When I arrived there, he was only a chick. Sakhu Tai would sit in a chair in the courtyard and teach him to speak as she chatted with the cook, Vijaya, or Raghu, the helper, 'Say, Mitthu—Ram, Ram, Sakhu Tai'.

The cook would laugh, 'My dear Bai! You are teaching him only your own name. Here, everyone is single.'

Wiping away the film of unknown sadness that fell on her face, Sakhu Tai had said, 'What to do, Viju? When I was a child, Aai-baba died of cholera. For my brother, who was much older than me and married, I was a burden. My vahini, my sister-in-law, never called me anything but a "whore". And even my worthless brother followed her suit—called me a whore, weakling or bastard. Eighteen years ago, they married me off for twenty thousand rupees to a widower who was a tuberculosis patient. Ten months later, he passed away, and his family threw me out.'

Sakhu Tai had grown quiet for a while. Nodding his head, Raghu kept saying, *Ho baba, ho baba* (O yes, O yes).

Turning Mitthu's cage around, Sakhu Tai had continued, 'I have remained alone since then and suffered a lot. I carried on with my little education, sewing, and housekeeping skills.

Since then, I have kept a pet parrot at home for company and entertainment. When one died, I bought another. All of them wished me "Ram, Ram, Sakhu Tai". The home didn't feel lonely anymore. He is only a chick, but soon he will learn to talk.'

Mitthu learned to talk in six to eight months. When the elder members came out in the courtyard, they stood before Mitthu's cage and coaxed him to say 'Ram, Ram'. Mitthu sauntered around and caught the bars of the cage with his beak. Then, fluttering his wings, he would instead say, 'Sakhu Tai, Ram, Ram.'

The resident would knock at the cage and say, 'You naughty bird, do I look like Sakhu Tai? Say, Karnik Bai, Ram, Ram.'

Mitthu would blink his beady eyes, move his neck side to side and continue his chant—'Sakhu Tai, Ram, Ram…'

Mitthu's little mind could only retain and repeat things he was taught. Similar to Rafu, who, too, would recite whatever he had learned by rote: 'When we meet someone, we say, "Namaskar"; when someone raises his hand before the synagogue, we touch and kiss his hands and say "Shalom"*; when you receive something, you say, "Thank you"; when you pray, you should cover your head and remember the tune of this song…' Beyond this, there was only a meaningless chatter!

'Rafu, today you sang in the annual day function at your school. Sing that song to Mama also,' Seema told him as she wound up her chores. He sang Kishore Kumar's famous Hindi film song:

---

*Although generally the meaning of 'Shalom' is 'peace', when combined with other words or in different contexts, its meaning changes. For example, here it means wishing someone 'hello' or 'good day'.

'Nanha sa panchhi hai tu, bahut bada pinjra tera
Udna jo chaha to kahan tujhe udne diya
Lekar tu pinjra ude, chale kabhi waisi hava...'
(You are but a tiny bird, but your cage is too big
You longed to fly, but we never let you go
Carry off the cage when strong winds blow.)

Rafu stammered when he spoke, tried to convey his message through mispronounced words, dragged his feet when he walked, flung his right hand forward, which was twisted at the elbow, and curved his lips as he smiled. But he used to sing the songs Seema had taught him correctly and perfectly.

He was put in Koshish, the school for special children. He always smiled. If someone asked him to sing, he would sing at once. Untouched by praise, criticism, embarrassment or admiration, Mitthu, too, chanted to everyone, 'Sakhu Tai, Ram, Ram.'

While singing the song, Rafu paused, turned Seema's preoccupied face towards him and asked, 'Mama, what is a "cage"? Tell me!'

Even Mitthu would blink his beady eyes and ask,

—Sakhu Tai, Prabha means what?
—Saaku Tai, Vimla means what? Sakhu Tai Ram, Ram.
—Sakhu Tai, Mary means what?
—Sakhu Tai, Sakhu Tai, Sakhu Tai, Ram, Ram.

Seema paused for a while. 'Cage? Okay, cage means a kind of mesh with bars in it. Like a mouse trap.'

'And bird means?'

'Bird? Oh! Birds are mynah, pigeon, and cuckoo that sing "koo, koo".'

'Okay. Has Nanu ever locked up the bird like he locks me in the bathroom? Was the bird naughty, Mama? Nanu is bad, he is hopeless. Shall I beat him?'

Rafu had learned to aptly use the abuses he received from others.

Seema shook her head and said, 'No. It's bad to say things like this. He is elder to you.'

'Then whom should I beat? The bird's nanu?'

'We don't even know who or where it is.'

Rafu thought for a while as he followed her. 'Mama! Is the bird crying? The way I cry in the bathroom?'

'Maybe, son.'

'Then, why doesn't he fly away to his Mama like Rafu.'

'His cage is locked. How will he go?'

Mentally a child but physically a young man of twenty, Rafu dragged himself around the house. Then, quietly, he came to Seema, who was washing clothes in the bathroom. He stood next to her and kept looking at her.

'What's the matter?'

He lowered his face in disappointment. His face was red. He stammered and said, 'Is Rafu also a bird, Mama?'

Seema looked at him.

A bird he was indeed, locked up inside the limited space of a cage. Walking back and forth, sometimes flapping his wings, sometimes biting at the finger in anger, nibbling what was offered to him, following words or behaviour taught to him, listening to instructions.

—Sakhu Tai, Ram, Ram.

As she carried a bucketful of wash to the balcony, Seema pulled Rafu to her, 'No, my dear, you are my darling Rafu.'

His face brightened a little, but he remained quiet. Seema was surprised. Rafu sat quietly on the bed in the room next to the balcony and stared at a fragment of sky visible from the balcony. She let him be and instead continued to put clothes on the clothesline. Busy with her chores, Seema didn't notice when Rafu came and stood by her. Watching the last rays of the setting sun, he whispered, 'Mama, are you also trapped in a cage?'

Seema knew that whatever she told this special child, he wouldn't understand. Still, she muttered, 'Who knows? Trapped in our own cages, we may be waiting for the change in the course of the wind!'

Rafu stood there holding the parapet, handing Seema the clothespins. When he gave her the last pin, he said, 'The wind has stopped, Mama.'

Seema looked at him suddenly. His face was as silly and innocent as before. 'Isn't it hot, Mama?'

Mitthu shrieks.

During the day, the door of Mitthu's cage would be kept open. He would perch on his cage. Sometimes, he would sit on the Neem tree in the courtyard. Sometimes, he took short flights, returned, and celebrated his arrival by alighting on the kitchen door and chanting, 'Sakhu Tai Ram, Ram.' But he seemed delighted to return to the cage. He would shriek, play antics, hang from the bars on his beak and make the tiny bowls of guava pieces, green chillis and rice tumble.

❁

While returning from her college friend Professor Nanaki Motwani's son's wedding the next day, when Seema sat in the auto-rickshaw, she remembered how overjoyed Rafu usually became on her arrival. She knew that the moment she entered the house, Rafu would hug her and complain, 'Mama, where were you? Rafu is scared of dark. He cried.'

Rafu would hover around her for a while, touch her cheeks, pat her hair, and run around. During that time, even Jyotsna Prajapati's stares wouldn't scare him. He wouldn't look at her; instead, he would smile sheepishly, assured that his mother was with him.

Professor Nanaki Motwani's son wedding took place on a Sunday. When Seema left the wedding at Mani Nagar for Gitanjali Society, the roads of Amdavad were almost deserted. Very few buses were plying. The house where the wedding took place had a similar ambiance. Everyone—the bride, the bridegroom, and all the people of the wedding party—was settled in front of the television.

The magic of Ramanand Sagar's *Ramayan* had taken over the country. When the wind chimed '*Jai Shri Ram*' (Hail Lord Rama), the sky lowered itself and echoed, 'Ram, Ram!' When the thin stream of the Sabarmati murmured 'Ram, Ram', the trees on the bank would bow and touch their ears in respect. All—nature and beings alike—had taken the superhero of the Hindu religion from the past and sowed his grandeur in the present. The seed will sprout, flower and flourish.

Lal Krishna Advani's Rath Yatra was yet to commence. The Babri Masjid, which was demolished in 1992, still stood intact on the bank of River Saryu. Till then, the seeds of communal violence, which had been sown in Amdavad during the 1960s, still hadn't received the conducive atmosphere to flourish.

Yet, when Seema came home that day, after climbing the same sixty steps she did every day, she found thick clouds of discontent and the signs of an impending storm spread all over the house. David's wife, Jyotsna Prajapati, had thrashed the twenty-four-year-old mentally challenged Rafu. 'Bastard, you pretend to be mad and insane? You, lecherous dog, I will teach you a lesson.'

That night, the entire neighbourhood was woken up by the noise. Their lights were switched on. Phones rang from one house to another. The sounds of footsteps climbing up the stairs could be heard. Then, there were knocks on the door. Samuel David opened the door nervously. David had been sent to Baroda for a temporary job. More than a dozen people stood in the drawing room of flat B-7.

Seema, Samuel or David never came to know why and how Jyotsna Prajapati had gone near Rafu, who lay bundled up in his bed with fear. They never came to know who had really got up to drink water that night. They will also never know if Rafu had mistaken Jyotsna for Seema and had gone to seek comfort from her. Or was it Jyotsna? They never knew how Jyotsna's blouse was torn, how she received scratch marks on her left hand or why she was breathless before everybody.

'You whore, bastard, bitch, this woman has an illicit relation with her own son, so he thinks of everyone to be like her.'

Switching off the *Ramayan*, Jyotsna Prajapati screamed at Seema, who had just entered her home. 'Bastard, these women can even have children with their male cousins. Don't they have any shame or dignity? These barbarians!'

This is exactly what Jyotsna had said to Seema when she came home that night.

How many times do we die in our lives?

Even before the predetermined moment of our death, who knows how many times we are killed slowly and painfully, as if bludgeoned by a blunt object. Deprived of our consciousness and feelings, is there anything left within us?

Sakhu Tai's Mitthu did not know death's leap, pounce, prowl, or paw. He only knew the terror of the cat and he knew of his trembling.

During the days of the Advani Rath Yatra, Rafu caught

a fever. He grew paler and weaker by the day. Meanwhile, outside, the entire nation was in the grip of the magic of Rama. And with the extra energy derived from this magic, a new society would be created.

Under the spell of this magic, lifeless bricks had come alive and begun a journey. Once endowed with life, the bricks understood that you could not create a commotion by walking, sitting, eating, or sleeping in queues. Queues cannot build pyramids, nor are they needed when charting one's escape. No, to create a stir, to cause a commotion, what is required is energy—the energy to create a tragedy, to frighten the non-Hindu communities.

And this made the old Jew, Mr Samuel David, living on the third floor, so insecure that he got up quietly one night and removed the mezuzah fixed on the left frame of the door.

The next morning, as Seema was leaving for the college, out of habit, her hand reached out to touch the mezuzah. But it was gone! She came back home. Jyotsna Prajapati jumped with joy, 'Good! The problem was solved without any effort. Damn it, the house looked so odd. Now, our gods and goddesses will live in this house.'

Rafu rushed to the door, touched the vacant spot, and returned, 'Mama, Mama, how will Rafu kiss the mezuzah now?'

Like Sakhu Tai's Mitthu knew fear, Rafu, a mentally challenged young man, also recognized his unsteadiness. But who has the energy to destroy the offensive, fanatic, confrontational culture?

Seema tried to calm Rafu, but the silly boy flung his left hand, ran towards the door, returned, and stood near Jyotsna. He lowered his eyes, raised his hand, and asked, 'Where is the mezuzah? Where is it?'

Only that, nothing else: 'Where is it? Where is it?'

Jyotsna stared at the stupid young man who was becoming weaker day by day, pressed her lips, and said, 'You, crazy bastard! I will tell you right now where it went, okay?'

How could this flawed boy understand such a confusing answer? He went to his grandfather with the same innocent face and asked, 'Nanu, how will Rafu kiss the mezuzah now?'

The unfortunate child-like man became the target of Mr Samuel David's fear, insecurity, ill treatment at home, and the sorrow of his disintegrating family. A frustrated Samuel David caught hold of Rafu's able hand and dragged him out of the room, 'It couldn't have been more unfortunate than to have this insane boy in this family!'

Rafu was examined by many doctors. Most days, David would climb the sixty steps to the flat carrying such a big boy in his arms. He would break into sobs when he saw Rafu lying still on the bed.

All efforts to increase David's self-confidence proved futile. In fact, words of assurance and trust only made him more distressed, helpless and guilty. Seema saw David standing at the threshold of dilemma.

Rafu's fate lay at Seema's mercy, and although it pained her, she had slowly started to accept it. However, it was David's uncertain future which frightened her.

Grunts of anger rumbled in their home, which now resembled an enclosure of wild animals. The animals confined to their cages roared in impatience.

'Seema, why is there no egg for my breakfast?'

'It's Tuesday today,' Jyotsna would say furiously.

'How does Tuesday affect me? Damn it, those of you who say Monday, Tuesday, get out of my home.'

'I will also see which goddamn mother's son dares get eggs in this house.'

'This is my home! Mine! It's not a charity house.'

'Did your son, too, come in charity? He has married me, not eloped with me! Do you understand, you old fogey?' Jyotsna would get as furious as wildfire.

'Misfortune spoils the mind. I regret the moment I let you into my home.'

'Just wait, worms will infest your body, and you will die.'

'And you think you have been sent to this world with the tag of immortality?'

Even that invalid Rafu hadn't been sent to this world with a tag of immortality. He would ask for the time at least ten times a day, have nothing on his mind other than eating and sleeping, run around the house dragging his feet; he would talk, laugh, and get angry with himself, never make any eye contact with others, try to copy everything Seema did. The Rafu, who was scared of his Nanu, Rosie, and later Jyotsna Prajapati, in the end, could not go very far.

❁

Insecure, afraid, and lonely, Mitthu has died in his cage. His feet are upturned, facing the sky, and his beak is open. His eyes stare beyond the bright sky towards who knows what.

Sakhu Tai's Mitthu's wings are spread as if he wants to fly away to a distant land!

Chapter 15

'Dhah jana tera maati da munnara
Birtha swas layo din rati
Jis deenh maut ne payi jhati
Swas mile na udhara,
Tera maati da munnara'
(Your earthen stove will fall into pieces
Day and night, you breathe uselessly
The day Death grabs you
You won't even be able to borrow a breath
This earthen stove of yours!)

As I stand, holding onto the railing of the veranda outside Room 20, I can hear Manjeet Kaur singing sweetly.

It has been a year since Vimla left. Her Canada-settled son had safely dumped her at some private mental clinic in Matheran and left. Who knows if Vimla has been able to adjust to the new and unfamiliar environment?

It is December again. Mary Varghese was with us last year, but after Vimla left, she, too, passed away in a few months.

'Please don't bury me, Miss Samuel.' This was her last wish.

Her funeral pyre had burnt noisily on the sandy confluence of the Mula-Mutha rivers of Pune.

Ever-active Mary had become quite slow of late. She would often just look out of the window of her room. Not seeing her in the lawn in the evening, one of us would go to call her, but she had an excuse every time.

'What's the matter, Mary?' finding her alone, I had finally asked her one day. 'You don't even come for the yoga class on the lawn anymore. And why do you look so worried?'

Mary stared at me silently. There was no sign of merriment on her face. She had neither winked nor hit me like she used to. She had only asked me to sit closer and had said, 'Miss Samuel, these days, I am bleeding a lot.'

'What?' It was all I could utter.

'I should have told you much earlier, but I thought perhaps I might get well with the help of Baba Ramdev and his ayurvedic medicines! But Miss Samuel, can a leaky pot ever be filled?' A permanent sadness had etched itself on Mary's face in those last days and it deepened at that moment.

She smiled out of habit, 'You see, I knew I was ugly, but even my relatives chose to be distant and aloof. At this stage of my life, I had wished to die peacefully, at least. Your company took away some of the loneliness in my life. But how can Mary Varghese ever have happiness? And I always yearned for happiness, Miss Samuel, honestly.'

I couldn't stay with her much longer, so I came back.

Mary Varghese, who woke up at the cock's crow, would chase us out to the lawn every morning for yoga practice. She would shout, 'You old hags if you don't move your limbs, they will become as stiff as rocks.' Then, pinching and winking at me, she would say, 'Don't you all want to become younger?'

Mrs Chitnis would say, 'Mary, you carry on being young. We will feel younger just by looking at you.'

The day would always begin with jokes and teasing. Mary would be glad to see improvements in Tara Nigam's knee pain,

Manda's stiff back, Rati Bharucha's sinusitis, Mrs Chitnis's insomnia, and my blood pressure. Her eyes would sparkle with joy. We hadn't known then that our improving health made her hope for a miracle for herself.

The next day, Mary came to my room herself. 'I am feeling better today. Let's go for a walk,' she said. I was relieved.

We walked towards the main road and reached the narrow, hilly track. All the way, Mary shared interesting, boring, horrible, sad, cruel and awful tales of her hospital life. As we talked, we reached quite a height. The hill had many turns, and the pathway passed a valley at every turn. But not all valleys were deep, and we could see small human settlements strewn all over their slopes. But, the slope was very deep and sharp at one of the turnings. If you looked down, you could see the mesmerizing, otherworldly, greyish-blue sea of mist flowing below. We sat on a fallen tree trunk in the flat plateau above the valley.

The evening was falling. The sun had climbed the hilltop and would soon start receding into the valley. And then, the valley would be filled with crickets chirping.

Mary left my side and walked slowly towards the sharpest edge, peeping below. Startled, I asked her, 'What are you trying to do, Madam? Do you have plans to jump?'

Mary seemed to wake up from her sleep at my question. Turning back, she came closer and stared at me. How transparent her face looked! I felt as though she had gone too far away at this moment, in these surroundings.

'What? What's the matter with you, Mary?' I stammered.

She pulled me up by my hand and dragged me to the edge. Pointing at the blue misty valley below, she said, 'Miss Samuel, do you believe in suicide?'

I looked at her in shock. Although I was trembling within, I wore a mask of restraint. Drawing her back, I said, 'Mary, it will be dark soon, and we won't be able to see our way. Come, let's go now.' A narrow track led us back to Parisar.

On the way, Mary remained quiet. She walked slowly and answered only in monosyllables. Parisar now stood before us. But before we could enter, she stopped and held my hand in her trembling one.

'Miss Samuel, you haven't told me your thoughts on suicide.'

Though very disturbed, I said calmly, 'Mary, the remarkable manner and courage with which you've led your life so far, wasn't it fulfilling enough that you are in such a dilemma now?'

Her face clouded with doubts. Then, it seemed she had decided to pour her heart out, 'I have seen innumerable people dying when I worked at the hospital. People never want to die, Miss Samuel. Despite the pain, suffering, and hell-like torture, they want to hold onto life as it slips drop by drop from their fists. They wait for a miracle, some magic drug, or incredible help. Then, when none of that works, they become emotional and beg God to pardon their sins, their wrongdoings and cruelties, and pester Him to save them. You might not have experienced how paltry they look. We used to laugh and make fun of them. But I hadn't experienced such horrible pain then.

'Now, I feel that perhaps, their desire to live wasn't as intense as to be free from the sufferings. Perhaps they—or most of them—could never distinguish between these two desires, who knows?

'But I want freedom from my pain; death doesn't frighten me, not at all. As it is, there was no sign of hope in this desert of my life. I just wish that my story comes to an end soon.

'I can't bear it anymore, Miss Samuel; the pain is so excruciating.'

She sat, leaning against the pillar in the veranda, and

closed her eyes. Walking on the hillside had exhausted her. Her pockmarked, tired face seemed to have plunged into the silent valley of pain.

As I watched her, I felt shards breaking within me. Was it my anguish for Mary's suffering or the fear of being left behind?

Next time, I accompanied her to the Sassoon Hospital because, by then, she had no strength left to travel alone. Earlier, she would lie to us that she had gone to meet her former colleagues at the hospital.

I remember it was 17 January 2005. Ameena knocked at my door quite early in the morning; it was very unexpected. She had a strange joy on her face, as one has after taking revenge.

'Did you read the newspaper?' she asked as she picked the newspaper from the table.

'No, I will read it while having tea,' I said.

'Arre, Seema, it says "Sabarmati Express and Godhra 2002" was only an accident. That's what Justice U.C. Banerjee and his team have announced. I am very happy. I want to thank Allah a thousand times. Many of our people, who were thrust into jails without any evidence or investigation and any fault of theirs, will now be released. Oh! I feel relieved after so long.' She smiled happily.

'Let us go out for lunch. It will be on me. I will inform Sakhu Tai.'

'I am going with Mary to the Sassoon Hospital this morning.'

She had perhaps forgotten about Mary in her excitement. She said quietly, 'Yes, that is more important.' Then, after sitting for a while, she left.

Mary had placed her file before Dr Neela Shahane. The cancer in her uterus was in the fourth stage. Mary had brushed aside the suggestion for surgery. Patting her friend Dr Shahane on her shoulder, she said, 'In the last stage, isn't it useless?'

Before I left her room, Dr Shahane whispered in my ear, 'She has hardly any time left.'

Before I could even react, the swing door of the doctor's room shut. I stood lost in front of the closed door. Mary, who was standing in front of me, somehow knew. She looked around, held my hand, and said with a smile, 'What is this, Miss Samuel? Are you scared to know that I have very little time left?'

She had caught me red-handed, but she was taking it all very lightly. 'I cannot be deceived in my life. In fact, a thousand and one times, I have seen similar gestures and words being used to convey such news. Now, it's my turn, isn't it?' She winked at me with puffy eyes. I felt like laughing and crying at the same time.

While returning, we took a train from Shivaji Nagar. It was a narrow-gauge train and the ladies' compartment was almost empty. The other one or two passengers got off at a smaller station.

We sat facing each other quietly. Mary, who couldn't bear the silence anymore, came and sat beside me. Slapping my thigh merrily, she said, 'Don't be so quiet, yaar. I am not going to leave you so soon.'

I smiled weakly and tried to lose myself in the scenery passing by the train window.

She saw me looking out. Taking a long breath, she said, 'How I wish even my train stopped at a small station after crossing these trees, hills, forests, and plains—at lonely places where passengers got down, sat on benches, drank cold water, rested, chatted, met each other and then returned home. My legs are tired of walking for so long, Miss Samuel. I have left loneliness behind, and I am moving towards darkness. And yet, it's too lonely out here.'

To lessen her sadness, I told her that all middle-class lives are as colourless as ours. 'We may or may not even remember the joys of comfort. Time flies in fighting melancholy or in trying to free ourselves from it.'

Before she could respond to my comforting words, her whole body became rigid. Mary tried to bear her pain, but her face was distorted. I made her lie on the berth.

A little later, when she opened her eyes, she saw me looking at her. She turned on her side and smiled, 'Yaar, I had no idea that this uterus of mine, which has remained unproductive all my life, would rebel so! Honestly—the hassles women must face! If there are more children, or if children come too late—say after thirty years—or even if there are no children, the danger is always there. I will certainly ask Him why He always wins, whether head or tail?'

By then, Mary was tired of talking. She closed her eyes and lay quietly. Perhaps she had even dozed off. I looked at her puffy face where her pockmarks had drowned and disappeared. Behind the shrewd image of Mary who lay before me, who knows how much sadness, deprivation and frustration were hidden! Has anyone ever known?

We carry our cries of grief and agony within ourselves when we leave.

'I have closed my eyes, but I am sleepless within.' Her eyes were partly open and blinking, 'What do you think when you look at me?' she asked.

'Nothing, Mary. I was just looking at you.' I gently stroked her forehead.

'Yes, you must see me, my dear girl. The end of the string of my life is about to slip off your hand,' she said as she snapped her finger.

Miss Samuel knew very well how the string of life slips off the hand. Every string she had ever known had just slipped off her grip and flown away. Every time, she had forgotten to tie a knot on the spool of string for safekeeping. The string would swim in the air with the kite, rise up and up, and soar far away in the sky.

The vein of Miss Samuel's forehead stood out. Her face was tense. A web of memories rose to her eyes. Her throat pricked. The two-faced djinn came swaggering out of the magic box.

Professor Prafulla Patel.

Miss Samuel had snapped the thread at once.

Although Miss Samuel had remembered very well that she had tied a tight knot on the spool. Still, the string had soared in the sky, and turned so destructive that it had cut and bloodied her palm. In the end, she had snapped the string at once. The wavering string hadn't been able to take the shock. It had stumbled at first, then dipped low, meandered, and flown away with the wind.

❁

In the beginning, Professor Prafulla Patel was happy to hear about David's closeness with Jyotsna Prajapati and had told Seema that her younger brother would probably settle down with her. He would always inquire about their relationship. And with time, Seema became more and more emotionally dependent on him, believing him to be a part of her sufferings and problems.

Seema would often run away to Professor Prafulla Patel and share her woes with him. Then, in her attempt to free herself from the terrible stranglehold of her problems, she would let herself get swept by his charismatic persona. But, by then, he had started to distance himself from her. As he continued to hear of her father's declining health, Rafu's death, David's departure, Jyotsna Prajapati's entry into the home and her increasing aggression, Professor Patel had slowly grown indifferent towards Seema. It never occurred to Seema that the play was long over and the empty stage had sunk into darkness.

Miss Samuel remembered her forty-eight-year-old self when she had first visited the widower Professor Prafulla Patel, the sober, dignified, reticent father of two married daughters. That was the first phase of their long relationship.

Seema had found his home well-maintained and tastefully decorated. On a small bedside table were framed photographs of his late wife and his daughters with their husbands. Professor Prafulla Patel did not waste much time pursuing her, and it never occurred to Seema that whatever happened between them was forced on her or planned.

All Seema wanted to do was continue in this dream world. All her hurts, abrasions and turmoil were washed away. The pure and virtuous Seema felt alive for the first time in life.

When Seema stretched herself lazily that day, Professor Prafulla Patel touched her nose and said, 'Always fall like a gentle spring on my rigidity.'

So, Seema, who always rushed to Professor Prafulla Patel, never knew when the stars became cold and turned into dead rocks.

Professor Prafulla Patel, too, never realized the intensity of Seema's deep love because of his male ego and superiority complex. His carefully suppressed desires, lying low at the bottom of his heart, suddenly rose to the surface, turning the waters murky.

So, on that special day, when she took the familiar, drowsy path with him, she hadn't anticipated waking into a nightmare.

Seema's fingers, which seemed absorbed in the song of love and longing, suddenly tightened at the heartstrings. With a clank, a string snapped and hit her.

Seema turned a long way back. Her feet stopped dancing. The music that was playing stopped, too. She felt jolted, much like she had years ago, when she had danced with Sohrab, and had been stunned to hear Tahmina's spate of abuses.

Shocked and taken aback, Seema had released herself from Professor Prafulla Patel's embrace. There was a touch of coldness in him. Green scum had started surfacing on the stagnant water. A pained Seema could see a fog in the growing distance between them.

'When your father and brother are no more, who will inherit the house?'

This was the breaking point in their seven- or eight-year-old relationship! Speechless, Seema had looked at Professor Prafulla Patel's face.

He had shouted with annoyance, 'Why do you stare at me like a fool? That worthless woman, Jyotsna Prajapati, will grab everything one day! Arre, shouldn't we pass on at least something to our two daughters?'

Seema had never found herself so alone, weary and down, even when B-7 was gradually becoming empty. It was such a sinking feeling! She came back to herself.

❁

'Where are you lost, Miss Samuel?' Mary had found me once again.

'You will get ample time later to be lost in thoughts. Listen to me now. See here, there's a strange restlessness within me! I escape outside only to find a forest growing there. Remember what Rama Aajji used to say? She was right when she said that if you are lonely within, there will only be loneliness waiting for you outside. Who knows, the sharp edges of time may have taught this lesson to Rama Aajji.'

She closed her eyes in exhaustion. There was a faint, tired smile on her face, which only reflected her suffering. She continued to lie on her side and drew her feet closer. The cold air from the window had spread her dry, curly hair over her face. I pulled out a hairpin from my bun and pinned her hair back. Then, I took out a shawl from the bag, covered her, and stroked her face with love. She held my hand and said in a choked voice, 'Neither my faith nor yours believes in rebirth, Miss Samuel. Otherwise, I would have certainly remembered you covering me with a shawl and your affection in my next birth.'

As I patted her and smiled at her, she pulled my face closer, planted a kiss on my forehead, and said, 'May God bless you.'

For the first time in my life, I winked at her just like she used to, hit her affectionately and said mischievously, 'At this age?'

Mary slipped into her usual roar of laughter, but the lines on her face had become taut with rocking waves of pain, and her face turned dark in agony.

I kept looking at the dark face of Mary Varghese, who lay with her eyes closed.

Why do the faces of Mary, Ma, Rachel, and Tahmina look so alike? Does pain have a universal colour?

Manjeet Kaur comes and touches my shoulder. She asks me in her Punjabi-mixed Hindi, 'Miss Samuel, why are you standing here, ji? Come in.'

'Next time…' I say and walk towards my room.

Chapter 16

Then even nothingness was not, nor existence,
There was no air then nor the heavens beyond it.
What covered it? Where was it? In whose keeping?
Was there then cosmic water, in depths unfathomed?

But, after all, who knows, and who can say
Whence it all came, and how creation happened?
The gods themselves are later than creation,
*so who knows truly whence it has arisen?**

Around 1500 BC, the Aryans arrived in India through North-western passes like the Hindukush. They opened India's literary history to the world, which was introduced to the Hymn of Creation, a hymn in the Rig Veda (around 1000 BC). However,

*These verses are a part of a longer—Hymn of Creation or the Nasadiya Sukta ('not the non-existent'), which is the 129th hymn of the 10th Mandala of the Rig Veda (10:129) and the oldest of the four Vedas and written around 1500-2000 BC. This hymn has attracted a large body of literature and commentaries both in Indian theology and in Western philology about the creation of the universe, which is still a major challenge for the modern sciences. It suggests possible answers to these questions but leaves the readers speculating, raising questions about the given possibilities in the end. The translation here is by A.L. Basham, who translated the Rig Veda in 1954.

they expressed severe scepticism towards the origin of the Earth, as explained in it.

But, in 2200 BC in the Ur town of Mesopotamia (modern Iraq), there was no doubt or confusion about the Earth's origins in the civilization established in the memory of Abraham, who had led the tribe of idol-worshipers propagating monotheism. Their beliefs in the primeval sea, the separation between Earth and sky, the creation of Man from the earth, and the notions of heaven and hell were clear and distinct. These ideas were later established in the Holy Bible by Moses, the descendant of Abraham, who laid the foundation of Judaism.

Dispersed and brought together again and again during different time periods, the most barbarous attack on the Jews occurred in their motherland Palestine (Canaan) in 70 AD when the Solomon Temple, built in about 516 BC, was looted and destroyed by the Romans. The heinous genocide which followed continued for days.

Watching the remains of the destroyed temple, some of the heartbroken Jewish tribes had cried and wailed as they had escaped. Together, they had promised that they would return to their own land one day, completely ignorant that they would enter a dark, deep slumber into which they would be lost for thousands of years.

This ancient tale of the Bene Israel has no historical evidence of its exact time period. Its roots lie in the history being passed on from one generation to the another of the Bene Israel.

Once again, I have opened the drawer in my table. Bobby's essay, published in a local English daily, is here.

When Bobby was dismissed from his job, he passed his unemployed days writing articles and opinion pieces for the

English and Gujarati newspapers. Since his subject was history, he expressed his opinions or commented on folk traditions, culture, civilization or their decline and fall with historical evidence. The name of one of his columns in *The Times of India* was 'Vatayan', which means window in Gujarati and Hindi. He had written this essay and sent its Gujarati translation to the Gujarati daily *Gujarat Samachar*.

However, the riot hindered its publication.

Eventually, the article was published, but Bobby never got to see it.

My hands shake and the pages tremble. I spread the pages on the table; my glasses slip a little over my nose.

Sometimes, such unexpected slumber becomes suffocating. All suppressed fears, apprehensions, doubts, hurt, hopelessness and uncertainties, and darkness lurking in the hollow of the eyes leaps up and occupy our thoughts, energy and life, depriving us of confidence, ethics and self-awareness.

We want to open our eyes and wake up; we want to check our shallow breath, and we struggle to get out of this frightening slumber.

The forefathers of the Bene Israel, who had landed two thousand years ago at the Konkan coast, may have gone through a similar slumber, painful, restless and terrifying. Their prayer books, belongings, their co-religionists, kith and kin—all had risen and fallen in the turbulent waves of the Arabian Sea and had gradually sunk into its foamy waters.

In their struggle to survive, these strangers to the land, who had only been able to save a few breaths, had hardly known that they stood at the mouth of a dark cave and that by the time they came out of it and into a ray of light, they would have lost who knows what else.

Around 70 AD (during or before the destruction of the Second Temple), these Bene Israel had planned to sell their goods in India and return home rich. But their vessel, riding on the stormy waves, had crashed against the rocky Deccan plateau and broken into pieces. Legend has it that only seven men and seven women survived the wreck. When they were washed ashore, the Sahyadri mountains (Western Ghats) looked at these survivors with surprise—they were men and women of different appearance, clothing, language, culture, and civilization. They had raised their hands to the sky, crying and sobbing and saying something, who knows what, in their language. These strangers would have been less miserable about their unusual appearance than with the niggling hunger which made them numb. Safety, shelter, occupation, society, culture and civilization were the subsequent steps they had to climb with great trouble because this new world was completely different and unknown.

The sun of the Mauryan dynasty had already set around two hundred years ago, and the entire Deccan plateau was in turmoil. But trade and commerce were not affected, so the incoming shipping vessels brought dates, wine, ivory, gold, pearl, copper, zinc, glass, and gold and silver coins from Ethiopia, Jordan, the coastal towns of the Arabian Sea or the southern towns of the Gulf of Persia. On return, they loaded their vessels with goods like indigo, aromatic herbs such as nard, diamond, hard turtle shells, turquoise, spice, and silk.

These strangers had nothing on them except the clothes they wore.

This must have hit them in the beginning. The common people used the barter system to buy useful commodities, whereas the elite class and traders used Greek gold coins. Then, Nishka (gold coins), pal (gold), silver coins (shatman) and zinc coins were also used. People in the lower classes of society used copper (kakini) and alloy metal (ranga). But how could these troubled and destitute strangers, these hidden, fearful outsiders, barter or buy?

To survive starvation and to find shelter, they may have made the first compromise with their self-respect and taken up any petty work.

As they knew of agriculture and olive oil production, they gradually took that up as their occupation.

At the turn of last century BC, the Saka dynasty ruled in South India or in Nasik in Maharashtra. But they were overpowered by the Satavahana dynasty in the first century AD. The capital earlier was Nasik, but Gautamiputra Satavahani made Paithan his capital. His descendants, Satkarni and his son, Vasistha, were strong supporters of Brahmanical rituals and treated the Eastern Sakas as 'cross-breeds' and the Greeks as 'fallen Kshatriyas'. Lower-class people worshipped their clan deities (peacock, crocodile, peepal, wolf etc.) and took up their names for their surnames, for example, More, Magare, Peepale, Vaghe, Ladage. Some worshipped stone idols of the goddesses Mengai, Manghrai, Songjai, Udlai. As Muslims and Christians would arrive later in history, it was important to have some idol or image of a god or goddess before them. These Bene Israel strangers had no image of god, no rituals for worship and no printed books.

Such an alien culture had to come to light. This was the first turn of events which distanced the Bene Israel, who had arrived from Palestine, from the masses.

In those days, varna (especially Brahmin) and the Hindu religion were the greatest identities and honours. But a large group of non-Hindus had gradually absorbed themselves into the Hindu religion as its lower sub-caste. This class gained political power, capability, security and status, wealth and authority; they got state security, comfort, and power.

But these people, whose forefathers were Abraham, Isaac and Jacob (known as Yisra'yel), who had escaped from Canaan, their homeland of 'milk and honey', to protect their faith, civilization and culture, did not convert to any religion or caste and did not follow the Hindu, Brahmanical way of life. So, even among the masses, they remained inferior and lived secluded on riverbanks or along the coast, took up small jobs to fill their stomachs, but refused to adopt Buddhism, like the Kushanas, Romans, or Sakas. And, because they had become a part of the weaker classes, they became ignorant and illiterate, unlike the Brahmins and Buddhist monks, who had the right to knowledge.

In the Konkan region of South India, the local languages Konkani and Marathi, derived from Prakrit, were spoken. They learnt these languages during their exile. Like the lower class, they slogged to earn their living. Since they were poor, they were resigned to their fate and depended on their rich benefactors and led a fretful and lowly life.

The pages of history continued to turn over. Calling themselves 'Israyels', this minority community continued to struggle day and night, slog hard, bear the burden of life and live in adverse circumstances. Perhaps in their struggle to survive, they gradually forgot Hebrew, their own language, their ways of dressing, customs and rituals, religion and signs of their civilization!

Human culture flourishes in the shelter of society; it needs the nourishment of others' company and understanding. Therefore, this minority community couldn't have survived in isolation and thus assimilated. All they could remember was that many generations ago, their forefathers had arrived from some far-off land, defeated by misfortune; that Saturday was a holy day in their religion, that it was a day of rest when they did not work; that the male infants should be circumcised on the eighth day of their birth. There were certain dietary laws that they followed—it was prohibited to eat fish without fins and scales and the flesh of carnivorous animals—though they did not remember which religion had said so. And, during joyous and sorrowful occasions, they chanted the first line of a prayer, though incorrectly and without knowing its meaning, 'Shema Israel…'

❁

Placing his thumb and little finger on his closed eyes and the rest of the three fingers on his forehead, Rafu would sit till Seema said, 'Okay, Rafu, start. Shema…"Shema" Israel…"Israel"… Aadonay…"Aadonay"… Elehenu…"Elehenu" (Listen, O Israel, our God is only one.)'

'That's all, Mama?' he would open his eyes and ask. After completing her prayers, Seema would glare at him, 'Shame on you, Rafu! Are you so sleepy that you can't even say the last prayer of the night?'

The innocent boy would smile and say in Marathi, 'Mama, is God watching us?'

'Of course!' Seema would say. At this, he would stare at the ceiling and ask, 'Why can't I see Him, Mama?'

'He looks at us quietly,' Seema had told him.

What she didn't know was that God was actually looking at him secretly.

Bobby worked on his essay diligently. Books on history, mythology, scriptures, Puranic tales, culture, and civilization were strewn on his table. He had even brought out his forefathers' old tin box from the attic. It seemed as if a magic box had been opened. Letters, festival greeting cards, bright and colourful birthday and New Year cards of the British period with good wishes written in English and Gujarati—'My dear son Sam'—were on his table.

Little Seema would quickly write her name on the greeting cards: 'This is my card. The one with a flock of ducks is also mine, and Bobby, that one with a bunch of roses is yours, and that dirty card in which a man in glasses stares—the way Danny stares—is his, so let's write, Danny.'

With his collection of yellow, crumbling newspaper cuttings about the Jews, old coins, badges, awards, certificates, degrees, and moth-eaten black and white photographs, around 150 years old, Bobby was trying to illuminate the path taken by the fellow members of his community—the Bene Israel, the pardesi, the foreigners—whom the people of Amdavad did not know in the twentieth century and believed to be Maharashtrians or converted Christians.

And yet, when communal riots broke out, the Bene Israel were thought to be Muslims when their pants were pulled down for scrutiny!

❁

It was slumber—a suffocating slumber. No ray of hope could be seen at all. Perhaps all their paths had turned back to misfortune and ill-fate.

For the first time, in the fifth century BC, there was a reference to India in the *Book of Esther* in the Bible. The Persian king, Xerxes I (Ahasuerus or Artaxerxes in the Bible) had established his empire from North India after crossing the Hindukush a little before 530 BC. Jews were scattered around 127 states of his empire, which spread over India to Ethiopia.

But it was in 1738 that a Christian missionary, J.A. Sartorius, first mentioned this minority community, which had settled in South India for two thousand years. Until then, they had remained unknown and ignored.

The few survivors may have thought it necessary to increase their numbers to become stronger and more confident when they married Indian women and included them in the Jewish faith. This progression seems quite natural and logical. Because of the changed geographical circumstances and hard labour, their racial features had been transformed by the genetic signs of other races. It is possible that during their long period of exile, some stray incidents of religious conversion may have taken place under adverse conditions, but this doesn't seem to be conspicuous.

When Christian missionaries on merchant ships started arriving in India in the first century AD, they may have found voiceless, mute, weak masses whose sole aim was to fill their stomachs and seek the mercy of the upper caste-class benefactors. Such humiliated people would readily accept the caste-less, compassionate faith in Jesus Christ so that they could have an identity. They could be transformed into a distinct group. But despite losing their racial characteristics, it had been engraved into the Bene Israel consciousness that their forefathers had left their home to protect their faith and community, so they neither became Buddhist nor Jain. Also, they did not follow the tribes that worshipped Vithoba, Khandoba Songtai, and Tuljamai, and did not help increase the number of the majority community. They stayed away from the Christian missionaries, too, and they stayed watchful.

However, over a period of time, they did acquire the culture of their surroundings, which is evident from their clothing, food, and speech—all of which have a Maharashtrian touch. But their women never got themselves tattooed, covered themselves, or committed Sati.

By adopting a similar way of life, customs and traditions, they managed to forge a bond with others and acquire the trust of the dominant community. This helped them in their business and helped them live their day-to-day lives with ease. Also, the most important safeguard was from the external assault—the persecution of the affluent class, the attack of pindaris and dacoits, or the danger of ill-treatment by the society in general.

It was around a thousand years since Jesus Christ had passed away. These minorities now adopted names such as Hasa-ji, Bana-ji, Elo-ji, Isa-ji, and Rama-ji (Ezekiel, Benjamin, Elijah, Isaac, and Rahamin respectively), while their women were known by Hindu names such as Hasu, Isu, Maka, Raju, Ranu, Kalbai, Dhanabai. They forgot their original names and the original traditions of their festivals; they even forgot their caste and religion. After suffering the heat of time, they could remember a vague dream-like story of how, during the last few centuries, the survivors had buried their dead perished in the shipwreck in the two mud mounds near Navagaon, that they could never go back to their own country, that they never converted to any other religion. But they did not remember which race or caste they belonged to.

This minority, the Shaniwar Teli, who assimilated with the local people, were a deprived and insignificant lot. They were about to disappear completely when an unexpected event occurred. Around 1,000 years ago, a missionary called David arrived in this Konkan region via Egypt and Malabar. He saw a community that followed strange customs and a mixture of rituals, chanted the 'Shema' prayer on every occasion, though incorrectly, followed dietary restrictions, practised monotheism and called itself the 'Shaniwar Teli'. They had perhaps left their homeland when the second great temple of Solomon was destroyed in Israel around 70 AD. Scattered in all corners of the world, this community may have descended from one of the tribes of Jacob's ten of the twelve sons—a forgotten race forgetting the world as it forgot itself.

❁

Bobby had titled his article, 'The Rise of a Forgotten Race'.

He laughed and said, 'Because I am a Jew, I have been working so hard on this article. Otherwise, who knows how many races appeared during different periods of history and during times of adversity, merged with the mainstream or just vanished, especially when the Sumerian and Babylonian civilizations were at their peak?'

Danny listened quietly. He said, 'To survive, it's important to have power and prosperity, which our forefathers did not have. It is by God's grace that we are still around.'

Danny was harsh.

Bobby looked at Danny thoughtfully. Then he said, 'Wrong.' He placed his hand on Danny's shoulder, 'Money and authority can certainly give importance and clout, but don't forget that they cannot give you respect and affection. They create circles of fear, and no one wants to be trapped in them, so they prefer to keep away.'

'Your argument is completely illogical,' Danny had said, now agitated.

'No,' Bobby was firm. 'Such people tend to become ruthless to safeguard their ego and power. Oppression, exploitation and fraud become their weapons. They are mentally sick, because they think everything they possess is perfect, especially their faith.'

'But what's wrong with it?' Danny blurted.

Bobby got up. Before leaving the room, he said, 'Danny,

if religion teaches us extremism and fanaticism in place of discretion, understanding and trust, it is wrong. If it makes our thinking narrow and self-centred, you should know that we are going against the religion.'

'I don't believe this,' Danny sounded angry.

'I am not forcing you to agree, nor am I trying to convince you, Danny,' Bobby said, leaving the room.

Today, when man is searching for the causes of illness and death through scientific research in genetic and stem-cell engineering, human civilization seems to be diving into the primordial past, trying to recover subjugation, oppression, religion, caste and exploitation. Some warn that Maharashtra is only for Maharashtrians, the others shout, Sri Lanka is only for Sinhalese, no, no, there is no place for people from UP and Bihar in Assam—the fanatic groups have their own opinion, and they come out to fight, face-to-face.

Whenever I read about such incidents and accidents, I am disturbed and look around for Bobby. But he is nowhere!

The Neem leaves outside the window murmur to say, 'You seem lost, Miss Samuel!'

I smile and pull up my glasses, which had slipped down to my face, back on my nose, arrange the fluttering pages, and continue reading.

The western plateau of the Deccan was unsuitable for industries or agriculture. So, the towns based on economy could not develop, and the Western Deccan was divided into local bodies and small states. As a result, people's faith depended on local headmen, kings, feudal lords and leaders whose responsibility was to supply soldiers to the state in case of war.

But since ancient times, the coastal region saw a lot of sea trade. From the Arabian Gulf to Babylon, Sumer, Alexandria (Egypt), Rome, Greece and China, goods were exchanged, so small settlements of foreigners came up in the coastal regions. After the eighth century, there was a huge increase in the arrival of Arab traders from West Asia, and, unlike other traders, they made the Western coast of India their permanent abode. Thus, they became friends and neighbours of this minority community.

The community seemed to emerge from a dark fog of loss of identity of two hundred years ago when they came to know that it was heir to the great civilization of Israel, that they were not Eloji, Isaji, Raju, Maka but Ezekiel, Issac, Moses; that they were Diana, Hannah, Ruth; that they were the Bene Israel and that the Bible was their holy book, which contained the history of their religion, the account of their generation, their customs and rituals, their great religious teachers and preachers and their commands and laws. After a thousand years of the dark past, they finally found the joy of being transformed into a 'distinct race'.

Although the social conditions were not favourable, and they fought off acute poverty, illiteracy, and marginality, the aggression and fighting spirit of their nomadic forefathers still flowed through their veins. So, most of the men took advantage of the situation and, leaving their low-paying jobs, enrolled in the local army.

Like the upper caste and the majority community, they, too, gradually acquired names indicating their native place. They added the suffix 'kar' to their village names—Navagaonkar, Shapurkar, Punekar, Awaskar, Chinchekar, and Kehimkar. After their entry into the armed forces, there was now a change in their lifestyle and capability.

The oil painting of a Bene Israel with his walrus moustache, 'achkan' or knee-length buttoned coat, pyjama, turban, and a walking stick or sword in their hand can still be found in old trunks in the houses of their descendants. A faint smile of bravery and changed status is evident on their faces. The mention of the regional leaders or the leader of headmen who joined the armed forces begins from the seventeenth century when the British hadn't reached the island of Bombay, but the Portuguese had already established themselves there for 150 years since 1509.

The Christian missionaries who came with the merchant ship were unfamiliar with the Bene Israel who had settled in the Konkan region in the distant South. Their purpose was fulfilled at the larger ports of Cochin and Malabar, from where they left. By that time, in 1923, Marco Polo had already mentioned the Jews settled on the Malabar Coast. The residents of the extreme South knew about the first synagogue built in Cochin in 1568 and were also familiar with those called the pardesi or foreigners.

The biggest change in the social and intellectual condition of the Bene Israel of the Konkan region was the arrival of the son of a Cochin resident, Ezekiel Rahabi, David Rahabi, who was sent to South India by the Dutch East India Company in 1768. He taught the Bene Israel about Judaism, took a few young men to Cochin to teach them about Jewish practices, and gave them the title of Kaji (judge in Arabic) so that they could return and teach the Jewish traditions to their people.

But most of the Jews settled in Konkan were illiterate, poor and backward. They had no religious book, even in their language, Marathi. In such a situation, in 1826, a preacher named Michael Sargon (a Jew who had converted to Christianity) came from Cochin. He started schools to educate them in small places such as Revdanda and Alibag in the Deccan plateau. In this way, the Bene Israels also became familiar with the English and Hebrew languages.

Although the Christian missionaries who came after 1813 enhanced the knowledge of this community, and provided the Old Testament in Marathi, and motivated the Bene Israels to pursue higher education, they were unable to convince them to convert because the seed of faith in Judaism, which was strengthened in them by Michael Sargon, made them stand firm like a wall against the American and aggressive Scottish missionaries.

As long as the Portuguese lived on the island of Bombay, not a single Bene Israel went near it for fear of their aggressive religious conversion policy. They continued to work for the Maratha landlords and under the Pant Brahmin secretary of the Bhor State, as well as the Muslim nawabs of the Janjira State along the long, 1,000-square-mile strip of the Konkan region. However, they were now more educated than the other castes in the local population and also knew about Christianity.

On 23 September 1668, Charles II of England received the island of Bombay as dowry from King John IV of Portugal when his daughter, Catherine of Braganza, married Charles. Bombay then passed on to the East India Company. The Bene Israels settled in the Konkan region quickly got themselves registered into the Bombay Army (the old name of the Company Army). They did not lose a chance to prove their bravery, courage and loyalty to the British.

When the educated and far-sighted class started working in offices, hospitals, education, warehouses, and ports, their women also came out to work. But the society looked down upon these women. Untouchability and casteism were still prevalent. The upper classes treated the Jewish women who moved in public without veils, those who worked in cinemas and the theatre or in offices, as inferior.

So, Bene Israel settlements were close to the economically

weaker people and 'mlechchhas' or people of foreign origin, which included the Muslims, people of mixed origin, and the Dutch, English, Portuguese, etc. When they arrived in Bombay, their first Jewish settlement came up near a Muslim colony in the Mandavi locality.

This arrangement was favourable for the Jews because they shared non-vegetarian food habits and some religious rituals (circumcision, calculating the days by lunar calendar and festivals) with the Muslims. Their ancestors and the seraphs of the Jews were the same as the Muslims, and, till 1205, this minority community of Jews had mingled more with the Arabs, Turks and Afghans who arrived in India with Alauddin Khalji and plundered the Deccan in 1296, a hundred years after Muhammad Ghori, than with their old Hindu neighbours.

Besides the sultans, khalifas, munsifs, ministers, ulemas, and nawabs, the common people, including artisans and servants, kept themselves away from the Bene Israel settlements. The influence of language and food was common. So, Islamic words were used copiously in the Marathi used by the Jews—words such as father, aaba, abba; synagogue, mashid, masjid; fast, roza; prayer, namaz; religious teacher, qazi, etc.

From their study of the Bible, they learned that the forefathers of Jews and Muslims were the same because the first ancestor of the Jews, Abraham, had a son by his second wife, Hazra (Hagar in the Bible), who was called Ismael and is considered to be the first ancestor of the Muslims.

Thus, Ibrahim in Arabic was Abraham in the Jewish Bible, Musa was Moses, Nooh was Noah, and Daoud was David.

Daoud...David. Azoba...David Reuben. Younger brother David. David...Daoud....Daoud Nawab.

Nawab Daoud. The grand mansion of Nawab Saheb; pigeons cooing over the parapets, window-sills, garrets, strutting with puffed feathers, beak touching beak, they fluttered and fought, fed, flew like patches of clouds, these white-and-grey, dappled pigeons. The thick bamboo screen on the doorway to the zenana or female quarters, from one end to the other, the silk and satin curtains flapped in the air; gorgeous, youthful, fair-skinned, laughing and giggling begums in their flowing wide gararas, short kurtis, and long dupattas; scented giloris or betel leaf cones in their mouth, their maids carrying betel boxes and basins used as spittoons; the overhanging expensive Bohemian or Venetian chandeliers, red, green, yellow, blue, turquoise, pearl white, ebony and white glass pots all around, in which burned flickering candles at night, when mehfils and mushairas where poems and ghazals were recited, song and dance performances held and films screened on projectors, lavish parties were hosted with delicacies like murg-musallam, biryani, kebabs, kofta, roasted fish, zarda, sewiyan, kheer, cashew nuts, raisins, almonds, pistachios coated with silver flakes and saffron! The light sea-green chiffon sari for Mama, lots of toys and toffees for Danny and Bobby. Danny was about eleven years old; Bobby was nine and Seema was six.

It was around the year 1946.

Papa had been promoted and transferred to Radhanpur in Gujarat. Ma and Papa got down at this small, deserted platform on a small-gauge railway station past midnight with their children and an office peon. It was raining cats and dogs, and the river was in full spate. Suddenly, the stone bridge on the river overflowed with knee-deep water. The family of Samuel David, wet and shivering, crouched under the thatched roof of the bullock cart. Once they had crossed the bridge, lathi-wielding dacoits with faces covered attacked and caught the reins of the bullocks. Ma started crying, and the children, too, sobbed in fear. The power and authority of Papa Samuel's government job were suddenly of no value. Just then, Nawab Saheb, in his carriage pulled by a caravan of horses, sped up and stopped next to them. As soon as his soldiers aimed their rifles at the bandits, they fled.

The acquaintance with Nawab Saheb went a long way. He would often gift magical toys to the children. Dauod Nawab had three legitimate wives but no children. The Nawab's chief wife—Begum Sahiba—treated Seema's mother like a friend. She would always take Seema in her lap and shower her with kisses. Seema felt suffocated. But she always got a handful of toffees, raisins, cashew nuts, almonds and pistachios! At her age, Seema had hardly seen so many things and in such quantities. At home, after much insisting, Papa would let the children have one toffee each, which Seema licked so that it lasted longer. Sometimes, he gave them a brass 'dhabbu' (worth two paise), or, if he was too generous, he would get his children salted groundnuts worth an anna coin with a serrated edge. All of them would get a fixed number of nuts. Danny would often snatch Seema's nuts away in some way or the other and make her cry. Bobby would wipe away her tears, stop her from crying, pat her and place his share of groundnuts in her small hands.

Perhaps he also gave his own years of life in her hands when he left.

Seema and Bobby would watch the opening scenes of films like *Badi Behan*, *Jwar-Bhata*, *Alamara*, *Ratan*, *Anmol Ghadi*, and *Dahej*, and fall asleep. In the morning, they would get up unhappy in their mosquito net-covered beds. Fascinated by the magic of the dream world of Nawab Saheb, though they could hardly understand the lure and harshness of the world, Seema would pester Ma to visit Nawab Sahab's place another day. Ma looked very pretty in her new sea-green sari. She told her mother, 'When I get married, Ma, give me this sari. So, wear it carefully and don't tear it.' Seema would hug her mother. Ma smiled at her innocent talk, kissed and hugged her with love. When Seema's mother smiled, her cheek dimpled.

Who knows where the Nawab Saheb is now... He took with him the twinkling fireflies in Seema's fists, the dreams in her clear eyes, and the butterflies flitting over her innocent face.

When the shreds of all Ma's saris wave before Miss Samuel's ageing eyes, her tight fists open and stretch in the darkness of night, and a forest of restlessness rises and falls and scatters the particles of forgotten memories.

Seema and Bobby would sing a sweet Marathi nursery rhyme: 'How sweet is the butterfly!'

Flower bird, flower bird. The bird of life, the pulse of life.

The bird of life leaves the body and flies away.

'*Rahna nahi des virana hai...*'

(No more do I wish to live here; this land is desolate)

Samuel David wanted to come back. He wanted to call back the bird of life. But the bird had flown. The empty cage trembled for a while and then became still. Holding the soil in a fist, hands rose over a deep pit six feet wide, and murmured, 'From the earth you came and to the earth you shall return', and dropped the earth on the soil in the pit.

❁

The Hebrew word 'Adamah' (Adam) means 'from the earth'.

History sometimes has abrupt turning points. A similar turn of events happened in 1599. When fate smiled on the masters of the East India Company in Surat, the large and easily accessible Portuguese port, Buan Bahia (Good Bay), fell completely into English hands in 1668 and became Bombay.

The fourth governor of this island, Gerald Angier (1669-77) was far-sighted and implemented his 'liberal' policy.

The Parsis settled in Gujarat were the first to take advantage of his policy and move to Bombay. A wave of Muslim traders also followed them, keeping in mind the rise in trading opportunities. Then, the Bene Israel community living in the Konkan strip also went to Bombay with their Muslim neighbours.

By then, the Portuguese, who tried every means of allurement and punishment to enforce conversion to Christianity, had left Bombay to settle in Goa. So, the Muslims and Jews, who were earlier afraid of enforced conversion, were now free from fear and went to Bombay.

Time is a flow. It encircles significant and extraordinary events and illuminates them. The circles contain a web of the complex problems of human civilization and also the shadows of errors. If the coming generation can dare to reach these dark caves and test them, it can brighten its future by looking at its own errors, misfortunes, indifference, joys and sorrows.

So, learning from its past failures, this minority community found a chance to profit when the right to emigrate under the East India Company was repealed. Because of the increasing pressure of the Turks, the Baghdadi Jew, Sassoon came to Bombay, leaving Baghdad. Bombay was then riding high on the crest of capitalism; therefore, when this trading family started their business, the Bene Israel with small capitals also benefitted.

The Sassoons opened a counting house and a carpet godown in Bombay. They also became money lenders. Soon, a situation arose in which, in the next twenty-five years, it was said that 'silver and gold, silks, gums and spices, opium and cotton, wool and wheat—whatever moves over sea or land feels the hand or bears the mark of Sassoon and Company'.

In 1875, David Sassoon's son, Albert Sassoon opened a spinning-weaving mill and the wet docks. He constructed forts and synagogues in Byculla and opened schools, reformatories and a mechanics' institute. Thus, he provided an opportunity to progress and prosper to the hundreds of poor, deprived and ignored co-religionists.

Thousands profited from this opportunity and progressed, but hundreds thought it below their dignity to work under their own people; they were jealous of their readiness and prosperity and nurtured their ego under the false pretence of self-respect. With time, they gradually stagnated in the same condition and circumstances.

Although they gradually overcame their inferior status, the Bene Israels weren't courageous and economically strong to purchase the properties left behind by the Portuguese and being sold at throw-away prices like the far-sighted, business-minded Parsis. Also, unlike the Parsis, they were neither professional, nor could they adopt the Western way of life. They were also not opportunist and extroverted. Therefore, some Parsi and Muslim families rose very high in social standing because of their education, prestige and prosperity. The Bene Israel continued to watch them silently.

An important thing, especially about the Muslims, was that they never shied from taking up any work. Hindus did not trade in leather, fish and meat. The Jews did not have any such inhibitions, but they thought themselves to be special and refrained from such work and, therefore, lagged.

Their sources of income were few, and their offspring more. Unlike other communities, they did not have ancestral homes, properties, or lands, nor were their forefathers collectors of revenue or members of the nobility.

Then, this large group of Jews who were employed in the Bombay Army left the place because of two reasons: One, because the Bombay Island Army was not in power, and the local prosperous communities looked down upon people of other castes and communities. Second, the continuing turbulence in the country. The Revolt of 1857 led to a simmering of casteism and, in such a situation, their senior Muslim or Maratha officials either terminated them or stopped their promotions.

They got frustrated and started leaving their jobs. Thus, unemployment and adversity re-entered their homes.

The Jews, already suffering poverty, were further hit when the Civil War began in America in 1861. The prices of cotton reached sky-high. Because of this, black-marketing, hoarding, speculative markets, and the share market rose, but due to the lack of initial capital, guarantors or mentors, not even the middle class among the Jewish community could do much, while the lower class was already in bad shape.

They shrank within themselves.

During their stay in the Konkan region, no other rule, king, sultan or peshwa, had given them any importance or showed any interest in them except the local ruler of Alibag, Raghoji Angriya (1790-1838). Therefore, till the early nineteenth century, when they settled in the island of Bombay and took up petty jobs or small trades, became soldiers in the military or worked as petty officials, the Bene Israel only faced poverty, the discrimination between 'pure' and 'crossbreed' in their community, and their fear and anxiety of whom to support when a conflict, brawl or clash broke out.

The helping hands who supported the Jews would withdraw their favour at their slightest lapse. So, this community was left to seek the mercy of power and authority from the majority community. On 23 December 1884, in Alibag, Maharashtra, the Bene Israel community settled there handed a written application to the widow of Raghoji Angriya and sought her benevolence: 'Our ancestors have stayed here and are aware of the respectable and sacred heritage, how could we even think of doing a detestable act of slaughtering a cow? We, the Bene Israel of Alibag, request you believe us that we haven't done anything like this, and it is the handiwork of an enemy who has spread this rumour. The whole town has stopped selling us food items. Even our little children are deprived of milk. We hope to receive justice and mercy from you.'

Similarly, in May 1882, a misleading article was published in a Gujarati newspaper about the rituals of the Jews: that the Jews of Basra consume Muslim blood. Hearing such a preposterous and false account, the Jews settled in Gujarat and Bombay trembled with fear, because in case of a clash or conflict or allegation, they would not be able to respond or face them. For, in 1874, they had closely seen a riot between the Parsi and Muslim communities, and also suffered its consequences because of their minority status. They knew the shadow of fear.

To oppress any small community, their poverty, unemployment and illiteracy is enough.

Who has the time to empathize with the problems, helplessness and loneliness of such a dwindling, timid community?

The Parsis arrived in India much later (716 AD) than the Bene Israels, but their Fire Temple was constructed in 1709 at the Nanabhai Lane in the Bombay Fort, whereas the first synagogue of the Bene Israels was built in 1796.

The Bene Israel settlements were displaced frequently, they would be driven away deeper, their cemeteries were dislocated, and then they would seek support from the Muslim cemetery to save themselves from more trouble.

I place the stapled pages of the essay on the table, remove my spectacles and lean back on my chair. My legs have become numb, sitting for so long. I lift my legs one by one and rest them on the bed. I feel a pressure on my heart. I feel restless and my hands tremble lightly. I want to close my eyes and be still, but I don't know what surge of emotions moves towards me!

Sitting before the only window of a ten-by-ten-square-foot room with my eyes closed, I wonder who I am searching for.

My long-passed forefathers? Bobby? My roots, or myself?

Am I subsumed in them? Does my own identity open up layer by layer like Bobby's essay? Are our courage, fear, frustrations, loneliness, attacks and counter attacks, selfishness, thinking, and helplessness a copy of the culture and status of a race or community?

What kind of copies are Rachel, Ma, Bobby, David? And David Reuben…Pappa…Azoba, my grandfather? Why is it that within the same family, when the colour of the words over a copy appears different, it becomes overbearing, oppressive or insensitive?

Aaza David's younger brother Moses. Ten years younger to his obscure elder brother David Reuben. A dreamer, humane, and a sensitive person.

Moses Reuben had thin, long fingers and a longish face with sharp features. He played the female roles of Taramati, Radha, and Rukmini in the drama-theatre. He ran away from home when his elder brother, the government jailor, suddenly came home one afternoon and saw his daughter Lily and Manoj's unblemished enactment of love in the presence of Moses.

A clear copy of the original appears on the surface and covered the blurred image. There is silence. The way the fearful, timid and scared Rachel was stunned.

Listening to filthy curses and abuses of Joel Garson and looking at the stunned Rachel, could anyone read that blurred copy?

I look out of the window. The sunlight is climbing, leaf by leaf. It will scatter in the sky by evening and disappear with the shadows. For some time, there will be warmth in the air; then it will disappear in the shadows of darkness.

Staring at impenetrable darkness, Sam had once asked Diana if Moses Uncle was also lost.

Diana Aajji had looked straight into my eyes. 'I didn't have an answer, or you may say that he might not have understood my answer.'

The toothless face of old Diana Aajji had opened and shut for air. 'He had lost his way and came to this earth like a wayward comet. He had brought along innumerable twinkling stars to brighten the home. After Moses died, David Reuben said, "That rascal only brought bad luck." But how? A caravan of birds came home with him; a thousand butterflies flew around him; the melodies of the sitar embraced his fingers; Lily and little Ruth rode on birds' wings and swayed in the air. How could gentle Moses bring bad luck?

'Then he had left as abruptly as he had come. It was dark, my dear. Because of the darkness, I couldn't find Lily, and Ruth was swallowed by time.'

The whisper of Aajji's sad voice still echoes in my ears and disturbs me. Has the journey that began with the story of Isaji Eloji now reached its final stage?

Ignoring the increasing heaviness on my heart, I pick up the pages and my glasses again.

Despite acclimatizing to the earth, water and air of this country, the Jews are in such a minority that they have no voice. So, they have no say in Indian politics or culture. Since they landed in this country, which gave them shelter, they have remained either mute, or short-sighted outsiders!

During British rule, the attitude the Parsis decided to adopt, the Jews also followed or tried to move a step ahead. Because of their growing mercantile activities and their relations with their English mentors and masters, when the Parsis showed their allegiance to the British rule, the Bene Israel community also quickly offered their services to the British.

And in 1887, the Golden Jubilee of Queen Victoria was celebrated. Like the Parsis, they offered salutations, expressed loyalty to the British Crown, and celebrated their economic gains.

Their only purpose was to emerge from their 1,800-year-old adversity and anonymity and create an identity. They were tired of being a mute community, even though they knew that the British were taking full advantage of them. So, they thought they could gain dignity and status in exchange for loyalty, and rid themselves of stressed conditions.

But things went wrong. This step of the micro-minority, poor, uneducated, timid community was objectionable to the Brahmins of Poona. 'You've been living in India, but you're loyal to Queen Victoria?' they shouted without hesitation!

This act of finding respect for themselves cost them dear. Newspapers objected against their behaviour. Afraid of this turn of events, the Bene Israels shrank within themselves again.

During the turbulent period of the nationalist movement, leaders like Bal Gangadhar Tilak, Dadabhai Naoroji and Sir Syed Ahmad Khan, who raised their voices against the British government, came from the Marathas, Parsis and Muslims, but the time when the nation was struggling, the important issues for these minorities were food, employment and security. The reason was that the British civil servants were treated as superior. So, unemployment increased, and economic and social security suffered a setback.

Those Bene Israels who did not let such adversities overpower them and mingled with the mainstream were better off than the others and progressed.

During this period, in 1884, the Bible and the Talmud were published in Marathi translations (by Mr Ezekiel Benjamin Penkar). Journals such as *Satya Prakash* (1877), *Israel Ashram* (1877), and *Bene Israel Race* were published, making this community aware of its practices. Not only this, but they became familiar with each other and with the upheaval in Indian politics.

Since the beginning of the twentieth century, the spirit of national consciousness flourished in India. Trying to break this spirit, the British partitioned Bengal in 1905 and gave birth to the demon of communalism. Urdu was made the court language in Bihar and Uttar Pradesh instead of Hindi. When the Muslim League was established in 1906, the British promoted the Muslims. In 1918, in the name of the Montague-Chelmsford Reforms, the Muslims were given a separate electorate. The British also tried to lure the Jewish community. The Bene Israel did not miss the opportunity to eliminate the feeling of humiliation and regret. They rejected the need for a separate electorate. The notice of this effect was submitted by the eight leaders of the community in Bombay.

But they knew that the migrant Muslims, Parsis, and Christians had strong organizations and codes of conduct. These numerically strong organizations had mutual and social commitment, they had support and security, and respect and recognition of society. India had imbibed their faith, culture and traditions, and they felt honoured by this.

Perhaps that is why, until the end of the eighteenth century, Christians, Muslims and Parsis thought of this micro-minority as a confused entity, dependent on its neighbours' mercy and fate. But neither they nor Indian society ever tried to understand that all the strength of this community was spent in finding ways and means to protect themselves from the onslaught of multiple social forces and struggling against poor economic circumstances. So, it was quite logical that they became introverted and self-centred.

Human history is witness, religions emerge by integrating completely new ideas, thoughts, and philosophy, but with the flow of time, their integrity is dominated by the mind of primitive man, and then, ghettos of sects and sub-sects appear within the same religion.

By the beginning of the twentieth century, when India became independent, in the face of population explosion, unemployment, health problems, nepotism and the rise in political clout, the white-collared, anglicized and prosperous Israyels started looking down upon their own poor, resigned and illiterate brethren and avoided them! So, this class could not keep pace with others and its own community and subsumed under a larger group of 'poor' people.

A huge number of this group were the first to migrate when Israel came into existence.

The educated middle class was progressing and was completely Indianized, but it knew that there were only some in the metropolitan cities who knew about Judaism and, even among them, some thought of them as converted locals or Maharashtrians. Conservative Hindus, on the other hand, were annoyed that these people hadn't become Hindus. And, if they don't want to convert, why don't they go back to their own country so that the exploitation of their country (India) could be reduced, and the local population got their rights? Foreign communities like these should be thrown out, or they should accept that they have a second-class status.

❁

I stop reading.

The pages of Bobby's essay were fluttering in Papa's hands. He had thrown the essay on the table and growled, 'What is this, Bobby?'

'What?' Bobby feigned ignorance.

'Do you think that you will be considered innocent even after writing about RSS leader Golwalkar?'

'The right to freedom of speech is for every citizen. It's not a crime, Papa. Why be afraid?'

'Wonderful,' Samuel David said, and picked up the papers again. 'You have exposed our helplessness, vulnerabilities, and short-sightedness, and that however insignificant and weak our history in this country is, we will dare to speak against you. You are not only hurting us but others, Bobby!'

'Aren't we Indians? This country is ours, too, and if some fanatics want to divide the country in the name of Indianness, we should bring it to light. The language used by my job interviewers does not represent the entire country, Papa!'

Highlighting the fear of the minorities, Samuel David had asked his son: 'Then, why did the people of this colony gradually become aloof towards us, Bobby? Try to understand, son, try to understand! Why do you have to hand a burning flame to the majority community, which is becoming more and more sensitive over caste and religion with each passing day? In this selfish, intolerant and indifferent time, people try to cover up their faults, create ficticious stories about their greatness, and rewrite history, but you...'

Bobby was restless. 'What, Papa? There are also well-informed people in this country who know about our contribution, however negligible it may be. They know the importance of Dr E. Moses*, the Mayor of Bombay in 1937, of David Erulkar, who was part of the defence team in the sedition trial of Bal Gangadhar Tilak in 1916 in the Bombay High Court, along with Mohammad Ali Jinnah and Joseph Baptista, of Gandhi-ji's doctor Dr Abraham Erulkar†, who was also the vice president of the Home Rule League. People know about the actors Nadira and David. Even now, our Bene Israels are in high positions and are engineers and doctors and serve the country. Why do you forget the poets and writers who write in different languages?

'Adverse circumstances, different environment and culture, meagre resources for life, employment and opportunities, the anxiety of the minorities and the challenge to preserve their religion…this is what I wish to write about.'

I close my eyes in sadness. Today, on 22 July 2007, I sit quietly in my room in Parisar and turn the pages of this essay again. I see the self-confidence of people like Bobby, who wanted to eliminate the fears and apprehensions of the minority community.

I feel as if I have been pushed from somewhere very high; I try to stop myself from falling but cannot. It's

---

*Dr Elijah Moses Rajpurkar (1873–1957) was the first person from the Indian-Jewish community to earn a Doctor of Medicine degree and the first to become a councillor in the Bombay Municipal Corporation in 1920. He is also the only Jewish mayor of Bombay.

†Abraham Erulkar (1887–1960) was the dean of Bombay University's Faculty of Medicine as well as the president of the Indian Medical Council. He was Mahatma Gandhi's personal physician during several of his fasts.

neither dark nor light. Beautiful Jyotsna Prajapati emerges from the deep, opaque circle and stands before me. She puts her plump, manicured hand with long fingers through the window bars before my face and shouts, 'You bitch, bastard, mlechchha!'

I try to escape her reach and turn back, but Professor Prafulla Patel stops me and laughs! To save myself, I want to hold Bobby's hand, but I see flakes falling off his confident face, and, in there, I see the face of the secretary's wife emerge. I fall and turn to look behind me, but find all the residents of Gitanjali Society clapping their hands and laughing, but there is no sound.

I see myself falling flat on the ground. I want to cry, but I feel it's not me but Tahmina crying persistently, like a howling dog.

Am I dying? I ask myself.

There is silence and an immense heaviness on my chest.

Taking a deep breath, I open my mouth to shout one last time, '...Bobby...'

I suddenly open my eyes. The pages I held carefully in my hand had fallen and my head is bent to one side. I rub my tender neck and steady my head. Picking up the pages from the floor and spreading them on the table, I wonder if it is possible for someone else to see the truth of our life from our perspective.

It is raining again. With every lash of rain, the trees shake violently, and water drops fall off the leaves, and the noise of the earth is stunned into silence and engrossed in hearing the pitter-patter.

Nature smiles at the sound of nature, but why does man, borne of nature, want to dominate?

The story of the Jews settled in India is neither glorious nor optimistic. It makes us sad. It disturbs us why their story is different from that of their co-religionists, who were also exiled from their country and settled in other countries, and also from the people of other religions living in India.

It is quite natural that when people belonging to this repressed and minority community reach a breaking point due to the constant pressures and start getting tired, they will dream of a miracle. Actually, miracles don't happen, but human beings may accept changed circumstances—scattered clouds and the warmth of happiness—as miracles. A miracle is man's desire to live, a daydream and life support. Miracles are like those pores in the closed walls before which we can stand and inhale deeply. It is like patchwork over fraying hope.

After World War II, Israel gained widespread recognition (14 May 1948), which opened up the magic door for these displaced, hesitant, economically weak, jobless, unsuccessful Jews or those who had dreamt of arriving in their homeland for generations. This was made possible in 1894 by the correspondent of the *New Free Press*, Theodore Herzl, who declared that the actual solution to their problem was to return to the Promised Land.

For nation-building and development, Israel needed morale, money and human resources, which was offered by those groups of people who had left sufferings, misfortunes, and humiliations behind in their host countries because they were all the offsprings and co-religionists of Abraham, Issac, and Jacob, because the whole country celebrated Sabbath, Rosh Hashanah (New Years' day), Yom Kippur (the holy day of seeking pardon), Pesaha (the day to remember Passover) or Hannukah (the celebration of the defeat of the Greek-Syrian oppressor Antiochus Epiphanes in the Maccabean Revolt), because there were synagogues in every town and qasbah, and every male Jew was circumcised on the eighth day of his birth, as Abraham promised God, without the fear of being lynched by a mob in communal riots.

Even then, many groups and people could not survive the harsh climate, compulsory military training (18 years onwards), communal living in camps, compulsory learning of the Hebrew language for all ages, collective work under supervision, and preferential treatment given to the Jews from affluent countries. Their loneliness became more acute in Israel, and they missed the madness and mayhem of their home in India. So, they returned and embraced their host country and cried.

The history of the Jews begins with sadness and pain. Adam and Eve were exiled from Paradise because Adam suddenly acquired forbidden knowledge. Adam's first son, Cain, killed his sibling Abel out of jealousy. The first forefather, Abraham, took them to Canaan (Palestine), but they had to escape from there and became displaced. Their magnificent temple was destroyed twice, in 590 BC and 70 AD. And, after 70 AD, the tribes of the ten sons of Jacob scattered like grains of sand to all corners of the world. They are known as the Wandering Jews in history.

Two thousand years ago, when the descendants of the Levi tribe somehow managed to reach the refuge of the Sahyadri mountain range and landed on the Konkan coast in Maharashtra to save their lives, religion, culture and tradition, they must have been people of good social standing and wealth. Over time, they became narrow-minded, dull, timid, fatalist and insignificant and stood on the edge of loss of memory. They kept their mistakes and failures to themselves and did not blame others for their misfortune. Perhaps, because of this, this micro-minority community survived—for renewed growth.

Generous and magnanimous, India sheltered them like a

huge, shady tree. But misfortunes never left the side of this minority community settled in other countries. For example, in Europe during the tenth century, the growing power of the Church held this community responsible for killing Jesus and indulged in their torture and genocide. In 1881, in Russia, a riot broke out on Easter Eve in which around two hundred Jews were killed, or during World War II, when sixty lakhs Jews were mass murdered. But India never sent away or tortured the Jews. They were never insulted for being 'Semitic' and got all the rights, like all citizens, from the Constitution.

Even so, in the atmosphere in which they lived and grew up, they were seen as outsiders. They never experienced the joy of being included. They were not humiliated, but the circles of human empathy and concern hardly touched them. The other ghettos of religions were not so indifferent towards them, but if they came closer to them, hardly anyone took notice. They were treated as they were, but they could never be one of 'us'.

Therefore, they always felt uprooted. They never felt the courage, concern or excitement enough to contribute to the Indian milieu, politics or culture. Perhaps because of this, many generations went to their graves, hoping to return to the soil from whence they had once come.

The Bene Israels settled in India probably felt incomplete, weary and sad. According to their Jewish faith, they believed that they suffered because God loved them the most. For 1,700 or 1,800 years, they remained shattered, suffering economic, social and caste disparities till they regained their lost identity.

Today, many of the Bene Israel settled in India are about to leave for Israel, in the hope of change, security and miracles for the success of the future generations. Even then, there are hundreds, like the writer of this piece, who honestly believe that only this country, India, blessed with six seasons, greenery, warmth, festivals and celebrations, languages, customs and rituals, traditions, saints and ascetics, babas and gurus, black magic and spirituality, soaked in different cultures, is their motherland. After being with her for centuries, their identity is bound to this country.

For such people, India is their Israel.

For a long time, my eyes stare at the blank space beneath the essay through my spectacles.

The writer believed that the essay was complete, but so many things remain unsaid; did he ever know? Who knows how many sounds of lost and forgotten stories there are in the leftover blank spaces around the words. The eyes of the people absorbed in these blank spaces stare continuously, their whispering lips disturbed—is there any answer to the queries stamped on their faces?

Words in themselves are never complete because they have neither beginnings nor endings.

The pages of this thirty-five-year-old essay are yellowed with age and about to crumble at the folds.

The way a body becomes brittle.

Rama Aajji would laugh and say, 'The layer of natural fat beneath the skin gives the body its charm, beauty and youthfulness. Gradually, time absorbs the fat. It also soaks the marrow, energy and enthusiasm. Look at me, my dear, how brittle I have become! Someday, someone will open the pages of my life, and I will crumble, too. This face, the laughter, these eyes telling the stories of joys and sorrows, will become mute like my photograph and just keep staring. I wonder why people preserve their photographs. I threw away all my photographs in the Mula-Mutha river. Now, nothing is frustrating.'

But my mind is in turmoil. I stand and then sit and gulp some water, but a restless roar rises and stops in my throat. There is no outlet. It's blocked. Perhaps the pressure is increasing because of this. It seems my rib cage will burst. Struggling hard, I open the door. Moist air fills the room. Outside, in the glow of darkness, there are the swaying shadows of trees. The sound of chirping birds sinks and fades.

In this wet weather, the time approaches night, framed in the door as you stand alone, Miss Samuel, what are you trying to forget?

Dragging my feet, I return to the table. I gently arrange the pages, keep them in the drawer and remove my glasses.

Who knows why the twelfth song of the Ecclesiastes, which was hidden under layers of the mind, comes to my lips:

When the street-door is kept shut,
when the sound of grinding fades away,
when the first cry of a bird wakes you up,
when all the singing has stopped;
when going uphill is an ordeal
and you are frightened at every step you take...
before the silver thread snaps,
or the golden bowl is cracked,
or the pitcher shattered at the fountain,
or the pulley broken at the well-head:
the dust returns to the earth from which it came,
and the spirit returns to God who gave it.

'Soul? What soul, Seema?' Bobby smiles and whispers in my ears.

I feel the stifled flood of emotions burst open, breaking all barriers in the stillness all around.

Chapter 17

There was a call from Parisar.

Atya had suffered a mild heart attack. Sakhu Tai had told us not to worry too much as she was much better now. 'Come over some time,' she had said before disconnecting the call.

Perhaps Sarah was in the operation room, and her phone was switched off, so they had contacted me.

Strange emotions swell up within me on the way—sometimes, anxiety, pain and discomfort, and at other times, frustration and annoyance. Mother and Sarah had wanted Seema to stay with them so much but, stubborn as she is, does she ever listen to anyone? She said, 'I have got used to living alone!' Sometimes, she would laugh and say, 'The mountains look more beautiful from a distance, Mili. When you come closer, the silence of their unruly wilderness is too scary, and all its mystery and romance transform into fear.'

She smiled, looked into my eyes, and said, 'Perhaps even I may face a similar silent forest.'

Lying on a single cot, covered with a light-coloured sheet, weak and frail Seema looks very quiet. When I touch her forehead, she opens her eyes. Looking at the anxiety etched on my face, she says, 'Silly girl! I'm fine, dear. Just wait and see. I will start running from tomorrow.' Then, a little warily, she says, 'Of course, I won't start running, but I will certainly walk.'

A wave of sadness clouds her face. She looks quietly at me for a while, runs her tongue over her dry lips. 'Whether at home or outside, it's all the same now, my girl.'

She looks out the window for some time and murmurs, 'All the outside noise echoes within and when the self-confidence, saved with great care within, comes out, it feels exposed and stunned!'

'Look, I am not at all concerned with this philosophical lecture of yours. If you create a fuss, Sarah and I will carry you home by force.' My tone is flat and rough.

Suddenly, she is silent. I look at the quiet and exhausted Seema lying on the bed. She has closed her eyes. Framed within the contours of her longish face with high cheek bones, her aged features look as still and peaceful as a painting.

Mother believes that I resemble Seema Atya a lot. The proportions of my nose, eyes and chin are exactly like Seema's when she was my age, and if I were of her age and lying like this, I would look exactly like her. But still, how strange is human nature that Seema, who is as soft-natured as me, likes Sarah's bold, carefree, rational and straightforward attitude to life, although, unlike Sarah, she couldn't follow them in her own life. I know this because I have often crossed the same lanes and by-lanes despite promising myself a hundred times to never glance at them. Could it be that responsibilities, duties and extreme sensitivity make you drift away, so you think only about yourself in the end? Who knows.

Sarah feels that I like being suspended in a web of uncertainties, and because I wander into uncertainties, I depend on others for my decisions. Is life so simple, clear and transparent? If it is, who would want to lead a life so predictable, dull and stagnant? The magic of twilight adds meaning to our lives, kindles the desire to move ahead and find the way, creates intimate, thoughtful and lively circles of joys and sorrows. If the glow of twilight indicates the meaningfulness of our life, the darkness is the hidden and unknown part of our destiny.

But Sarah laughs at my thinking. She believes that there is no such thing as destiny. There may be coincidences, adversities, and one's own incompetency, but destiny? And Seema feels that our lives depend totally upon our temperament and mindset. Honestly speaking, I am unable to understand this view. There is no complexity in Sarah's views, but then, I always found Seema to be confused.

I agree that my mind has a complex web of queries that entrap me repeatedly, and probably because of this, on certain occasions, I have hesitated to make decisions. But how can we recognize the truth of our decisions—whether they are beneficial, right, and uncomplicated?

If you miss this frame of reference, you are bound to face the same twilight, the same webs of queries.

Mother was always very disturbed because of me. Even sad. She would frequently call up Seema and say, 'This girl wants to marry outside our community. If she married within the community, at least the honour of the family would have remained intact.'

Seema had rebuked my mother, 'Will you come to see what Mili's children are doing after your death?'

Mother had cried. Consoling her, Seema had explained, 'Dolly, there is an appropriate time for every decision, it shouldn't be wasted. Don't impose your decisions, doubts, dilemmas or close-mindedness on others. Let them be free. You will also feel relieved.'

I had remained quite uncertain, even when I had loved and married Srikant. Although Srikant's nature, personality, intellect and increasing interest in me and my religion had fascinated me, I was surrounded by apprehensions. The differences in cultural values, and the customs and traditions of our families, and the barrier of religion seemed difficult to negotiate.

Srikant would laugh: 'My dear, what matters most is love. Everything else is secondary.'

After more than eighteen years of marriage, looking at Seema lying silently, I think how 'the secondary' turned the warmth and value of human relationships cold and dry. As if I was being dragged on a set groove. At such a time, the bright canvas of life before me would dim.

Sarah is bold. There is also no threat to her boldness because she never relates life to domesticity. So how would she know the meaning of grief, sorrow, regret or passivity, which arose out of adverse circumstances? How could she know the pain of giving one's piece of sky to others just to get ones space? What has Sarah to say about the shattering of our shared life of days, nights, months, years, and eternity?

She laughs and teases me, 'Don't ask for your share, just grab it!'

I remember my childhood days. Grandpa was a miser. When he took us out, he would make us walk very far, saying, 'See that white house, you just have to walk till there.' On reaching there, he would say, 'Oh, not this, the other one!'

How could we know as children that Rafu was mentally challenged? That's why he would throw himself on the ground and cry. Grandpa would lift him in his arms. Sarah would cry, too, and hit Grandpa. She was the younger of the two and wanted to be in his arms. In the end, Grandpa would hire an auto-rickshaw.

How could I know what it meant to lose one's father at the age of three? But Ma, sitting lost in thought, ignoring little Sarah who cried piteously, Mamma (grandmother) wailing and muttering, Aunt Rosie's rebuking us all the time in irritation and Nanu's (Grandpa) silence, had left a sad imprint on my tender heart. To stay quiet, not to complain, to accept whatever came to me as my share and to be wise beyond my age became a part of me. There was no dearth of self-confidence, yet I could never show confidence in my life.

Perhaps because of this, I gradually became an introvert. I shrank to leave space for others. And now, after growing up, my anger, hatred and fight to achieve something in life seem so ridiculous because—can we get what we desire with these? I feel that in this world, what you receive from others depends on the amount of concern, affinity, respect and love they have for you; and respect is the most important of all.

Srikant has flung himself out of my circle. However, Sarah feels that I suffer from the disease of suspicion. When our sensitivity is hurt, it staggers, and the chain of attachment snaps. The weak link doesn't break off, suddenly. No one knows how much heat, friction and stress of struggles it endures before it becomes weak and fragile and reaches the verge of collapse. Severing or uniting, both these conditions deprive it of its original state.

Seema believes in giving life a second chance, while Sarah prefers instant decision-making. In fact, what does Sarah know about grief, depression, complexities, hurts, ordinary concerns or sadness arising out of following a set groove? What is there in life for her besides taking care of her mother, loving and arguing with Abeer, pampering her pet dog Roxy, exploring the unknown territories of her patients' minds and bonding with Seema?

Has she ever faced and tolerated someone saying, 'Seema was quite a flirt'? How would she know how someone is made to disconnect from her own thoughts, society, values, temperament, traditions and religion? Not intentionally, perhaps, but by ignoring her mind and heart.

Seema knows the noise of struggles. She knows the suffering of Rafu's living and leaving. She remembers the passion of love and the terrible sorrow of losing it to chance or circumstance. She has hidden the sorrow of separation and her loneliness from her whole family. Perhaps because of this, she sank so deep into silence. But no one has the right to speak about a woman of any profession, caste, community, class, or interest in such a frivolous manner.

A fine barrier separates Srikant and me like a film of cataract between our eyes. He looks vague and hazy to me and it irritates me when I see him speaking with women.

My elder daughter, Shubhra, watches my restlessness, discomfort and confusion. Sometimes, she comes to me, touches my forehead with her young, soft, sensitive hand, and says, 'Forget it, Ma...' But Srikant's disapproval of my frugal ways, thrift, frankness and baffling decisions, hurt me like hammer-blows. Probably, when he made snide remarks—'Don't be mean like your people', or 'You won't die if you accompany mother to the temple', or 'You are a woman, after all', or 'Don't meet with this woman or that man too often, they don't have a good reputation', he exerted his authority as a husband. But even after heated arguments, he would not relinquish this right, and blamed me of being irritable. Offending someone's sensitivity means throwing a stone into a stagnant pool of water. How could someone become as inert and lifeless as a stone to awaken the circles of sensitivities in others?

In such a situation, I struggle like a blind person and hold fast to God's support. I know He will help me and lead me to the right path. But for Sarah, that is an illusion. Ma is completely absorbed in this 'illusion', so, Sarah's thoughts don't reach her consciousness. Seema's beliefs only create confusion. She denies the existence of God, but has faith in divine justice and miracles! She follows customs and rituals out of habit. Isn't it ridiculous? What if she is told that there is nothing like divine justice in this world because, if there were, then the deprived, truthful, honest, hardworking and the oppressed wouldn't feel suffocated. Therefore, our destiny is to flow in the sea of faith and believe in one's karma. As the current diminishes your strength, you get carried away by it.

I feel I am neither atheist like Sarah, nor irresolute like Seema. God is a thought, He kindles the flame of faith and provides a peaceful shelter. Perhaps Man negotiates all the ups and downs of life with the support of the Invisible. Or else, would not life's intense sufferings have uprooted him? God may have been conceived for emotional support.

It is very strange. Our small community of Bene Israels in Pune is very organized and pious. But when the Marathi newspaper *Saamna* questioned our need to have two synagogues in one city (Pune), as we were now only a quarter left of our original number, and because the Lal Deul (Red Synagogue or Baghdadi Synagogue) in the Cantonment was already there for the foreign and white Israyels, after initial murmurings, our community finally gave up its claim and agreed to have only one.

Although the issue was raised only for the sake of ruffling feathers, Srikant and his family members supported it, and I was expected to agree with them. This was another moment of anger and argument. When I told Sarah, she had laughed. 'So what? Hardly any people go there. Frankly speaking, where is the need for another synagogue? You worry yourself unnecessarily.'

Wasn't this another blow to the uneasy minorities? 'Why these ghettos of caste?' Sarah asks, but is it possible to imagine a society without caste or religion, however happy it may appear to be?

I wonder if the graph of David Uncle's mindset would have been different if Grandpa had fought with Akram's father that day. Or, if Danny Uncle's medical store had thrived, the frayed patches of family relations arising from financial crisis wouldn't have been exposed in this way. If we were the same as the majority community, Papa wouldn't have had to stay out late in the evening for private tuitions, Ma would have got a job, Seema wouldn't have been taken for granted and then quietly thrown out of B-7, Gitanjali Society.

I wonder if the grounds are prepared only to create misfortunes for us. It took years to prepare the ground in Gujarat. Only then could crops grow. Weeds were cut; they were either buried in the soil or burned. Only then did women like Ameena Iqbal Rizvi leave their ghettos, accept defeat in life, and become silent. Seema had to search for a shelter, Rati Bharucha wanted to change her surname for it reminded her of her city, Manjeet Kaur sought solace in the *Shabad*, and I searched for myself—I didn't want to forego my identity.

I sit reclined on a chair and watch Seema sleeping quietly under the effect of medication. I don't know how and why, but I suddenly burst into tears. I wonder how the whole life of some people just goes to waste. And what refuge could David Uncle have found, if any?

Seema had shared a deep bond with Papa, but could she save the future of her ten years younger brother, David? Dividing herself among Rafu, David and Nanu, could Seema save anything for herself?

With closed eyes, I start murmuring Psalm 121 from the Old Testament:

'I lift my eyes to the mountains—
where does my help come from?
My help comes from the Lord,
the Maker of heaven and earth.'

'Okay, He will help you, but right now, let us persuade her to accompany us,' Sarah murmured into my ears from behind. Later in the evening, Seema sat on the bed, supported by a pillow. Her face looked weak, which she wanted to hide, so she had started talking. At night, following the doctor's instructions, she took a light meal and was somewhat ready to accompany us in the morning.

But in the morning, she refused. 'I'm all right now; the next time you come, I will come along.' She had postponed her plan. All the members of Parisar had supported her decision.

Before I leave, I open the drawer of Seema's table and pick up the envelope with Papa's essay, 'You've read it so many times. Let me also read it for some time,' I say with a smile. It's better to remove the cause of mental stress.

Her face suddenly turns pale, as if the dream of an intimate memory had shattered. Before she can speak, Sarah embraces her and says, 'Seema, how many times will you read Bobby? Why don't you read the two of us sometime?'

When we turn around to look at her as we leave, something seems to linger on her face.

Standing at the gate of Parisar, Seema seems to be running after her younger self and calling out to her.

Chapter 18

The morning of the retreating rainy season is spread out in the sunlight. Occasionally, a wandering cloud smiles as it nestles in the sunlight. I sit on my favourite bench. Behind, there is the same old flowering periwinkle bush. A small lawn is in front of me. The first half of the day is about to end, so the residents leaving their rooms are quiet.

Sudha Akka comes quietly and sits beside me. 'You know, Miss Samuel, I can feel my body becoming weaker day by day, and my mind also seems to be following the same path. Often, when I sit on the toilet seat, I forget to get up. Only when my feet turn stiff do I realize I have been sitting there for very long. Then, I feel like laughing and crying, but I don't do it knowingly, do I?'

It is very surprising that Akka has not asked or said anything about food today. So, I ask her, 'Do you know what Sakhu Tai will serve us today?'

Looking at me, she smiles cynically and says, 'What is there for me except eating, sleeping and sitting, my dear?'

I gently mock her, 'Why? Don't you always sit brooding the whole day?'

'Yes, dear! Do not judge us by your standard,' she makes faces and mumbles.

'I don't want to remember what has gone by at all.'

'Every day, I strike out a day of my life. Like me, thousands of women grow old every day and one day die unheard. Where was the time to think about myself? But now? Time spreads before me like an ocean, but now, there are heavy padlocks on the doors to emotions and relationships. They don't even open, however much you knock, my dear.'

I cut her short, 'Forget it, Akka, don't we have love and closeness here?' Then she gives me her toothless smile, 'The reason I have survived.'

A thick cloud stretches over us, and we keep looking at it. It seems so close that if we lifted our hands, we could touch it as it went by. The shining green leaves of the trees seem hidden under the darkness of the clouds.

Suddenly, a cold breeze blows and scatters the cloud. The cloud turns into a fluffy cotton ball and swims away. As it leaves, it releases a gentle drizzle. But before we can leave, the sunshine has spread gently.

'The world is like this, Bai.' Looking at the bright sunshine, Akka says, 'Neither sunshine, nor clouds, nor this rain shower are mine.'

Holding her hand, I ask, 'Why do you talk like this today?'

Without context, she says, 'People called me Kaushalya. I had four sons. Their names were also in the same order—Rama, Laxman, Bharat, and Shatrughan. Only the story of my Ramayana is upside down. All of them sent this wretched widow into exile forever.

'Don't mind my saying this, but you have never felt the upheaval inside a mother's heart. Even at this old age, during my deep sleep, I feel the throbbing of a baby in my empty womb. During those times, my breasts, which now sag and touch my stomach, become slightly hard and taut. Then, during those midnights, my weak, wrinkled hands rise in the darkness to lift my baby. There is only a dark night around.'

It seems Akka's face has melted and begun to flow. She blinks her eyes and looks like a lost bird. 'Forget everything, Akka, that's the only way out,' I console her.

She sits quietly, looking at the patches of sunlight on the lawns, filtered through the leaves of the trees. Then, taking a deep, long breath, she says, 'I had thought my days would pass with the little ones. But was there even a corner left for this old, wretched, weak, uneducated mother, who intruded everywhere like a useless object?'

Sudha Akka becomes breathless as she speaks without stopping. A thin line of spittle dribbles out of the right corner of her mouth. Wiping it away with the end of her sari, she continues, 'Children these days have no space for their parents. Just look at Mrs Kulkarni, Rama Aajji, or even your friend, Mrs Chitnis. It's the same old story everywhere.

'Have you ever been to Sandhya, the old age home for men, a little way from here? I know someone there. He is a retired professor. I go there quite often.

'Those poor men are even worse off than women.'

'Why, I think both face the same condition, Akka.'

'No, dear. A woman at least has a sense of fulfilment through her womb. She knows how to live for others, and has suffered the pain and humiliation of living in a subordinate position. Man has no such experiences. In his youth, he roars like a lion and walks like a cheetah, but a widower becomes so lonely, handicapped and wretched that he is unable to live with his tormented self and breaks. Because the women who pampered his ego, made him feel honoured and tolerated him have disappeared, he looks like a lost child.'

Sudha Akka is not very educated. It doesn't seem right to argue or contradict her. She lives in her own small world. The joys and sorrows of her world are also limited. Obviously, then, her ideas of life and death are conventional.

She says, 'Tell me, Miss Samuel, how could someone long to be reborn in one's family, where one has received such contempt, insult, and mental agony? Wasn't one life enough to bear such insult?'

Akka strokes her aching knees and then walks away.

I keep looking at her receding figure and wonder what it is that helps human beings to survive.

What will help me survive?

'The strength of your character, compassion, and consciousness, Seema.'

'How is that possible, Bobby? I am so tired now.'

'So, what's new in that? Fatigue has been with us since the very first day of our existence. It is just that we don't notice it. We are always ready for the rat race. Then, we were trapped in that same labyrinth. In our pursuit, if we encountered the marich, the mythical golden deer of deception, startled, we stopped.

'The struggle and bitterness arising from this deception seems to drown us. Only the depth of your vision will sail you across, Seema. Everything else is futile, superficial.'

'Superficial. Yes, you are right, Bobby.'

'Whom are you talking to, Miss Samuel?' Mrs Chitnis asks, coming closer to me.

I look over my shoulder sadly. The leaves seemed to touch me in a strange and gentle way.

'Oh, I was just talking to these leaves, Mrs Chitnis.'

I move a little on my bench to make space for her.

For some time, she stares at the lawn and sits quietly. Then, turning to me, she says, 'Even I used to talk a lot to myself.'

She smiles sadly. 'I don't know what has happened to me now. This continued heaviness scares me. My desires, thoughts, frustrations, complaints, everything seems to disappear through doors and windows, Miss Samuel.'

Then she sits quietly, looking at the moving clouds. A very thin web of distress appears on her face, and she tenses.

'What happened, Mrs Chitnis?' I touch her shoulder and ask.

'It's all over,' she speaks, staring at me.

I look at her.

'You know, I have started forgetting these days, more frequently since the last few months. Earlier, I would forget names, places, Miss Samuel, but now, I even forget the faces of very close people and my connection with them. A little while ago, Sudha Akka was sitting in my room, but I couldn't recognize her until she said as she left, "This old hag Sudha Akka must have bored you a lot." I am so scared, Miss Samuel.'

Her eyes are vacant, and her voice is moist with pain. She seems lost. After some time, she shakes her hands before her face as if trying to clear away a web. Her voice becomes hushed. As I strain to listen, it seems she is talking to herself. 'I sit blankly for hours together. And my book? It remains stuck in my hand. I tell myself, what do you think, Shanta? Your train has already arrived at the station, but there is no railway track ahead.

'What are you saying, Mrs Chitnis?' I interrupt her.

She checks herself at my query. Her face looks strange, as if she is straining hard to remember. Then circles of familiarity surface. 'These days, I even tend to repeat my daily chores. Sometimes, I brush my teeth twice, even thrice, in the morning. I often forget if I had tea today or the day before. When I go to take a bath, I keep sitting there. Am I moving towards Alzheimer's? I am so afraid, Miss Samuel.'

I shiver and think—it was not only her; I was scared, too.

A ghostly image of loneliness hovers over the trembling shadows of Mrs Chitnis's wisdom. All the frustrations in her heart seem to have devastated her.

How these old people, sitting in homes, on verandas, in a corner, on benches, in parks or in old age homes are thrown out of their homes, left to live alone and melt into nothingness.

A question suddenly strikes my mind.

Has the time of fall arrived? Has the despair of loneliness won over Mrs Chitnis's self-confidence and intellect? Can I help her in any way?

Am I also not moving on the same path?

I have no clear answer to any of these questions. All I can do is console Mrs Chitnis by saying that this was quite natural at our age. Forget about the past and search for yourself.

She nods her head, smiles weakly, and walks away.

Looking at her faltering steps, I remember a Sumerian myth that Bobby had once told me.

It is believed that Nammu Devi holds an essential place in the creation of the universe. Nammu Devi represents the ancient water element, which gave birth to a divine mountain. The base of this mountain was 'Ki' (Earth), and the summit was 'Un' (Sky), and both were united. 'Enlin' (God of Wind) was born from the womb of 'Un', which separated the Sky and the Earth.

There were other deities too, besides the God of Water, Enki, and the Earth Goddess, Ninmah. These deities had to face a lot of hardships. So, to alleviate their troubles, they sought help from Nammu Devi.

Nammu Devi ordered her son, Enki, to arrange an army of slaves to help the deities. Thus, Enki created the first humans out of the clay produced in Nammu's body.

Seeing her husband's work, Enki's wife, Ninmah, told him

that she would also create humans and give them good or bad fates, as she deemed fit. Enki challenged his wife that despite their fortunes or misfortunes, he would find a befitting place for every human being that Ninmah created.

Ninmah created a woman from clay who could never become a mother; Enki placed this barren woman in the harem. Then she made a man who was sexless—he had neither male nor female genitals. Enki made this asexual person a sentinel to the king. As the Earth Goddess continued to create different creatures, Enki found each a place.

In the end, Ninmah became so obsessed that Enki had to take back her power as the creator. In her obsession, she had created insane, disabled, and sick figures, and, at last, she had made a human figure who could neither walk properly nor speak nor hear, neither eat nor drink nor even think.

Enki couldn't find a place for that pathetic, old creature.

Looking at Mrs Chitnis's receding figure, I think, *'Have we reached that state of the Sumerian imagination, where our destiny is uncertain, and our place in the world is lost?'*

I feel a slight shiver of sadness. My heart is restless. Everything around me has disappeared from view. It feels impossible to sit for long. So, I get up and go to my room.

I hesitate in front of Mrs Chitnis's room. She is blankly staring at the ceiling, completely unaware of the moving scenes on the television screen.

Slowly, I enter and stand by her. She is startled even by my slow movements. 'It's me, Mrs Chitnis,' I say. For some time, a shadow of confusion swims on her face, and then, shifting on her bed to give me space, she says, 'Come and sit.'

We watched the TV for some time, and then she picked up the remote and switched it off. The silence is deafening. Outside, the receding cloud suddenly bursts forth with rain.

'There is quite a popular song these days. Have you heard it, Miss Samuel?' she asks me, staring outside.

'Which one?' I stop, then ask her again, 'From which film?'

'I don't know from which film it is, and I won't be able to sing it properly, the way I had sung it at the college annual function. And for the first time, Madhav had held my hand and said, "You are such a matchless beauty with a wonderful character and sweet voice…" You know?

'How misled we are by such delusions, aren't we, Miss Samuel?'

'You were telling me about a song.' I change the topic.

'Okay, I will try to sing a few lines.

'In the song, the daughter requests her mother to send her Baba (father) to bring her home as the month of Shravan has come. So, the mother tells her daughter that her Baba is too old to do that. "And my brother?" the daughter asks. "Your brother is too young…" In this way, the daughter asks about the other relatives, but everyone is too busy or has reasons not to go fetch her.

'In the end, the daughter tells her mother in frustration…'

Mrs Chitnis clears her throat and sings with a little tremor but in tune:

'"*O Mother dear, send me my childhood then*
As the month of Sawan has come."

'Her mother answers:

"*O my daughter, your childhood is gone, dear*
The month of Sawan has come…"'

Mrs Chitnis can't sing any further. With a sob, rests her head in my lap and cries. Gently stroking her head, I let her cry for some time.

After some time, she calms down and wipes her tears. She puts on her glasses, looks at me and says, 'Forget about the childhood, Miss Samuel, even our old age is about to leave us. How will I cross it like this? The wilderness of forgetfulness is spread all over. Will I be lost? It's very dark here.'

'Everyone has to overcome their own darkness.'

Sitting on a chair in the familiar corner of my room, I think.

The dull grey of the evening makes the silence of Parisar greyer. The heart struggles to go out somewhere. The feet are numb, the body sags and the heart mumbles. How can one escape in this condition?

How far could Moses, Azoba's younger brother, go?

That faded image, left far behind, was etched in a corner of the memory.

'It's too dark here.'

This was the last line of his letter.

A face had emerged from that faded letter when Bobby and Seema had opened that crumpled piece of paper.

A longish face, thin and delicate fingers, long, artistic hands, dreamy eyes, fair complexion, and tall and sensitive image—this was Moses.

'I know even this letter will remain unanswered... Still...

Lily? How was she lost?

And Ruth?

Was she also your own? Who was she?

Human nature is very complex. Sometimes, it rebuffs, scars, and destroys its own near and dear ones so that its authority remains unchallenged. Roaming within its labyrinth, it believes this is the ultimate truth.

Is it not important to see the truth from others' perspective?

I used to feel stifled. Dada, your cruel nature, oppressive behaviour, rash decisions, and the trap of religion, caste and honour used to frighten me.

Let me speak out today. After my mother and Aaba's death during the outbreak of Cholera in Pune, I was tossed into your home like a falling star...but I could never breathe easily.

I wanted to live in the stories, but there were no windows to let the dreams in. With the shower of rain, ants would grow tiny wings. I would roam among mountains, forests, underworlds and rivers with Lily and little Ruth. Then, you would come, pour kerosene oil and put a burning matchstick on the mounds of ants.

We trembled with fear when you shot the mynahs, parrots and squirrels, whom we watched with curiosity as they pecked and nibbled at guavas, mangoes, papayas, custard apples, and pomegranates, hanging on the trees in the courtyards. They would fall, panting at your feet, hurt by the pellet bow. You roasted them in the wood fire so happily, and the aroma arising from their tender flesh brightened your face. Then, you would howl with laughter when you forced us to eat that meat.

A terrible roar would rise within me, and I would close my ears. You said it was all a farce.

Isn't this life a mix of strange acts, scenes, characters and curtain calls? Those acts and scenes presented on the stage, change once the curtain is drawn and the characters also change with the changed circumstances. Some come onstage, and some go behind the stage.

After I had escaped from home, I had thought that the curtain call of my life would be at the stage of the Parsi Theatre. But how could it be possible? The role of the hero is important in every act, his presence is necessary, but a minor character like me just fills up space on the stage. Why else would the old Portuguese gentleman of the theatre company take a poor fellow like me under his wing and tell him that his ancestors, too, were Jews and were converted forcibly? In that intoxicated state, he would even embrace me. He would cry and say, 'Moses, we are brothers.'

And then what can I say about Suleiman Bhai, who lived in the Aambeypur village in Konkan? It seemed God himself spoke through his voice. He was the life of theatre. He had once lent his voice to a fakir's role in the first scene of Heer Ranjha *and had sung passionately—*

The Sun and the Moon will perish one day
So will the Earth and Sky,
The mighty rulers of the universe will perish, too
What hope then holds for you?

Evoking sharp feelings of mortality in us with his melody, Suleiman Bhai had lived with the Bene Israels of Konkan for hundreds of years and even treated me like a brother and friend. Yet, even then, he could not bear that his younger sister, Rehana, loved me.

Mr Antonio and Suleiman—crossing the boundaries of disgrace and friendliness, one of them had tried to take advantage of my helplessness brazenly, and the other had strangled my love and stabbed me in the back.

How can I forget that after shooting Manoj's dog, you had aimed at me?

Blind alleys have only one exit.

I was kicked out of the drama company. I wandered for a long time. Everywhere, I could feel Rehana's big and innocent eyes, staring at me. I tried to reach out to her, but only the wind howled.

It's too dark here, Dada.'

That letter, without an address or closure, is still in my diary. When someone speaks of his own darkness, I find all darkness is similar.

In my declining years, I see a steep upward climb before me. My heart trembles with fear. Even an enlightened woman like Mrs Chitnis has stumbled because the bond of attachment pulls her back, the pain of humiliation pricks her heart, and the path seems lost in the fog of memories. The path is indeed difficult.

I try to convince Mrs Chitnis and myself that a path goes out through this fog.

I can hear Kishori Amonkar singing somewhere within...

Main kaise aaungi Sawariya
Teri unchi atariya

(How shall I come, my dark-hued beloved? The parapet is too high.)

Sitting quietly in the silent room, I can hear the waves splashing in my mind. I sigh, 'How shall I come?'

Rama Aajji stands in the middle of the room. She looks at me and smiles sarcastically.

'I know the last stages of life is difficult, but won't you reach out to Him?'

I look around the vacant room with open doors. Night falls silently. The wind has carried a dry yellow leaf inside; it trembles and falls to the ground noiselessly. From the hollow in a tree, a skylark twitters, and then there is silence all around.

I close the door. Then, before lying down, I mutter as I put out the lamp, 'Now what is there to be afraid of, Rama Aajji?'

Chapter 19

Today, I miss Ameena very much, though she passed away on 22 August 2006, last year.

I had woken up to Sakhu Tai's loud banging at the door. At first, I couldn't understand what was happening! I opened my eyes, lay on my back and composed myself, then realized Sakhu Tai was shouting, 'Miss Samuel, Miss Samuel…'

I looked at my watch. It was five in the morning. Sakhu Tai had left, running, but other footsteps on the veranda were growing louder. There were murmurs, whispers and sighs. I stepped out of my room.

In the dim darkness of the receding night and the coming dawn, I could see a crowd before Ameena's room.

Something seemed to crash within me. I stumbled. Ameena? It seemed my mind had stopped working. As it is, in adverse situations, our mind brakes for a while to absorb the heat of the moment.

On a cot near the window, Ameena lay peacefully. A little froth had dried over her lips. Her hand was stretched towards a glass of water kept on the table. Her throat had probably dried up because of an overdose of sleeping pills. The signs of disconnect, confusion and oddness visible on her face for the last few months had vanished. It looked very soft, small and intimately peaceful. On the left side was a framed family photograph with Ameena and Iqbal's granddaughter in the middle.

The chapter titled Ameena had ended.

I remember the day of 28 July 2006. The newspapers had reported the incident that occurred on 27 July at the Jama Masjid in New Delhi, when sloganeering and a protest march against Israel took place after the namaz. Statements and photographs of posters and banners were also published. The newspapers also reported similar processions being taken out in Lucknow, Allahabad, Aligarh and Amdavad.

As I read the newspaper, I remembered portions of Bobby's article, which had to be removed at Papa's insistence. His article mentioned that the famous intellectuals and scholars of the Jewish community, who are less than one per cent of the world population (nearly one fourth of one per cent), had differences of opinion regarding Israel's independence.

In 1930, the great scientist and thinker Sigmund Freud had written in alarming tones about the misguided faith which would turn the remains of Harold Wall (named after Harold, who aided the reconstruction of the First Temple built by the famous Solomon) into a national memorial. He said it would assault the sensitivities of the native residents, and he did not sympathize with this mindset.

Similarly, in 1938, Albert Einstein had protested against the campaigns for a separate Jewish State, saying that he was afraid of the damage it would cause to Judaism because this mission would give birth to narrow nationalism.

While reading the newspaper, I realized how true these honest disapprovals had turned out to be on the touchstone of time and how Israel's independence, attained in 1948, resulted in unrelenting violence. Also, how the domination of religion and politics surpassed humanity, making life insignificant.

It was too depressing. I sat quietly and stared at the newspaper. Then, as I had picked up my towel for my bath, Ameena suddenly rushed into my room. She had stood before me, a newspaper in her hand. Almost chucking it to my face, she said, 'Did you see? Did you see what devastation Israel is up to?'

With utmost calm, I took the newspaper from her hand, kept it on the table, nodded my head and said, 'Yes, I read it just now.'

She sank on the bed. Her face was flushed with anxiety. Biting her lip, she said, 'Looks like the whole world is ganging up with George Bush to fight Islam.'

Her flushed face, bright eyes, hostile temper and probing manner took me back to the past. I smiled gently, 'Okay.' Is the blast over?

'Why did you smile?' She spoke fast and spit came out.

I became tense and murmured, 'Arre, just like that, Ameena.'

'Of course, why won't you laugh? Your country has won, isn't it?'

'What nonsense are you talking?' I retorted with irritation.

She started trembling. I tried to console her, but she jerked my hand away. Looking into my eyes, she said, 'Do you know about the biggest concentration camp, Auschwitz built in Nazi Germany?'

'Yes.'

'Then you must also be aware that the camp has been preserved as a symbol of racism, intolerance, vandalism and genocide because it was a witness to the most heinous and torturous murder of sixty lakh Jews during the Second World War.'

I came closer to her and touched her shoulder. She was

so annoyed that she pushed me and moved away. 'Keep off,' she said angrily.

I got up, sat on the chair in front of her and looked out of the window. 'Don't look out, look at me and say, isn't the killing of the innocent people of Iraq cruel? Shouldn't Lebanese cities like Tyre and Jbeil also have similar concentration camps as symbols of racism and barbarism?'

'Yes, you are right.' I made a feeble effort to agree.

Her face grimaced with hatred. She stood up suddenly and started pacing in the ten-by-ten room.

'At least those sixty lakh Jews knew that death stared at them. But those studying in schools, playing and talking in homes and in courtyards, seeking refuge in relief camps and hospitals, walking through the so-called humanitarian corridor from Al-Arida to Beirut, hoping for life, were they any different from your Bible's first men and women? Expelled from homes, settlements, and countries, these people are even deprived of food, water, and medicine.

'For months, I have been watching the horror and tyranny of Israel on television. Today, my heart almost burst as I remembered Godhra. I remembered the 1993 riots in Mumbai after the Babri Masjid's demolition, during which the families of my two brothers died. Why are Muslims always targeted?'

She suddenly bursts into tears. Her hiccups made her look insane and deranged. When I touched her, she looked at me. There was no sign or glimmer of familiarity in them.

'Ameena,' I said softly, but she panicked and moved away and whispered hoarsely, 'Don't kill me, please don't kill me.'

Then, she left the way she had come.

Looking at the ray of sunlight entering the empty room through the open door, I thought that perhaps the web of human relations is woven in such a way that it traps time.

Since that day, I barely saw Ameena outside. She had food in her room or skipped meals. A dark shadow of sadness and depression was always evident on her face. If she saw me, she quickly ran into her room and peeped at me through the crack in the door.

There is a small park outside Parisar. It is not well-maintained. Some children play there. One evening after my walk, I went into the park and saw Ameena quietly sitting alone on a broken bench.

I quietly sat next to her. She frowned at me and turned her face away. It was getting dark. A cloud of mosquitoes hovered over us. The constant chirping of crickets had made the atmosphere heavy. I held Ameena's hand, 'Come on, get up. Let's go'. I got up.

She kept sitting and looked at me. But she did not remove my hand from hers. I don't know what she saw in my eyes and what I found in her face, but with eyes brimming with tears she said, 'Everything looks so gloomy, just like this garden, Seema.'

She got up and without turning back, walked on. As I watched her go away, I saw a fourteen-year-old girl standing at the door of our classroom. With a suppressed smile, she asked, 'May I come in, Sir?'

It was our history period. Karim Sir was teaching us about the lineage of the Mughals. Everyone looked at Ameena. Standing in her salwar-kameez with a dupatta draped properly, a fair, tall, strong and beautiful girl was asking permission to come in. All of us, dressed in skirts and blouses or frocks, looked at her with jealousy and curiosity. Dressed in the school uniform of a chocolate brown checked kurta and a white salwar, the girl came and sat next to me.

She hardly took ten minutes to adjust to the new surroundings. Then she took out her notebook and on its last page started her game, her never-ending game.

Ameena. And yours?
Seema Samuel.
Christian?
No, Jew.
Okay?
…
Do you know about the Muslims?
Just a little.
I know a lot about your people.
What do you know?
Your mosque is at Khamasa Gate, isn't it?
It's not mosque, it's a synagogue…
Arre, it's all the same!

'Stand up, Seema.' Karim Sir had ordered. 'What is going on? She has hardly been here for fifteen minutes and you have already started talking? Tell me, what you have written?'

But when this newcomer tore off the page, how and where she hid it, nobody knew. Yet, as soon as class was over, she got up quickly and took out the pieces of paper she had sat on and said, 'Poor thing! How badly crushed these are!'

That was Ameena. By the time we went home that evening, she had become a good friend. I came to know that she had three elder brothers, a younger sister, her father, who had been transferred to Amdavad, and that her aunt's house was in the lane behind our Khamasa Synagogue, that Muslims also wear a skull cap like us when they pray, and believe in a formless god. And yes, Ibrahim, their first ancestor, was also the ancestor of the Jews, who call him Abraham.

I could never forget the way that fourteen-year-old girl had suddenly kissed my cheeks with emotion. So now, when she looked at me like a stranger and begged 'Don't kill me!' it hurt me like a splinter struck through my heart.

I knew that the splinter of pain would always haunt me.

Since that day, Ameena, who had disappeared into her

room, was hardly seen outside. On 15 August, it had rained since morning. The sun and clouds played hide and seek. When the rain stopped for half an hour, Sakhu Tai quickly hoisted the flag and we ate sweets and batashas, but Ameena was nowhere to be seen.

The rain continued to pour from the night of 15 August. By 21 August, there was havoc all around. In the lawn, water had risen up to the ankles. Water dripped from the rain-soaked bent branches and leaves of trees. Residents of the old age home sat gloomily, dozed off, or watched TV.

Sitting on the stairs of the veranda, oblivious to the growing clatter of rain, I was nowhere because on that afternoon, the suffocating silence had left my heart, and a void had filled its space. There was a strange emptiness, strain and restlessness.

I felt as if someone was sitting next to me. I looked up and saw Ameena! May this droplet of time stay on the tip of the leaf eternally, I hoped.

'Today, we'll have dinner together.' This was her first remark. Without saying a word, I pulled her and kissed her cheeks. She smiled softly.

Outside, it continued to rain. The evening continued to melt slowly. The silence of Parisar continued to tiptoe around. Twenty women growing old in twenty-odd rooms continued to drown in their emptiness. And I continued to sit and look at the silent Ameena and the rain.

Now, the droplet on the leaf lengthened and fell into the pool of water below.

'At the end, all theologies, devotion, God, or virtues seem so hollow in the turmoil of an ordinary person, don't they, Seema?'

For a moment, I tried to understand her mental state. Then I said, 'It's not so, Ameena. All these inferences depend on the mental state of the person.'

'And what is the mental state of a person?'

I couldn't answer immediately.

'Shall I tell you?' She said, looking at me. 'The mental state which you blame is created by the breaking of trust and faith. Which means we are moving in a circle. And this is the only truth of an ordinary person like me.'

'Why be so depressed and hopeless, Ameena?' I could only say this before she interrupted me and said, 'Long ago, I had read somewhere about a character from ancient Mesopotamia in 2000 BC, who had said, "Death awaits me, and I feel as soon as I am free from this imprisonment, I will see my much-awaited home." Then, I had thought it was such absolute nonsense because no one wants to die, but...'

Suddenly, she was quiet. I said, 'But Ameena, it is a fact that human desire to live surpasses all its negativities.'

'Maybe...' She said only this as she got up as the sun set on 21 August.

The cook had come out of the kitchen to ring the dinner bell. During monsoons and winters, the bell rang early. It was around seven-thirty in the evening.

'I know today's dinner will be delicious,' Ameena said with a smile.

I laughed and said, 'Gone are the days when we had spicy and oily food, Ameena! Now, whatever you eat, imagine you are having delicacies like halwa-puri. What new could there be?'

Even now, when I remember her answer, I shiver. Walking ahead of me, Ameena looked back at me. Then she had held my hand and said, 'It's so painful to go on living, Seema, isn't it?'

That day, I had thought her comment was in the context of the food, and I had found it so strange and senseless. But today, when I think of the late night of 21 August, I feel Ameena had reached that last turning on that lonely road, beyond which the only thing left was to disappear forever.

Chapter 20

He came out silently from behind the Neem tree in the corner. His face was vacant and emotionless, unlike his nature, so that Seema Samuel couldn't recognize him at first.

September was about to end. Here at this height, the blasts of summer are hardly felt, and greenery and silence keep the temperature low.

Miss Samuel was resting under a patch of sunlight on the lawn of Parisar when he came before her. She thought if she ignored him, he would leave, but she couldn't, so she looked at him.

He came silently and sat next to her.

'Parisar is becoming emptier, isn't it, Seema?'

I am startled. Will I also see Seema changing into Miss Samuel if I watch myself from a distance? Where is Seema? Where is everyone else? Was the fading and disappearing of Rama Aajji, Mary Varghese, Vimla, Sudha Akka or Ameena from the scene a part of this larger picture?

When Vimla left Parisar, dragging her feet behind her tall, strong, and noble son, she looked like his maid servant in her crushed cotton sari.

And Sudha Akka, she had lost so much weight that she looked like a reed. Her younger son may have given her the final rest in peace at home. Who knows what destroys someone slowly?

His stare disturbs me.

He is quietly reading the lines on my face.

Looking beyond me, he mutters, 'Empty rooms will fill again!'

I start thinking—somebody will say, 'Miss Samuel's room is vacant', and a new sadness will enter that room.

I see him leaving silently. Then, he stops, turns back and says, 'Life passes in a very haphazard manner, doesn't it?'

I had probably nodded in agreement because I glimpsed a strange compassion welling up in his eyes. His lips trembled. I wanted to reach out to him, but he had already left by then.

I think I heard him murmuring, 'We hardly get time to change our lives.' But he was nowhere.

After walking on the grass for a while, I sit wearily on a bench in the corner and watch the sunlight fall on the green hillocks. In this quiet qasbah life seems pretty still, and the sun is also a part of that stillness. Smiling to myself, I lean on the back of the bench. It looked like a picture—hills and mountains, sun, Parisar, bench, lawn, trees, saplings, grass, a few houses on the hills, spiral roads and I, leaning on the bench.

Suddenly, a photographer stands before me with a camera slung around his neck and a tripod in his hands. He claps for everyone to get ready for the shoot. From here and there, everyone arrives. Dressed in an English suit and tie, Pappa sits among them. In one hand, he holds a carved walking stick with a gold handle, and his other hand is placed firmly on the arm of a high chair. He wears a pair of spectacles with a semicircular lens in a frame of rolled gold. From his breast pocket peeps a gold watch with its gold chain attached to the buttonhole. He raises his eyebrows and his dignified countenance reflects power and position. His pretty wife, Diana, stands next to him. The end of her Parsi-style embroidered sari touches her high-heeled sandal. Her forehead is adorned with curled locks, similar to those of the film stars Nadira, Rubi Marius and Nadia Hunterwali. She wears dangling earrings but her face looks tense and nervous. Moses stands close to her. He is Pappa's younger brother. His hair is ruffled, the white shirt sticks out of his long half-pant, and he wears white sports shoes without socks. He seems to look at—who knows where! Next to Pappa stands Samuel. Tall and lean with sharp features, he is smartly dressed in a shirt and trousers with a tie; his eyes are fixed above the camera. Lily and little Ruth wear two long plaits each and sit on the floor. Ruth's hand seems to play with her long, wavy hair and she has a soft and gentle face.

The photographer adjusts the camera on the tripod, covers it with a black cloth, and hides his face beneath the cover. Then, he lifts his left hand and calls out, 'Ready?' He presses the shutter and the next moment, he smiles and hands me a black-and-white photograph. I am amazed at how quickly the photograph was ready!

I look at this old group photo intently. What's this? I can now see Ma, Papa, Bobby, Rachel, Rafu, Rama Aajji, Ameena, Vimla, Mary, Rati Bharucha, young Seema, Mrs Chitnis, Sakhu Tai, Raghu, Tahmina, Sohrab, Sarah and Mili in the photograph. I wonder how long they had stood with us!

Then I see the photograph fading. I quickly put on my spectacles to spot myself in the photograph but I can't. While I search, some of the people leave the photograph, and some faces become so blurred that they seem out of focus…young Seema is absent too! I keep searching for faces in the photograph when my eyes finally fall on one. In a frilled floral frock, and braids tied with ribbons and a lot of mischief in eyes—I think this is me, but when I lift my finger from my photograph, I see it is Ameena, dressed in a sari. I am scared. Where am I lost? My heart races as I wonder. My hands perspire, and my body is bathed in sweat. I shout in agony—'Where am I lost? Where am I in the photograph?'

Manda wakes me from my nap. 'The sun is too hot, Tai. Come inside. It isn't November, it's September.'

'Yes dear, September will end, and this year will also end, then this decade, then this century, then one more millennium and the era. Everything will end,' I say as I get up. Manda looks at me strangely and then goes to the kitchen.

Climbing the stairs of the veranda, I repeat a line from Ghalib's couplet,

Hota hai shab-o-roz tamasha mere aage...

(Every night, a spectacle unfolds before me)

❁

Accustomed to seeing and suffering spectacles, do we ever separate truth from illusion?

A spectacle had fluttered in Seema's consciousness.

'Paro, will you remember your Deva?'

Seema moved faster to catch hold of that letter. But, the spectacle rushed faster and turned into a train departing the station.

Five minutes were left before the train departed, but there was no sign of Raghav. Seema was leaving for home. It was the last day of her stay in the hostel. An account of an entire year of affection, promises, togetherness, trust and completeness.

By the time Raghav could reach the platform, the train had already given the green signal. Breathless as he ran, he reached Seema's third-class coach, smelling of perfume. He embraced Seema and kissed her forehead and cheeks many times.

When the eighteen-year-old Seema returned to her seat, her face was flushed. Shock and disgust were evident on all the faces around her. But Seema noticed all this much later; at that moment, she seemed to be flying along with the train like a bird seeking shelter. She wanted to build a nest. She wanted to bring the eggs to life. She wanted to see the little ones growing up and then watch them disappear in the wide azure sky. Why should she bother about the feelings of her fellow passengers?

So, when Seema opened her tight fist, she saw a gem sparkling there. She opened her palm. The gem seemed to wriggle in its slumber. A hundred rays broke from it…

'Paro, will you remember your Deva?'

Seema touched the gem with her eyes, and her eyes seemed to turn into a blue lake in which the gem swam gracefully like a swan.

That summer was very harsh. Over time, the lake turned murky and then dried up. Seema wrote many letters secretly, but every letter turned into a fish that writhed in the drying lake. Then the water started reeking of dead, rotten fish.

The stories of Paro and Devdas don't take place on railway platforms or turn into a lake. They sometimes lie hidden under an old folded newspaper in Seema's almirah and gradually turn into yellow crumpled paper, which Seema remembers while leaving her home. She smiles bitterly at the spectacle of the past and moves on.

❁

These spectacles are like games.

As I climb the first few stairs of the veranda, I become breathless. Holding the parapet, I take in a long breath and look at the empty veranda.

'Spectacle…' I mutter.

'What spectacle are you looking at, Miss Samuel?'

I look up in surprise. Manjeet Kaur stands before me.

'Spectacles change their location. The performance ends and leaves behind a fluttering desolation.' Manjeet Kaur says as she places her hand on my shoulder and leans against the parapet.

I smile. 'Spectacles only leave desolation behind, Manjeet Kaur! Time, place, and performers change, but do grand shows ever worry about them?'

'Yes, you are right.' She says as she heaves a sigh. For some time, she is quiet and stares at the empty veranda. Then, she says, 'I lost my two young sons in the 1984 riot. Avenging Indira Gandhi's assassination became a spectacle, then in 1993, the Babri Masjid, too, became a spectacle, and then in 2002, a spectacle at Godhra and now, every day, we witness the spectacle of the Bal Thackeray family.

'Twenty-four years have passed, Miss Samuel, since we arrived and settled in Poona. But even today, we haven't found a sense of belonging anywhere!'

She turns slowly and returns to her room. I watch her leaving. Sardar-ji passed away last year. Those who depend on others for support all their life, how forlorn they look when left alone.

But people like me look like wanderers, too. Probably, we look more confused because our age defeats us.

I return slowly to my room. My heart feels heavy with an unknown burden. The residents of Parisar are walking in the lawn. The gardener is planting winter saplings in flower beds. I sense the wheel of life moving and the day is about to set.

I don't know why as I sit on the chair and lean back, I remember Lakshmi and her curse. How could the family of retired Subedar Isaji Eloji or Isaac Elijah of the Tenth Native Infantry Regiment of the Bombay Army forget Lakshmi's sufferings?

Chapter 21

Sarah tells me flatly this morning that Abeer got married a few days ago. The same old reason—his widowed mother had refused food and water.

The girl chosen for him was Ketaki, his eldest sister's daughter.

I listen to her, stunned. Sarah chuckles, 'Seema, why do you look so shocked?' Then, with a mocking smile, she imitates a famous dialogue from a popular film: 'Yaar, *bade bade shehron me aisi chhoti chhoti baatein hoti rehti hai*! (Such small things keep happening in big cities!)'

I feel my head spinning. I draw back, support myself on a wall and rest my head. There is a void before me.

Sarah had called quite early in the morning: 'Seema, tell Sakhu Tai to keep extra food for two people. Mili and I will reach around one in the afternoon.'

Before I could ask or say something, she disconnected the call.

Mili asks, 'Seema, are you all right?' touching me with concern. I open my eyes, look at Mili, and nod.

'Why are you so affected by everything, Seema?' Sarah asks.

Running my tongue over my dry lips, I say sadly, 'You won't understand, my dear; you are too young!' She immediately counters, 'It's of no use, worrying like this, Seema. You won't be here to worry about me when I grow old and as of now, I am capable enough to take care of my life.' Sarah is clear as she replies candidly.

After a brief silence, she continues, 'What pained me most about Abeer's marriage was that despite being together for so long, he needed another companion. But, this often happens, Seema—that even people who may have similar mindsets encounter terrible situations and choices, and the mind looks for a simple and uncomplicated way to find peace. So, Abeer's decision to marry wasn't that big of a crime, as was his dishonesty. He had left, saying that Akka was extremely ill, and then he married in full splendour and brought home Ketaki, a bride thirteen years younger than him, and he avoided me for days together.

'I was surprised, Seema because we had been together for almost fifteen years. He told me that I wouldn't have converted to Hinduism, I wouldn't have changed my name, but his mother was firm on having a traditional marriage and did not want a crossbreed to keep the family name going. Could any argument or query be left after this logic, Seema?'

Mili is quiet throughout. Sighing, she says, 'Only you can be so bold, Sarah. Look at me; though I married outside the community, I couldn't save anything of my older self. I pray like a traditional Hindu woman; I have even installed the idol of Lord Ganesha and immerse it in water every day. I cook Maharashtrian food and also follow all religious customs, rituals and festivals. My children have Hindu names, and even my name would have changed, had it not sounded like a Hindu name. On top of that, there were debates about how one synagogue was enough or even none, in my presence and within my earshot.'

'I feel so tired, Seema,' Mili says, resting her head on the table. She continues, 'Even if there was no compulsion to follow or not to follow caste or religion, the vulgar display of your identity being altered is so disturbing.'

'Now, if I say something, you will be offended, Mili,' Sarah counters immediately. 'Feeling disturbed and sad is also a kind of display. Blindfolding your eyes and moving round and round like a buffalo is not life. There are small trails, lanes, by-lanes, pathways, and horizons, and new worlds to watch out for. All you need is patience and courage.'

'I don't know,' Mili says sadly, 'I feel as if I am like a broken line: start, stop, start, breaking, exhausted!' Her voice chokes. Staring out, she sighs again, and says, 'I don't know why my heart continues to be so miserable.'

It feels as if it was not Mili but Diana Aajji speaking, holding my hand, 'I am tired now, my daughter. I don't know how long I have been trudging.'

Why is Mili so tired at this young age?

And Sarah? Will she also suddenly be tired one day?

Why do only women get tired so easily?

Outside, the sun is at its peak. A strange turmoil and anxiety overwhelm my heart. I stand, staring at the two sisters.

'Don't worry about me, Seema,' Sarah says as she gently pats me. She sits near me and adds, 'I have so much work that I can drown myself in it. The world is full of greater sorrows, Seema. How long can we hold on to our petty ones? All we need is sympathy for the sadness, pain, and disappointments spread all around. There are endless ways of doing that.'

'And loneliness? Old age?' I suddenly blurt out.

'Ha! Rubbish, useless. Why should I think about it now?' Sarah grimaces.

This is Sarah, one who lives with such ideas and mindset. She is sensitive but unemotional and practical. I silently pray to God to save her from the dullness and greyness of life. Let her find something that doesn't tire her.

There is a deafening silence in the room. The ceiling fan whirs slowly. The sunshine outside begins to fade. Now, I think that all the while, Mili was trying to be brave because, a little later, she started pacing the room.

She walks to me and then goes out onto the veranda, returns, sits on the chair, and rests her head on the table. I can't stop myself. Knowing her reserved nature, I finally ask, 'What's the matter, Milcah? Why are you so restless?'

She stops and slumps near me. She looks depressed and bored. Resting her head on my lap, she avoids my gaze and says, 'Seema, do you remember Ustad Barkat Ali Khan Saab's thumri…*Tum Radhe bano Shyam*.' (O Shyam, become Radha.)

I am startled. Long ago, this rare thumri in Raga Pilu was played at home, at B-7 in Gitanjali Society. Ma loved it. Bobby often sang it. The lyrics of the thumri compelled us to transform ourselves, and it had stuck to our lives.

Mili lifts her face, looks into my eyes and says, 'How I wish, if not the whole world, at least Srikant understood the meaning of this song. I tried very hard. Half my life is over now, working and looking after children, relatives, and household. The children have grown up and are lost in their worlds. There will be no one, neither here nor there, for me. And who understands this better than you, Seema? How helpless is the old generation with each passing day, estranged and cast off by this selfish and insensitive young generation? Who knows where this free, impudent and caste-ridden society will stop? Will I then be trampled by them, disowned by my own community and by Srikant's?

'Radha's pain will always hurt me. In such a situation, our minuscule community, which is scattered along the margins of society, hardly has an authentic history, Seema.' She sighs, 'I shall find my salvation only in a place like Parisar.'

It feels as if something has crashed within me. Sarah must

have looked at Mili in shock, although I hadn't noticed this. I collapse on the bed.

It is dark for some time, and then, slowly, I see light. The sisters are bent over me, and Sarah sprinkles water on my face, muttering indistinctly all the while.

'I am okay.' I whisper weakly, trying to smile.

No one says a word for some time, but Sarah could not bear the silence. She looks angry and pained.

'Great!' she says, looking at me sarcastically, 'What an act it was, Seema! You decide to stay in this Parisar and not with us, that's fine. You teach us to be bold and courageous in making our decisions, which makes sense, but when we tell you about our choices, you faint and fall. How could you be so weak, Seema? Don't you know there is hardly any space left in our cemetery in Pune, which is why many Israyels have wished to be cremated by fire or electricity? There is no memory after death, isn't it, Seema?'

It takes a lot of effort to convince the two sisters that my emotional and physical condition is fine. Also, Dolly wasn't well—this was a genuine reason. Only then do they agree to leave me. I bid them goodbye at the gate. When Sarah's red Santro disappear at the curb, I come back and sit on the stairs of the veranda.

It is now evening. Mili's moksha terrifies me. But why?

Long ago, Mrs Chitnis had asked me, 'What do you think of salvation?'

I had smiled and said, 'Well, there is no place for salvation in my religion, but I am surprised that even an enlightened woman like you believes in a spiritual and superstitious notion like salvation.'

'Why? It is a natural and traditional belief for me. But

why speak of me? Even Mary Varghese, a Christian, thought it better to be cremated so that all her pain, illusions, ambitions, mistakes and sorrows of this life were consumed by fire and her soul found deliverance; the soul didn't have to wait for the Final Day of Judgment and wander among the cycles of life and death. And, Miss Samuel, isn't it surprising that despite being a non-Hindu, the shadow of our culture had such a deep impact on Mary that she was convinced to find salvation this way? As for me, I am a Hindu and I believe in moksha.'

I remembered the many lives Mrs Chitnis experienced in a single life and my own and all the people who surrounded me and stared at her.

Perhaps Mrs Chitnis saw sarcasm and bitterness in the sharp lines on my face and said, 'Do you think I am wrong?'

'You tell me, Mrs Chitnis,' I asked openly, 'Who among us has committed such a grave sin to live in this old age home and sink our roots here at our age?'

She continued looking at me. There was sadness on her face. I took the conversation forward. 'Good or bad, heaven-hell, moksha, or life after death, these are all windows to our mind, Mrs Chitnis! As for me, the decisions taken by my free will and in a sane state of mind are moksha. Even if they may not result in happiness, it is deliverance anyway.'

She thought for a long time, and then said, 'I think you are right, Miss Samuel. For me, salvation also means keeping my dignity intact without being humiliated, and when I go to bed, the pangs of sadness do not gnaw at me! The burden of memories is there, but we don't see ourselves as broken or miserable.'

Today, when I see Mrs Chitnis staring at the wall for hours, searching for herself, it feels as if time has snatched away her share of moksha.

That's why Mili's idea of salvation has made me sceptical. Mili won't know that when little Seema in her two plaits peeps out of my wrinkled and dull face in the mirror and smiles, a light emerges from some other birth.

Or, perhaps, I am scared of Milli's darkness.

Hansa Chitre comes out of Mary's room. I see Mary on the veranda. She smiles and asks me, 'Miss Samuel, "my house" is occupied now, isn't it?'

She used to call her room her house. She didn't mean its expanse. It was rather the warm feeling of belonging and trust that that empty space provided. 'This is my home Miss Samuel; that was a damn morgue,' she would sometimes say when she was sad. She would say, 'Miss Samuel, houses shouldn't be kept vacant because empty houses turn into ruins. You will see, even my home will be filled as soon as I leave.'

Yes, Hansa Chitre has filled Mary's home.

But sometimes, even houses full of people gradually turn into ruins; you only watch helplessly.

❁

Seema remembered well how, after Mr Samuel David's retirement, the birds of the colony had stopped making their nests in B-7. Earlier, when people used his government telephone, they would arrive like birds with twigs of grass, bringing birdsongs and fluttering feathers. Even the neighbours who used to come to Mira Ben's (Miriam) house to learn the recipes of snacks and savouries like chakli and puranpoli, now avoided her and stopped coming.

Amdavadis who were on the fast-track of growth and development had learned to be tight-fisted with money and also knew how to splurge lavishly. People who used to travel on cycles or buses now had scooters and, occasionally, a Fiat car was parked in front of their houses. Those who had first arrived and settled in this colony admired Samuel David's Rexine sofa and ordinary pinewood dining table. But now, they had golden temples and silver chandeliers in their houses. Their homes had two telephones, and were huge and extraordinary-looking. Seema had often found her father in dirty pajamas, staring open-mouthed and wide-eyed at the newly constructed apartments.

At home, Samuel David was getting weaker day by day. Rosie's anger and disrespectful behaviour and Danny's detachment and indifference were becoming unbearable. Rachel and Bobby had already drowned in the sudden deluge of misfortune, Danny and Rosie, who initially perched on the high parapet like birds, flew away into the vast sky. The deserted house needed just one final shove of Jyotsna Prajapati's aggression to collapse.

Seema remembered the first time she had met Jyotsna Prajapati. Those were happy days for David. He was becoming sincere in his job, and when Papa brought the issue of marriage before him, he avoided it for a few days and then, one day, opened his heart to Seema.

'She is a good girl, beautiful and honest. She works as a clerk at my office. She cares for me a great deal and tells me that if I marry her, she will take responsibility for all our problems,' he told her.

Seema had found David's trust in Jyotsna Prajapati quite strange, but she was more concerned with David himself—he was finally on the right track. On her first visit, Jyotsna Prajapati had shyly touched Papa's feet and then turned to touch Seema's feet, but Seema had hugged her. She had kissed Rafu and stuffed his hands with two Cadbury chocolates.

When the same beautiful and shy Jyotsna Prajapati started destroying their home soon after that, the weak walls echoed with a terrible sound. Surrounded by these walls, old Samuel David, ageing Seema and innocent Rafu fluttered here and there helplessly.

This young one, scared of the darkness of his past, was hardly capable of nurturing any dream of his future. He could only remember things he had learned mechanically or his natural needs.

How could this naïve, innocent and dreamless Rafu see the cracks in the walls made by the rumbling noises?

He would obviously be trapped one day.

Despite witnessing all this, the retired Under Secretary Mr Samuel David was in no hurry to leave the home. Jyotsna Prajapati would scream, 'Why don't you die? Coiled up like a snake on our chests—you fogey! That bastard, impotent son ran away, leaving him behind for me.'

'Is death in my hands?' Samuel David would murmur in a weak, sad voice.

He would narrate his sorrows to Seema. 'My life-breath is stuck in David. How I wish, if he had given me an heir, I would have died in peace. Someone to carry the family name forward, the clan of Isaji Eloji.'

Seema couldn't control herself, 'You want an heir from Jyotsna Prajapati? From this wicked woman and your crazy son? Do you think a son born of them will carry your name forward and preserve the tradition of the Jews? Forget this wishful thinking, Papa, and leave this world with dignity. You are tired now.'

Seema was breathless as she spoke.

Samuel David looked at his ageing daughter and said in a sad, sinking voice, 'David, my son, David, come back.'

Standing at the last leg of the journey of his life, tired, sick and sluggish, Seema kept looking at her father. Was he the same man who had once scolded his young daughter, who was studying in the tenth grade, for paying five rupees extra for the school fees? 'I walk miles to reach my office. I never have tea and snacks worth even two rupees because they are a waste of money. I can bear my hunger. When you return from school tomorrow, you must have those five rupees back, do you understand?'

One thundering shout from Samuel David was enough to suffocate all life at home. He loved only Rachel. And she left. He would argue with Bobby. Bobby, too, went away. Rafu always reminded him of Rachel's misfortune, so he could never love him, and he saw him go, too. Vigilant and reserved on the outside, Samuel David gradually became empty within. And when his youngest and dearest David left him, he was utterly hopeless. He tried to lord over Seema, but both of them knew the truth.

Seema knew that he couldn't slap her the way he had once when he had discovered Raghav's precious letter to her. He thought it was his duty to rummage through the wardrobe, purse and bags of his children in their absence.

'You shameless girl!' He had thundered as he slapped Seema on her face. 'Did I send you to study or to play the love game? How deep are you into all this? Do you even know these Hindu boys? They want only veiled, old-fashioned women in their homes. Which world do you live in, Seema?'

Seema had thought of eloping with Raghav, but Papa was right. Miss Samuel remembered that yellowish, moth-eaten letter hidden under the newspaper.

Seema could hardly forget her 'Deva'*, her lover, or that

*'Deva' was the nickname of Devdas from the Bengali writer Sarat Chandra Chattopadhyay's novel, *Devdas*. Set against the backdrop of rural Bengal during feudal times, it is the story of a doomed love affair between Devdas, Parvati (Paro), the daughter of his middle-class neighbour and Chandramukhi, a beautiful, kindly courtesan. The story has seen multiple

sharp niggling pain or even Papa Samuel's terrible anger. Happiness may or may not bring the sunshine of good cheer, but the bruise of a hurt carries with it a heavy cloak of darkness.

❁

Coming out of my reverie, I realize Mili and Sarah may have reached home by now, and here I am, sitting on the steps of Parisar and wandering who knows where. In your declining old age, your steps take you forward, but your heart and mind run after the past. Then, finally, one day, they split ways. Perhaps this is why a dense cloud of heaviness continues to envelop our hearts.

Holding on to the railing, I stand on my weak legs and walk towards the veranda. I feel a young Ameena suddenly step out and stand in front of me. She shows me a piece of paper and smiles. I look at it closely.

Written on it: 'I am Ameena, and you?'

Me? Who am I, Ameena?

---

adaptations in the regional languages of India. However, the three most popular Hindi versions of Devdas were released in 1936 (K.L. Saigal as Devdas), 1955 (Dilip Kumar as Devdas) and 2002 (Shah Rukh Khan as Devdas). Of the three, the reference here is to the 1955 version of *Devdas* featuring Dilip Kumar, Suchitra Sen and Vyjayanthimala.

Chapter 22

I have returned to my room. It is quiet and dull as always. Surrounded by a table, chair, cot, window, doormat, curtains on the door, a fan hanging from the ceiling, a small television set, a transistor kept in a niche in the wall and a steel almirah, is a seventy-year-old woman. Me, Miss Samuel.

4 April. The year 2010, and a receding evening.

Before leaving, Mili had read out a poem by Wisława Szymborska to me.

I don't want
The waves of the ocean to rise and fall at my will
I don't want
The forest to change its colours for me
Sometimes green
Sometimes blue
And sometimes brownish
But I don't even want
To return
To this beautiful world
again
I want to give up my right,
My right to exist

She had kept looking at me after reciting the poem. Then she had patted my shoulder and said, 'You know, Seema, Sarah and I have made our last wish: to be cremated instead of being buried. I want to give up my attachment to that six-foot grave.'

Will Mili, too, follow in the footsteps of Seema?

I am very disturbed, and there is a deep sense of anguish as if I have been engulfed on all sides and the suffocation is slowly closing in on me. I am soaked in sweat. I don't know what to do. I rest my head on the pillow and lie down quietly. But the distraction is gradually rising. It seems as if the stress will penetrate through my ribs and overflow. I open my mouth to breathe in like a fish, trying to draw life-giving air from water. What restlessness is this?

Gradually, the confusion subsides, and I feel a strange calmness. As I toss and turn in bed, I feel myself stepping into the darkness spread outside the window. There is no light anywhere, only a dusty, narrow pathway which meanders and stops in the flash of light near a house.

It's an old-looking house.

This house, with many rooms and corridors, belongs to a Parsi gentleman, Baba Rustamji Daruwalla, and sits at the end of a middle-class qasbah. This locality is known as the Parsi Colony. The roads are tiled with slabs of hilly rocks on which horse carts, bicycles, donkeys, horses and, occasionally, motor cars ply.

There is a huge and shady tamarind tree just a little way away from the house where the colony begins. Seema's school is at the other end of the colony. Crossing the entire Parsi Colony, she comes out of the Baniya quarters, enters the quarters of the goldsmiths, crosses the Desai and Patel quarters and reaches her school, which is just a little before the river bank. The only cinema hall in that humble middle-class qasbah was situated quite close to her school, where she had watched the film *Jagriti* and had cried all through the film.

Her mother had scolded her when she had reached home swollen eyed—'Poor wretch! Why did you go to watch this film if you would cry so much? How will you live with such a weak heart, Seema?'

But Seema continued to live even after her mother's scolding was silenced forever like a delicate earthen pot quietly falling to pieces by the riverside when all songs had become silent.

As she plays with her two long braids, Seema has several questions within her, but she can't find the answers to them, or they are beyond her comprehension, like she could never understand why her friends stopped coming to her house. When she asked her best friend, Reeta Desai, she gave her a funny answer: 'Your father tickles me too much.' How could Seema understand this? And when she had asked her mother about it, she was scolded, and she didn't know why her mother fought with her father that night.

Seema could never understand why Danny always gave her a sharp look when she discussed her homework with her classmates, Varun, Mahesh or Uttam. At her age, she could never understand why every time her father was transferred, he wouldn't get government accommodation, why they had to live in a house in a Parsi or Muslim colony located at the end of the town, from where her school would be extremely far. And then, why did her mother tell her to introduce herself to her Hindu friends as Maharashtrian? When Seema asked why, her mother told her that her friends wouldn't understand her 'Jewish caste' and wouldn't let her enter their homes, thinking she was untouchable. At this, Seema would think it would have been so much better if she were a Hindu. At least she wouldn't have had to face such problems. She always felt a tug of sadness as to why her Jewish community was different from the majority community.

She never anticipated that this distinct identity would change her life one day.

She felt that perhaps she could understand a few things, but everything would slip out of her mind too soon and disappear. And that is why Papa and Danny did not like her. But without bothering herself by them, and without caring a damn for the world, she loved her school, the sparkling white sand on the river bed, the roadside shops selling lemon juice, peanuts and other eatables at the entrance of the cinema hall. She also loved the two white-turbaned guards standing at the entrance and her classmate Raman, who was once sent out of the classroom by Saiyyad Sir for singing a few lines from a vulgar song during the antyakshari song competition.

Then? Then Seema started growing up. Everything was left behind—the school, that middle-class qasbah, Sohrab, Abdul Zaidi, Raman, Reeta, Urvashi Desai, Jalu Gazdar and yes, that Rameela Patel (who farted during PT class, and all the students had burst into laughter). When Seema asked, 'What was that, Rameela?' she had responded with a straight face, 'It's only rice and dal exiting the wrong way!'

Everything was left behind. The houses became smaller and started turning into ruins and, one day, they were abandoned. Walking on that narrow dusty pathway one day, Seema had quietly entered this ten-foot-by-ten-foot room.

I leave my bed with great effort. I pick up the glass of water from the table and take a few sips, but there's no peace. Holding the iron bars of the window, I look outside for that dusty pathway. Outside, the murmurings of night feel like whispers.

while the sun, or the light,
or the moon, or the stars, be not darkened,
*nor the clouds return after the rain:**

In the darkness of the night, looking out of the window into the silence, which clouds am I thinking of?

I slowly turn back, and with stumbling steps, I crash on my bed. A small circle of light from the hazy night lamp hangs from the ceiling. The circle looks like a silver coin placed in a palm. Seema wants to reach out and take the coin, but Sohrab laughs and chides, 'Crazy girl! This is a dinosaur's egg. Don't you know that dinosaurs have become extinct from the earth?'

Seema laughs and says, 'I know it, Sohrab. One day, everything will vanish from this earth, but not these voices from this infinite universe. Not even mine. And you know, Sohrab, how many lost and forgotten voices and signs exist in those gaps around our lives, which echo in the space surrounding this earth. But who has heard them? Because then, the sounds of the grinding stones and the chirping of birds and all songs become silent, then all the sounds enter the core of the universe, leaving this life behind. The exits of life are then shut.'

Slowly, the stress eases out, I feel weary but strangely peaceful, as if my memories are dissolving. The stress in the mind is losing its grip. It is peaceful and tranquil, as if all sufferings have been left behind. How peaceful is this stillness, what a quiet peace! It looks as if the footsteps have stopped, and my heart leaps ahead of me, a silent dim light is spread before me, and I am slowly hypnotized by it.

Looking at the dark, still night, I feel as if the distant twinkling stars are moving. They will leave the face of the sky for some far-off place just as Seema left hers, leaving behind

---

*Ecclesiastes 12:2.

the space in which she existed. Now, I can clearly hear the murmur of the earth's movement.

I enter a speechless silence. It feels cold. The mist starts enveloping me, but I continued walking. A female figure, wrapped up in a cloak of mist, is walking ahead of me. She is silent like a picture and flows like the wind. I walk faster to catch up, but she silently walks ahead. Stop! I call out to her, and she stops for a moment and looks back. Do I recognize her? Perhaps I am hallucinating. She continues walking and I follow her as if tied to her by a string.

What kind of hypnosis is this, Seema? I ask myself but don't get an answer.

The image walking ahead suddenly stops, and I stop behind it. There is no mist around, and the dim lights, too, have disappeared. I look around. It is neither day nor night, dark nor light, clear nor hazy, land nor sky. I am standing in unknown, strange, and unspoken surroundings like a lost soul.

Where do I want to go? I question myself. There is silence. I am flowing like the wind, surrounded by high mountains. There is a vast stretch of sand ahead of me and the ocean full of dancing blue waves, but there is no noise.

Is this a painting?

In this silent environment, I slowly move towards the unmoving image. When I reach her, I ask, 'Who are you?'

Slowly and silently, the image turns towards me. A cloud of sadness covers her blank face. Then she raises her right hand.

I lift my eyes to see where her forefinger points.

On the silent ocean waves, next to the mast of a stationary ship, I see Isaji Eloji holding the hand of dreamless, vacant-eyed Rafu, standing like a still portrait. Who knows what unknown horizon they were gazing at!

Glossary

Aaba: Father.

Aajji: Marathi word for grandmother.

Akka: Tamil word for elder sister.

Aaza/Azoba: Marathi word for grandfather.

Abbu: Urdu word for father.

Ammi: Urdu word for mother.

Antyakshari is a spoken parlour game played in India. Each contestant sings the first verse of a song (often Classical Hindustani or Bollywood) that begins with the consonant of the Hindi alphabet on which the previous contestant's song ended.

Bai is term generally used to address women, used widely across India. During earlier times, bai was used a respectful suffix for women from the royal family. In Marathi, especially in villages, 'bai' refers to a Teacher.

Batata is the word for potato in some variants of Arabic and some Indian languages, including Gujarati, Konkani and Marathi, and Portuguese.

Bhajan refers to any devotional song with a religious theme or spiritual ideas, specifically among Dharmic religions, in any language. The term 'bhajanam' means reverence and originates from the root word 'bhaj', which means to revere.

Binaca Geetmala was a weekly countdown show of the top songs from Hindi cinema. It was popular and had millions of listeners.

A **Chabutra** is a tower-like structure found in India that provides nesting sites for birds, especially pigeons.

Chakli is a savoury snack from India. It is a spiral-shaped snack with a spiked surface. Chakli is typically made from flours of rice, Bengal gram and black gram. It has several variations, depending on the types and proportion of flours used.

Dhansak is a popular Indian dish, originating among the Parsi community. It combines elements of Persian and Gujarati cuisine. Dhansak is made by cooking mutton or goat meat with a mixture of lentils and vegetables. This is served with caramelised white rice, whole spices, and caramelized onions.

Djinn, in Arabic mythology, is a spirit inhabiting the earth but unseen by humans, capable of assuming various forms and exercising extraordinary powers. Belief in them was common in pre-Islamic Arabia, where they were thought to inspire poets and soothsayers.

Gulal or abir is the traditional name given to the coloured powders used for some Hindu rituals, in particular for the festival of Holi.

Halwa is a type of confectionery originating from Persia and widely spread throughout the Middle East and South Asia. The name is used for a broad variety of recipes, generally a thick paste made from flour, butter, liquid oil, saffron, rosewater, milk, cocoa powder, and sweetened with sugar.

Ikka or tonga is a one-horse carriage used in northern India. They were commonly used as cabs, or private hire vehicles in nineteenth-century India. They find frequent mention in colonial literature of the period.

Israyel is another word for Jew. It is derived from 'Yisra'yel', the given Hebrew name of Jacob, the patriarch and the traditional ancestor of the people of Israel.

The **Kaddish** is a hymn praising God that is recited during Jewish prayer services. The central theme of the Kaddish is the magnification and sanctification of God's name

Derived from the Hindi/Urdu word for 'cut' (circumcision) **Katua** refers to a man who is circumscribed. It is an oft-used derogatory slang used for Muslim men in India.

Khichdi is a dish in South Asian cuisine made of rice and lentils with numerous variations.

Kirtan, derived from a Sanskrit root meaning to call, recite, praise, or glorify, put simply, is the act of praising and glorifying some form of divinity.

Lal Deul (Red Synagogue or Baghdadi Synagogue): Ohel David (Tabernacle of David) Synagogue, also called Lal Deval or Lal Deul is a synagogue in Pune, India. It is located on Moledina Road. Its construction was started in 1863 by philanthropist David Sassoon and completed by his successors in 1867. Built in the English Gothic style and designed by Henry Saint Clair Wilkins, this red brick and trap stone structure resembles a church. It has a 90-feet high obelisk with a clock at the top brought specially from London.

Mezuzah is a piece of parchment inscribed with specific Hebrew verses from the Torah, which Jewish followers of Rabbinical Judaism fix to the doorposts of their homes, on the right side of the entrance. A mezuzah declares that the people who dwell here live Jewish lives.

Minyan is the quorum required for Jewish communal worship that consists of ten male adults in Orthodox Judaism and usually ten adults of either sex in Conservative and Reform Judaism.

Mlechchha: During the Vedic period, 'mlechchha' was a Sanskrit term used to mean foreigner or someone with incomprehensible speech and unfamiliar behaviour. Over time, in the deeply segregating caste system of the Hindu religion, the term became colloquially used for people who existed beyond the Hindu caste system and were usually meat eaters, thus making them impure and untouchable by the Hindus.

Natya Sangeet is a form of Indian Classical and Semi-Classical music. The name literally means 'Dramatic Music' or 'Musical Dramas' and are also popularly known as Sangeet Natak. It is also one of the two popular forms of vocal arts in Maharashtra.

Pani ke Batashe is a kind of street food in India. It has various names throughout the country such as pani puri, golgappa, phuchka etc.

Patra ni Machhi is an Indian dish originating from Parsi cuisine, which is made from steamed fish topped with chutney and wrapped in a banana leaf.

The **Pindari** were irregular military plunderers and foragers in 17th- through early 19th-century Indian subcontinent who accompanied initially the Mughal Army, and later the Maratha Army.

Poha is flattened rice originating from the Indian subcontinent that is usually served as a breakfast dish in many parts of the country.

Puran poli is an Indian sweet flatbread that popular in South India and the state of Maharashtra.

Historians have variously translated the **qasbah** as 'small township', 'commercial mart', 'between a village and a city' and 'garrison town'. Colloquially in today's world, it means small localities in a town or city.

Raita is an Indian condiment consisting of yogurt, spices, and diced or grated vegetables or fruits.

Rasta Peth or Succath Shelmo Synagogue is a ninety-six-year-old structure built by the Bene Israel community and situated on the Rasta Peth lane in the heart of the city of Pune Maharshtra. The old name of this road was Jew Lane. A large Jewish community lived on this street in the late nineteenth and early twentieth centuries.

Sheol in the Hebrew Bible is the underworld place of stillness and darkness which lies after death.

In British India, **Subedar** or subadar was the second highest rank of enlisted Indian soldiers. The rank was otherwise equivalent to a British captain.

Tevilah is a full body immersion in a mikveh, the bath used for the purpose of ritual immersion in Judaism to achieve purity.

Thumri is a North Indian vocal form and is based on the romantic-devotional literature inspired by the bhakti movement. The text is usually derived from the Radha-Krishna theme and is of primary importance.

Wali Dakni, or Wali Mohammad Wali, was a classical Urdu poet from India. He is considered by many scholars as the father of Urdu poetry for being the first established poet to have composed ghazals in Urdu. During the 2002 Gujarat riots, Wali Dakni's memorial tomb in Shahibaug, Ahmedabad was vandalized by a Hindu mob and replaced with a makeshift Hanuman temple by the Hindu Administration. Later, the tomb was completely razed and a road was constructed overnight.

Yama and Yami, in Hindu mythology, are a divine pair of twin creator deities. Their relationship is connected to the concept of time in several ways. In one story, Yama's death is considered the first death in the universe. To help Yami cope with the grief of her brother's death, the gods created night. This is how time and the cyclical change of day and night was conceived.

Zamzam is a well located within the Masjid al-Haram in Mecca, Saudi Arabia. According to Islamic narratives, the well is a miraculously generated source of water, which opened up thousands of years ago when the son of Abraham, Ishmael, was left with his mother Hagar in the desert.

ALSO IN SPEAKING TIGER

THE DRUNK BIRD CHRONICLES

Malay Chatterjee

Allegro Armstrong Braganza, the eponymous avian chronicler of this novel, is immoral, immortal, irreverent, intelligent, irritable and often drunk. Born in the forests beyond Shillong, he was a foul-mouthed friend of the eccentric Englishman Gareth Armstrong; then coarse companion to his daughter Rachel who married a talented Anglo-Indian piano tuner named Emilio Braganza; and finally avuncular anchor to five subsequent generations of this expansive British-Goan family who travel across India and the globe to further their various quests—Orlando in Cambodia studying the architecture of the Angkor Wat, Bella learning translation in Portugal, Maria in Almora furthering her dance ambitions under the tutelage of Uday Shankar, and Asifio in New Delhi continuing the family's thriving music shop in Connaught Place. Through shifting tides of fame and fortune over a hundred years, it is Allegro who remains their constant and reliable port of stability.

Wickedly funny and full of surprises, Malay Chatterjee's *The Drunk Bird Chronicles* is a sparkling debut that will be read and enjoyed for years to come.

ALSO IN SPEAKING TIGER

THE LADY ON THE HORSE AND OTHER SECRETS

Ramona Sen

Spanning over a century, *The Lady on the Horse* tells the story of five generations of a family in Calcutta. Starting life as a khansama in an Englishman's house in 1900, Dipendra Nath Lahiri dreams of acquiring the wealth and status of a zamindar. His wife Pritilata's skills as a seamstress—much sought after by the memsahibs— become the means, and by 1919, their tailoring business, Lahiri & Sons, has made them fabulously rich and they've bought a grand mansion, Lahiri Bari. Their progeny can live a life of leisure, at par with the white sahibs Dipendra Nath and Pritilata had once served.

But with time, Lahiri Bari also becomes the house of many secrets and contested legacies: of injustice, betrayal, love and pain. What was the unmentionable 'thing' that happened between Neelratan Lahiri's wife Ishwari and the black-as-a-crow Kanailal—the revolutionary who wanted to burn down the Raj? Two generations later, what is the mysterious connection between Pixie and the maid's daughter, Ayesha, who grow up like sisters? And what was the oldest secret of them all—what turned the demure Pritilata into a rebel who rode out of her mansion on a magnificent horse one day—never to return.

Set against the backdrop of the freedom struggle, the Bengal Famine and Partition, this sprawling family saga explores the insidious implications of class and caste through the lives of people thrown together by blood ties and fate lines. At the heart of the story is the idea that everything which happens in the present has its roots in the past—every generation will be shaped by the legacy it has been bequeathed.

With a rich cast of characters and lyrical prose, Ramona Sen takes us on an exhilarating roller-coaster ride through the trials and tribulations of one family—and the passionate loves and bitter enmities that shaped their fortunes.